I0885854

SHIRT KINGS

PIONEERS OF HIP HOP FASHION

by Edwin PHADE Sacasa
and
Alan KET

SHIRT KINGS
PIONEERS OF HIP HOP FASHION

© 2023 Dokument Press, Edwin PHADE Sacasa & Alan KET
Paperback edition
Printed in Poland 2023
ISBN 978-91-88369-78-9

Authors: Edwin PHADE Sacasa & Alan KET

Foreword: MC Serch

Text: Andre LeRoy Davis, Alan Ket, Edwin Phade Sacasa & MC Serch

Photo: All photos are copyright by Edwin Phade Sacasa / Ultimate Hip Hop Experience collection, 1998 with the exception of photos provided by Mel at 1 Minute Photo, Ernie Paniccioli, and Paradise Gray

Graphic Design: Noah McDonough

Editor: Björn Almqvist

Cover photo: Shirt King Phade and Nike with Ivania from Marcy Projects, by Mel Simone

First published in 2013 by Dokument Press, hardback edition.

Dokument Press
Årstavägen 26, 120 52 Årsta, Sweden
dokument.org
info@dokument.org

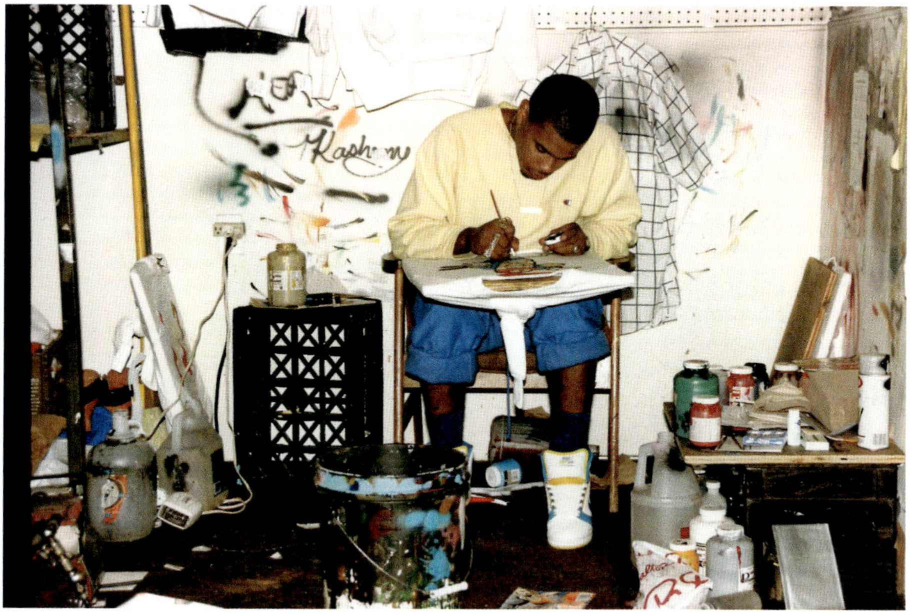

Dedicated to the memory of Rafael Avery aka Shirt King Kasheme

King Kasheme, 1987.
Photo by Paradise Gray. Courtesy of The Paradise Collection.

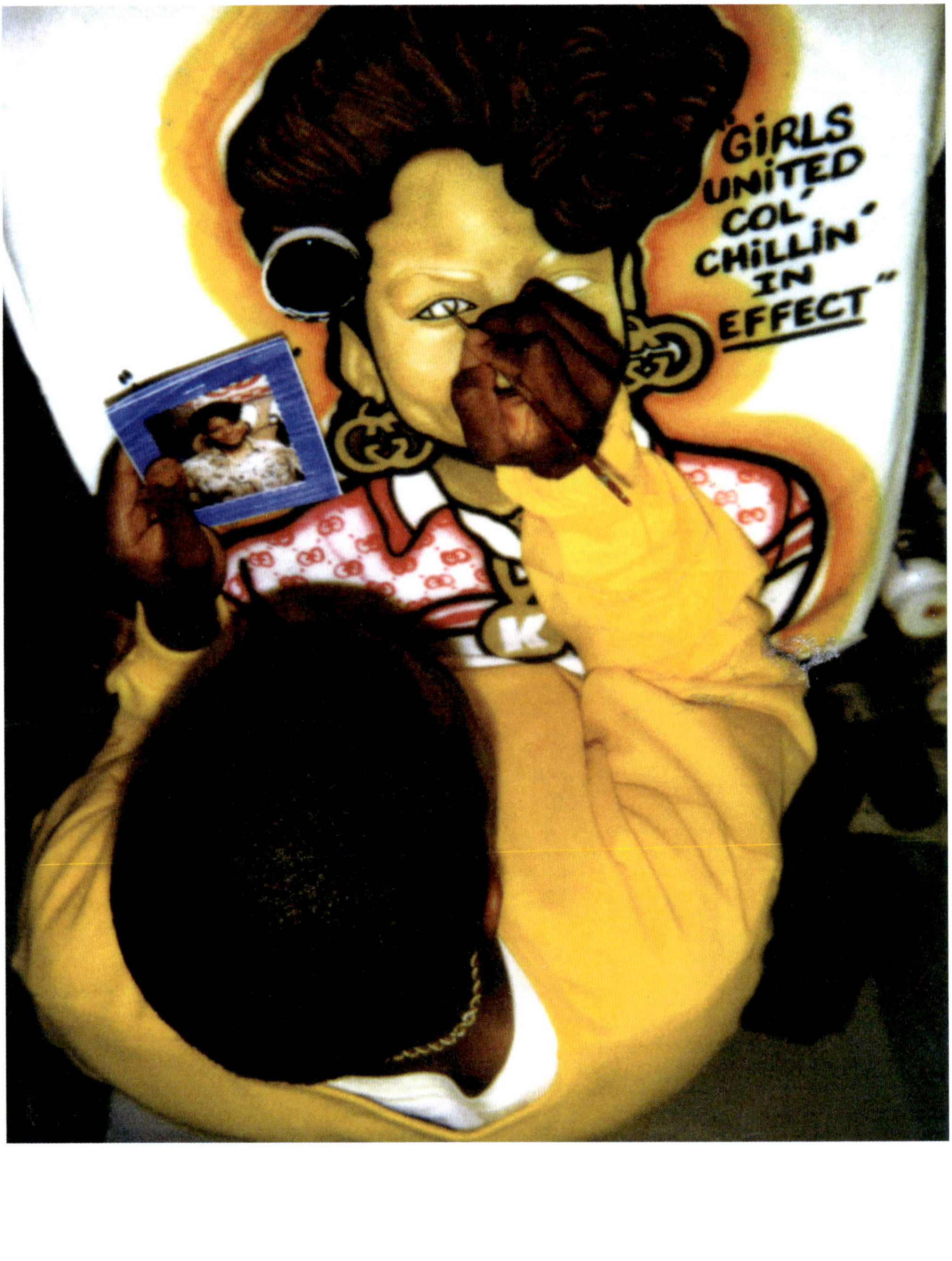

Nike hand painting at the shop in the Jamaica Coliseum, 1986.

TABLE OF CONTENTS

FOREWORD
HOW YOU LIVING HOBBES?
By MC Serch

Hip hop was the soundtrack of my youth coming up as a teen in Far Rockaway Queens. Many of you can share that sentiment; maybe not the location, but the sentiment. With the music came the attitude, the style and the fashion. For us Queens residents hip hop culture and fashion was layered with the sounds of local Queens artists who went global like Run DMC, LL Cool J, and other tri-state area artists like Spyder D and Sparky D, to name a few, who would all get our fashion fix from the Coliseum. The Mecca of fashion in Queens is what my friends and I from 'The Rock' called it. We would go to Doughty Boulevard, hop the bus to Jamaica Boulevard, and walk over to 'See 'em at the 'Seum'. There were the greatest looking females in the whole city there, as well as the hottest styles of Nike, Adidas, Puma, Ellesse, and Lotto, all in mad flavors. They had the Coca-Cola shirts and pants first; the Benetton knock-offs that looked mad official, and there in time for you to see it on Thursday in the Benetton Store, and buy it on Friday on 'The Ave' (Jamaica Avenue). But if you were either one of two things: A rapper that thought you had a hot record, or a dude with some bread, you went downstairs, past the gold tooth spots, next to the barber shop, to see Nike and Phade, from The Mighty Shirt Kings.

I saw my first Shirt Kings shirt when I saw my dude from my local gold tooth spot, at the Flea Market on Rockaway Boulevard, having one made for him. He was a dude I admired 'cause he had his own business at like twenty years old. He got me open to what they were doing in the Coliseum.

When I first put out my records on Warlock Records in the early 80s and then with my partner Tony D at Idlers in 1986, I was starting to get a little rep. I was in the Latin Quarter (a nightclub nicknamed the LQ) every week and would see the Shirt Kings hanging out and they would show me love. One time Phade bought me this pink drink and told me to drink it fast and then go dance with some girls in the middle of the dance floor. One week I would see Paradise, who ran the door at the LQ, with a fresh Shirt Kings joint with his face looking like a Pharaoh. The faces always looked like you and not what they thought you looked like.

I would hang out in the Shirt King's shop and they would play my record when I would show up, people would give me pounds and show love. They made me a fan of theirs, and they treated me like a superstar, then one day it came: my first Shirt Kings joint. It was of a penguin character with my glasses on, and after that one came the one with my face on it, in my Avirex jacket. Then it was the famous Calvin and Hobbes jeans for the *Steppin' to The A.M.* video, with Calvin screaming, "How you living Hobbes?", which also happened to be a line in the record that my partner Pete Nice spit. It was so butter. Then came my denim jacket, and then it was over. Soon after that the times changed. Style changed and we drifted apart. It was a moment when things changed for all the right reasons but not the right timing.

But the Shirt Kings were creative. They made clothes and logos and stayed in the game. I would see them out every once in a while and they would show me what they had been working on. They had a body of work that was iconic and that many would be proud to have designed. The guys from the Coliseum were now the men from the Shirt Kings, and I revered them.

I have worn their clothes at shows in Detroit when I was the morning show host at WJLB. I would come out during the Return of The Legends concert and do the running man. All of the hip hop fans that were in attendance would hear *The Gas Face* and I would come out with the glasses and the clothes that I wore back in the day. It looked tight, I mean I looked TIGHT, but it felt right.

My kids today look at my videos and look at the boxes of memorabilia I have from touring. In those boxes is every Shirt Kings piece of clothing the guys ever made me. They love the clothes and I tell them the story of the Coliseum — what it was like to know that your Shirt Kings shirt was done, how it felt to put it on, and what it was like to know you were going to be seen. My kids see it. I never stopped seeing it, which is why I kept it. In this book of memories I hope you get to enjoy seeing it as much as I did.

Enjoy the pages,
MC Serch

The Shirt Kings with MC Serch at their birthday party, January 21, 1987.

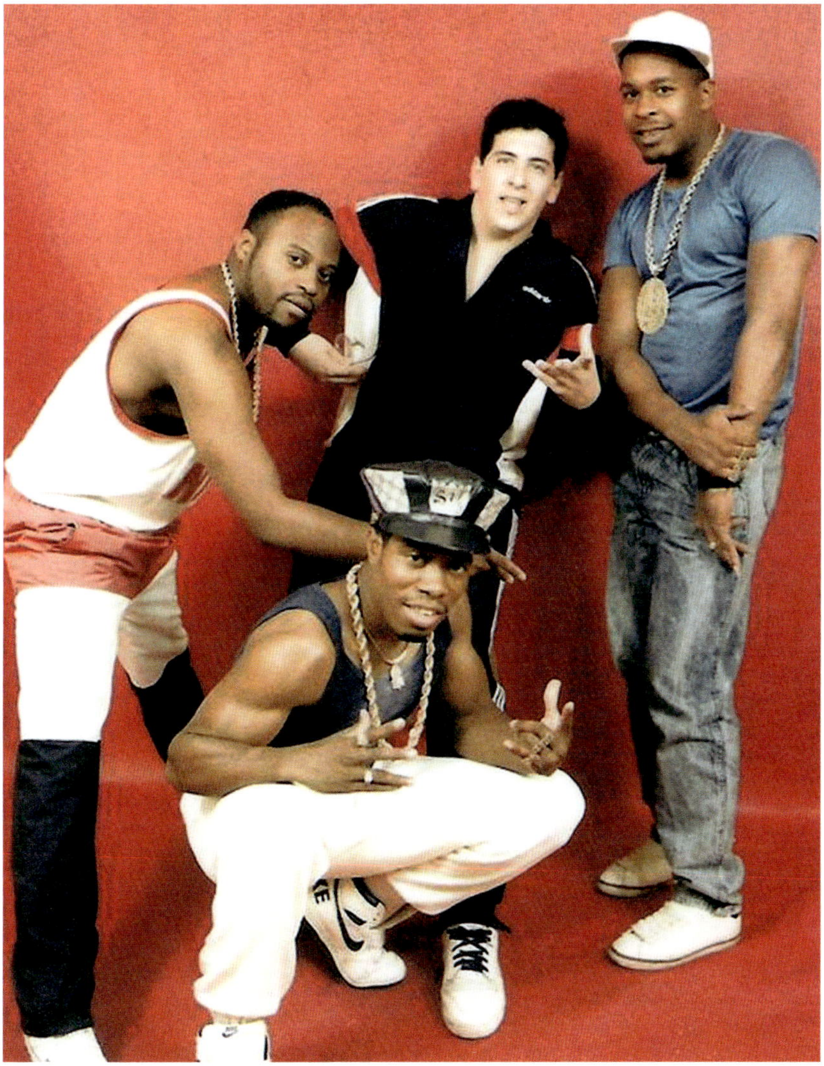

INTRODUCTION

THE ULTIMATE HIP HOP EXPERIENCE

By SHIRT KING PHADE

In 1972 my family moved from East New York, Brooklyn, to 3055 Bouck Avenue, uptown in the Bronx. It was a big move for me and the first step towards a commitment to hip hop culture; a culture I did not start, but I watched it grow from its initial inception.

My mother noticed that I loved to draw at the age of five, when we lived in Brooklyn. She would buy me Disney coloring books and she also exposed me to the art of Peter Max. His psychedelic paintings reflected the times, what was going on in politics or sports. Peter Max had a direct influence on my style.

My older brother (Fly1, Ex-Vandals, INDs, BYB) quickly became the man with the ladies. So I watched him and mimicked him. He had a big influence on my rites of passage and on survival in the world we now know as hip hop. I listened to all his stories about a dude named Kool Herc and the Herculords, Sha Sha — the famous break dancer, along with the Nigger Twins. In those days we were our own superheroes. Our lives mirrored Marvel and DC comics. Bruce Lee came into the picture and every one was kicking and Kung-Fu fighting. I witnessed gangs terrorizing as we were rushed on to the school bus to avoid cuts and bruises. Spikes, chains, swords, brass knuckles and razors; whites against blacks, blacks against latinos. It was crazy, but against that backdrop I saw my brother and his crew always gearing up to go tagging up. I remember watching fifteen to twenty guys and girls gather every Saturday to go racking paint, then to the train yard. I wondered what this was all about and eventually went one time. They tagged on every train while people were sitting there, getting ink on people's business suits; for me it was the ultimate hip hop experience. It seems like everyone back then was a writer. The whole projects used to go, big or small, to tag up while the train was in motion.

DJ One-Time and DJ Doc la Rock encouraged me to apply to the High School of Art and Design in New York. One-Time showed me how to use acrylics on jackets and pants, see he was also known as Kaos One, a king of the 6 trains and now turned DJ. He and Doc allowed me to become one of his record boys (someone who had to know the titles of the vinyl and pass them from a milk crate where they were placed in order of importance or party mood). I passed the test for the entrance into the High School of Art and Design and was introduced to a whole new world. Especially going to the third floor bathroom. It was like being on the train, tags were everywhere.

So many artists were at Art and Design high school, A&D as we called it, and it had all the top subway writers. I got a little intimidated and quickly joined the photography dept. There is where I hooked up with my boy Todd who hailed from another part of the Bronx. Then Rafael from South Side Jamaica, Queens, Clyde from Marcy Projects, Bird from Brownsville and Dean from Bushwick. We played the A&D lunchroom religiously. Always banging those Bronx beats on the table while someone kept up by rapping. At the lunchroom table we planned out what graffiti pieces were to be painted on the side of a train that weekend. But I never got invited. I would just hear about the aftermath of the train tunnel experience. I vowed to get really good.

How did I derive my name? My first tag name was Phase 3. I had often heard my brother and his crew speak highly of Phase 2, who is legendary and mysterious. He was the one to aspire to in graffiti. In basketball it was Julius 'Doctor J' Erving and in boxing it was Muhammad Ali. I desired to be great so naturally Phase 3 was the name for me. But the veterans over at A&D thought differently. One day as the dust and weed smoke filled the third floor bathroom with a thick cloud I emerged next in line to tag up on the wall. When I was through I heard nothing but silence. I thought, 'I must have achieved some sort of status!' Nope! At the lunchroom table Daze, Jae 5, and Dee2 let me know that writing a legend's name is a no-no. So, I began to go down the alphabet and stopped at the letter D. I added a two to the back of my name to mimic Phase 2. I did not want a father to my style, so I claimed two spots (Phade 1 and Phade 2). Any other Phade would be a fraud because I was hitting the trains hard — like a job with benefits.

I did my first Phade piece with an outline that my mentor, Adam, gave me at the lunchroom table. I always had the gift to scale any picture to any size and replicate it to its exact specifications. When I met my next mentor, Kase 2, executing his outline was the big test. He was one of the originators, after Phase 2 and Riff 170, and a true style master. So I had to rise to the occasion. Armed with a Kase 2 outline, I proceeded to lay down fire to the side of the number 2 train parked in the middle track at 225th street in the Bronx.

So what's so special about the 80s? For me it was the graffiti cars swirling through New York City like canvases painted for the world to see. It was watching school comrades transform into the next generation of graffiti artists and joining the Rock Steady Crew. Getting calls to mentor and giving out the wisdom I got from Kase 2 and Butch 2. Going to clubs like Harlem World on 116th street and Lenox Avenue, Broadway International, T-Connection in the Bronx, Disco Fever, P.A.L. 183rd, Galaxy, Skate Fever, Skate-City in Brooklyn, Roseland USA and Empire Skating Rink in Brooklyn. Watching the Old Gold Crew from Brownsville, Brooklyn fighting with their hand skills. Hearing the Supreme Team Show on the radio.

Opposite page top and bottom: A young Phade with Anthony Riley in High School, 1981. Detail of a Phade and Karado #6 train car, the Bronx, 1980.

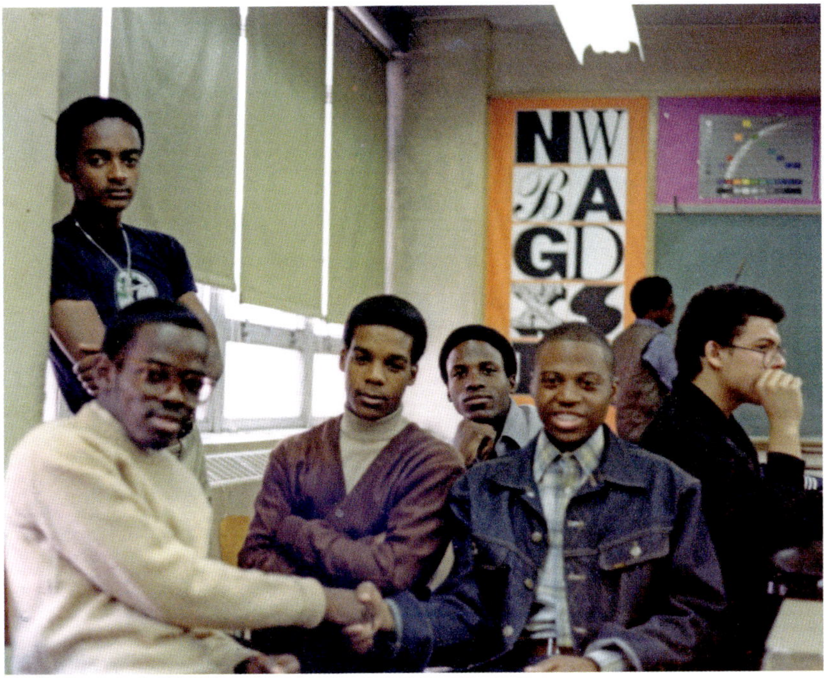

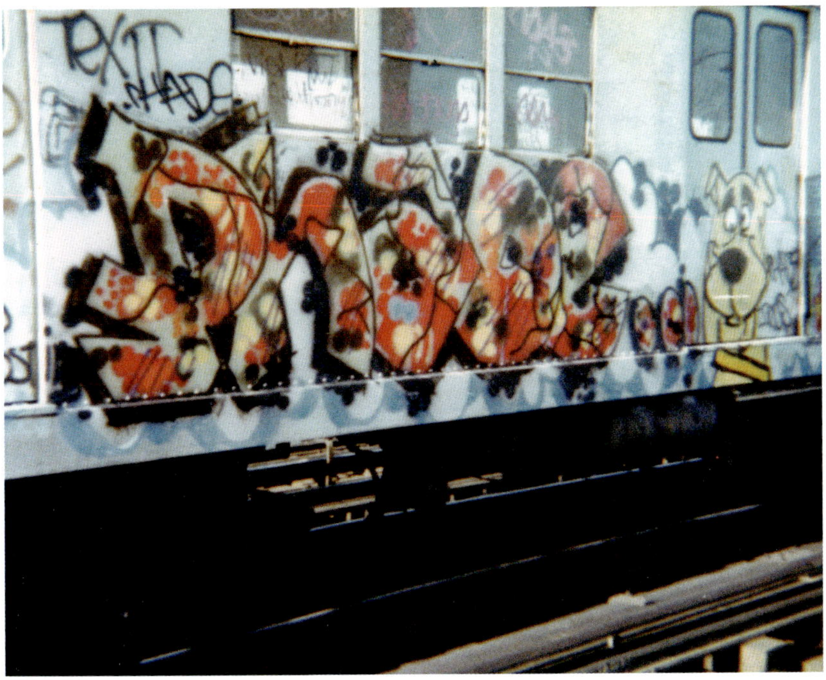

Mr. Magic and Eddie Cheba late night on the radio. Listening to hip hop with a hanger for an antenna to get some bootleg station. The clubs became my big boom box where I could hear the music I was used to hearing in the Bronx and see the artists perform. Hearing Run DMC for the first time at the Roxy skating rink on 19th street in New York City. I felt like a panther gathering with all the beautiful black and latino people. And by getting invited by Lil Seen and Doze to come out, I was thrust into another world.

I thought hip hop was over for me when I signed up for college. But instead a new era began. The Roxy had let me know that hip hop was very much alive with or without me. Movies were being planned, history began to get documented, and documentaries were being filmed. I was still a graffiti outlaw by nature so I kept my distance from being in the limelight. Since I had an understanding about one's exposure and exploitation, the media did not sit too well with me unless someone was talking money. The entrepreneur in me kept me cautious.

It was in 1984 when Georgie aka Sound 7 taught me how to airbrush. He insisted that I learned because I had shown him some good techniques on the trains. He never forgot it and felt compelled to return the favor. So with airbrush in hand, I began to fuse my experience with graffiti and my surroundings and put them on blank white t-shirts. Unlike the airbrush artists that were working at the carnivals and fairs who never expressed or reflected what I saw daily, I set out to make a statement. I would combine all of my worlds into a wearable piece of clothing. Standing on the corner of 125th street and Lenox Avenue selling "Money Making New Yorker" t-shirts was my introduction to business.

On 125th street selling airbrush and silk-screen designs was where my entrepreneurial foundation was being laid down. I hired three young cats from my projects to help. They had that hustle in them but none could help with the actual design. Soon, the demand became overwhelming. I had to get a team. I went to Harlem first, to Darryl Ferguson's crib. We went to the High School of Art and Design together and I heard he was doing shirts as well. He was hand-painting cartoons and cars with acrylics. He tells me, 'Yo, I got this from you. You used to come to school with the graf going down your pants!' He reminded me that my boy Nike was nice with characters. Darryl and I did a couple of collabos but that was it. He always kept asking me where my boy Nike was. Then it hit me, I needed to go out to Marcy Projects and find my high school buddy.

In 1985 Nike's building in the Marcy Projects in the Bed-Stuy section of Brooklyn was like a gallery, a hand-painted heaven. He painted the Hulk, Thor, Human Torch, Silver Surfer and a host of other cartoons all over the walls. In Brooklyn it seemed like they appreciated your skills as the local talent, there was so much community support. In the Bronx they would have exed that out quickly.

When finally arriving in Brooklyn, Nike is nowhere to be found and I am commissioned by this mother to help her out and find him. She tells me that his friend Rafael (Kasheme) has access to his whereabouts. She gave me his number and I called him and journeyed to Queens.

South Side Jamaica, Queens was fascinating to me. It was hood but surrounded by private houses. Coming from the projects in Brooklyn and the Bronx I never understood what people who lived in houses were mad at. Maybe mortgage rates? Most of the families hailed from Brooklyn so they had that BK swagger, a love for the uptown beats and music, hustle like a Harlemite; Queens was unique. Everyone was God-Body (Five Percenters).

I began to notice how crack's tentacles had invaded the South Side. Kasheme smoked recreationally and it hurt me since I knew the devastation it wrecked through the Bronx where I

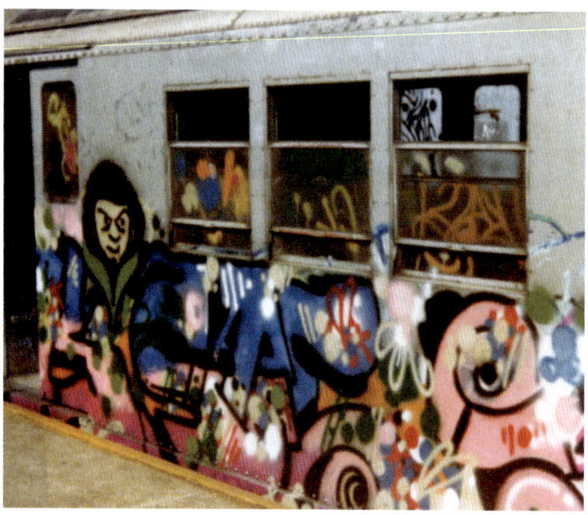

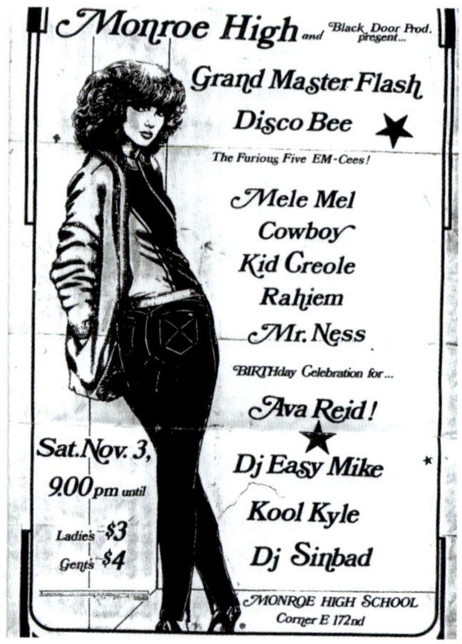

Above: A Monroe High School party flyer by Anthony Riley, 1981.
Left: Detail of a Kase 2/Cue/Phade end to end, the Bronx, NY, 1981.

was awakening every morning to a sea of used vials of crack in the streets. When you walked in the urine stench buildings you could slip on the little bottles strewn everywhere. It was 1985 and the epidemic was now hitting home and my boy was indulging. So Kems 5 and me would beat Kasheme's ass every time we went out to Queens, this is what love does. Understandably, as I walked around with Kasheme explaining how I was getting money uptown, but now wanted to incorporate Nike to get to the next level, he became very excited. He wanted to get down as well, and perhaps use this to escape his addiction.

Kasheme was friends with Jam Master Jay and Jay's close friend, Luvvy, so the very next weekend Luvvy took us to Jam Master Jay's house in Hollis Queens. Now here I was standing face to face with someone who's music was being listened to over the boombox for years. I pulled out my sweatshirt samples and Jay immediately ordered two shirts. He wanted black sweatshirts with a gold chain around it, one for him and one for his son. He went as far as to mention that we should go to 'The Ave' (Jamaica Avenue) to get our product into the mall and he offered to help us out financially. We took his recommendation and at the same time it sparked Kasheme to buy his own airbrush and start practicing with it.
I showed Kasheme how to airbrush with the set he purchased with his last unemployment check. As Kasheme began to lose buddies to the crack game he made the choice to go forward with his life as a Shirt King. We had several chances to get financed by the drug dealers, local ones we knew who saw the potential. I stressed to Kasheme that it was a bad idea because if they go down we go down as well. First Tyheim was found tied up and murdered gangland style in his basement. Then Unique was killed in a hail of bullets at his spot in Brooklyn. After this, Kasheme's fascination with the drug dealers was gone and he made the decision to airbrush and sewed up his projects, the notorious 40 Projects in South Side Jamaica, Queens.

Yet, I was still on the hunt for Nike who was a master with characters. Finally Kasheme contacted him and the three of us: Nike, Kasheme, and I launched our business in the Jamaica Coliseum, after scouting out all other possible locations in the area. We brainstormed together for the name of our new business. I was already a king on the trains (King Phade) so it was natural to blurt out shirt kings, meaning the best at our craft. June 1986 is the said birth date of the Shirt Kings renamed, The Mighty Shirt Kings of South Side Jamaica, Queens. Nike hand painted for the first year, staring at the airbrush like a piece of foreign land out the corner of his eye.

Upon opening, as promised Jam Master Jay came through with at least fifty dudes from Hollis, walking down the avenue, into the Coliseum and downstairs to see us amidst the blaring boom-box sound with Public Enemy's *Rebel Without a Pause*, Eric B and Rakim's *My Melody*, Kool Moe Dee's *Go See the Doctor* and Super Lover C's *Do the James*. The rest is history.

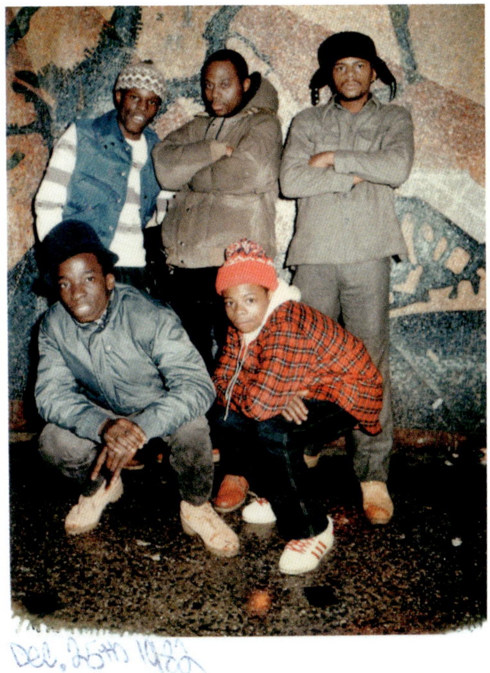

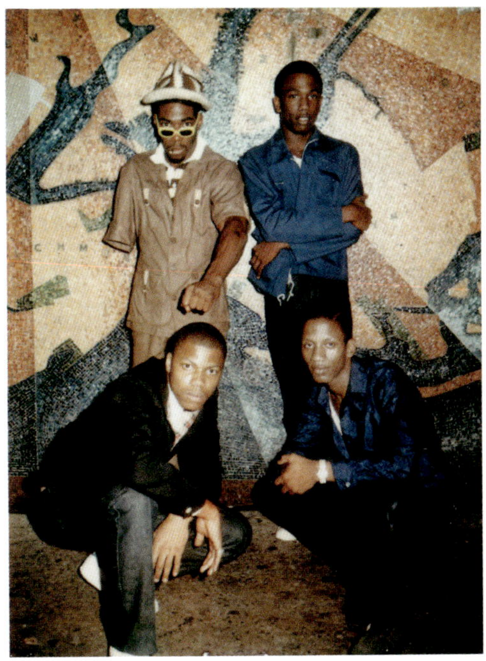

Top: 110, Phade, Pop, Big Earl, and Chrissy Black, 1982.
Above: Kase 2, Cue, Butch 2, and EC 3 - The TFP crew, 1982.

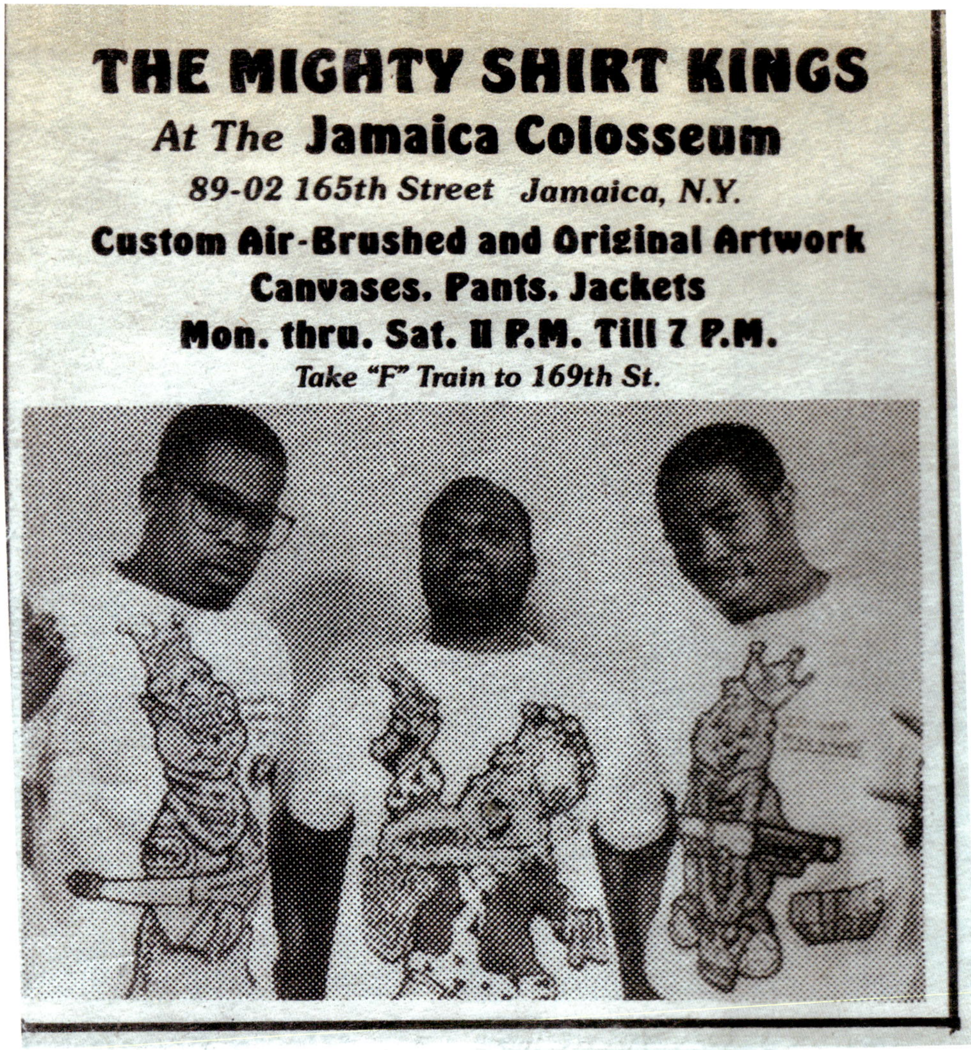

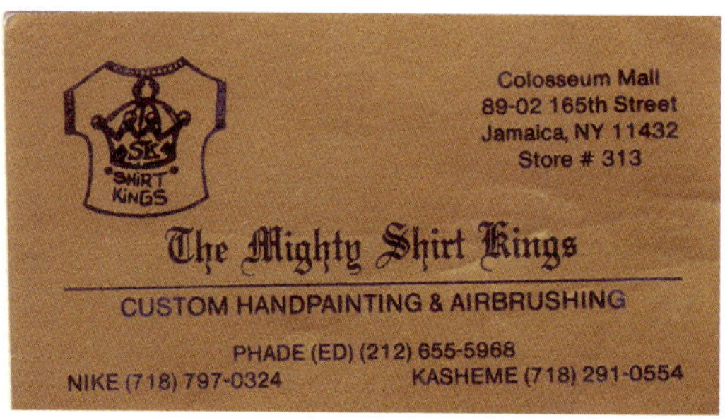

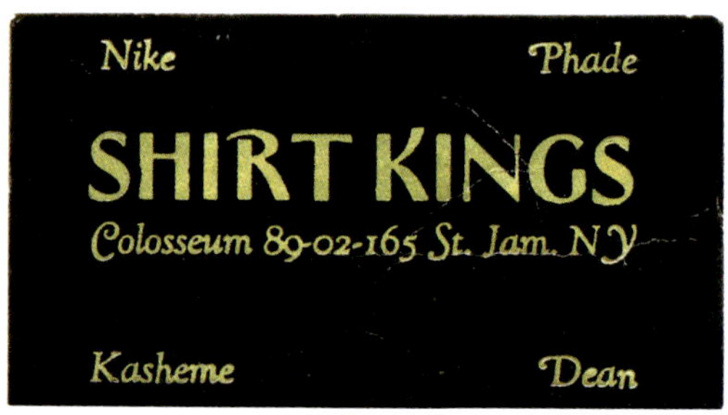

This page: Vintage Shirt Kings ad and business cards, 1980s.

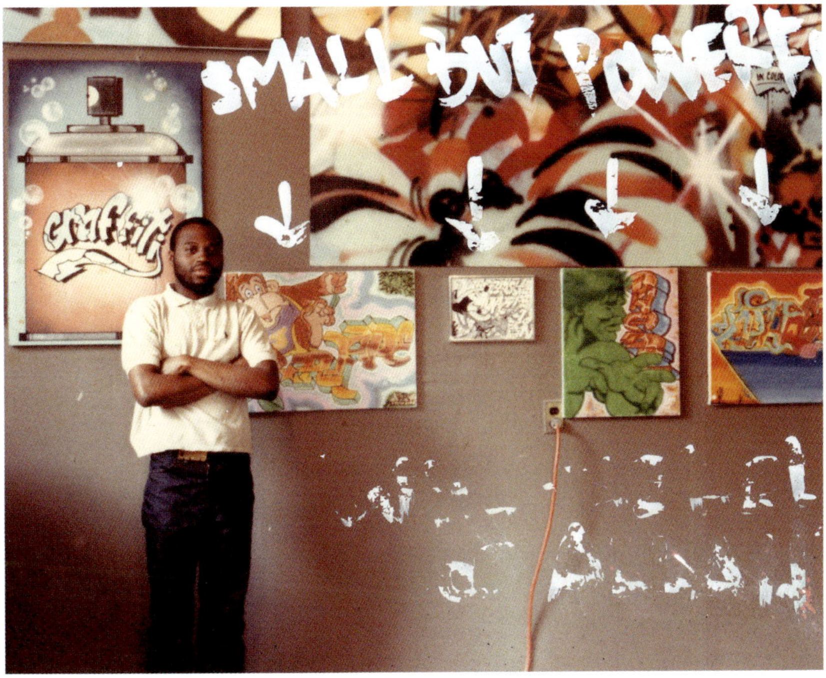

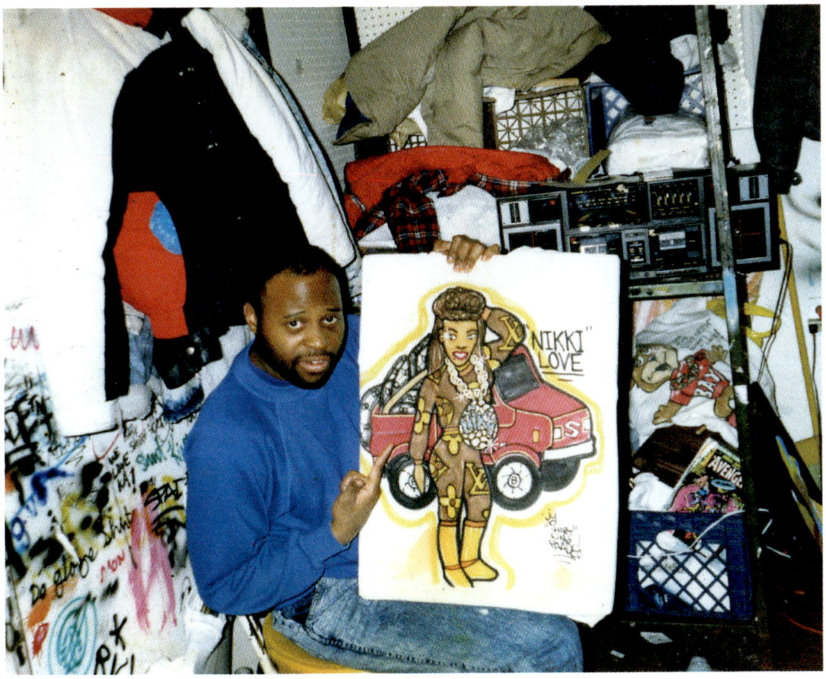

Top: Phade at his first art exhibition, 1980. **Above:** Phade with his Nikki Love design, 1987.

URBAN FASHION'S ROOTS

By Alan Ket

Blacks and Puerto Ricans in New York City have always had a fly side, a get dressed up to impress side. Different eras of course had different dress codes as much as different occasions did then and still do today. The Shirt Kings book is a fashion story as much as it's hip hop history; it's an early moment in time in the evolution of the 'urban' fashion business and in the entrepreneurial and creative spirit of both the graffiti and hip hop movements.

We have all seen images of 70s New York fashion in films like Saturday Night Fever where rocking flared bottom jeans, platform shoes and gold chains looked cool and made up the disco look. But as rock music and punk rock grew, there was also a trend of making your own t-shirts that took off with the invention and mass production of the iron-on decals. This customization of shirts, and that of the punk rock and outlaw gang movements, showed that do-it-yourself style was possible and better than the store fashion of the day. The tough gangs in the Bronx and all over New York had specialists among them that knew how to modify jackets, sew and make roc-a-block name patches as well as add studs, chains, and other ornaments to complete their look. The flamboyancy that existed was present to make teens look dangerous, and it worked. This was not lost on the kids and was quite influential for years to come (anyone remember Africa Bambaataa and Soul Sonic Force's outfits?).

By the early 80s young people were rocking tight Lee jeans with Le Tigre shirts to go with their British Walkers. Sneakers were considered most important and many looks started from the feet up. Starting with the color of for example your Puma Clydes and build up the look to match. T-shirt graphics were limited and it was mostly athletic brands or surf brands that made their way to the east coast via stores like Macy's or VIM. For the most part the b-boy and b-girl aesthetic that existed was simple, clean, and affordable. The extravagance took the form of small gold chains or leather coats. Park jams and clubs were where you would see young people looking their freshest.

Phade's high school alma mater, Art and Design, played an immense part in schooling him and connecting him into a world of train painting, outlaw art, and hip hop music. His good fortune of being surrounded by the city's soon to be top talents (Daze, Pink, Doze, Lil Seen, Marc Jacobs) put him in a DIY mindset and he became driven to create. Graffiti writers with talent got training by painting trains and turned to adorning their jackets and jeans. This took off and now there were teens all over New York clamoring to have their names designed by the popular painters in their neighborhood. The trend soon moved to shirts and the customization of the iron-ons continued but now it was crew names and Playboy bunnies. This was Phade's start and the start within the hip hop movement to be heavily influenced by the artistry of the graffiti writers that lived in the same hoods.

Sergio Valente, Jordache, and Calvin Klein were popular brands at the time, and it seemed like the Brooke Shields commercials and other ad propaganda from the time worked. We all wanted to look great and straight out of the TV ads, and quite possibly to avoid the realities of the disparity between the poor, middle, and upper class. No one wanted to be poor and much less look like it, so the collective decision was made to dress it up and hide it. Aspiration was at an all time high. We wanted out of the hood even if only thru a luxury fantasy. It didn't come easy for many and it was key to take care of your fresh fashion. Jeans went to dry cleaners, b-boys scrubbed their shell toe Adidas with toothbrushes pulled from back pockets, and mothers and grandmothers everywhere were on alert to hang dry the shirts.

Meanwhile the streets embraced the b-boy aesthetic, but swallowed up those that were not tough enough and alert enough to protect their gear. If you were caught on the wrong block, bumped into the wrong thug, or just had some bad luck you could easily have your jacket or sneakers stolen at knifepoint or gunpoint. Fashion thievery was at an all time high, and it was by any means that some went out to get it. I believe that most of the drug dealers that came out of the 80s simply did it so that they could have money to shop and look fresh. The Shirt Kings can surely attest to that.

The other motivation for the freshness and the flamboyancy was to attract the opposite sex of course. Herein lies the push to even more excessiveness and the luxury label hype. Everyone wanted to look like a million bucks and those that made money and led the way were the drug dealers (names like Supreme, 50 Cent, Alpo, and Rich Porter come to mind). They had the means to purchase the brands and to commission designs from Dapper Dan and the Shirt Kings as well as the purchasing power to acquire the luxury cars and trick those out too. Us regular folks worked our jobs and saved up for the fashion in order to not be left behind.

Opposite page: The Shirt Kings at their shop in the Jamaica Coliseum, 1987.

The Shirt Kings style of airbrush design became a fashion statement made popular by the hottest rappers and deejays of the day. It seemed like overnight that their designs were everywhere from Just Ice's record to The Audio Two's popular album to the stage of the Latin Quarters where all the best emcees were performing weekly. As the Shirt Kings business took off their style was copied across the Northeast and they themselves expanded and covered Miami. Pretty soon they had deals with rappers and singers alike to provide the wardrobe designs for tours and music videos. They were in a sense everywhere.

There were many brands and designers that were influenced by the Shirt Kings and it is no wonder that one of the early 'urban' brands was Fubu also out of Jamaica, Queens. Soon brands like the Shabazz Brothers, Karl Kani, Sir Benni Miles and others entered the market and mass-produced clothing designs. The era of customization was dying down, but the impact that the Shirt Kings brought to the fashion world is undeniable.

Enjoy the trip down memory lane.

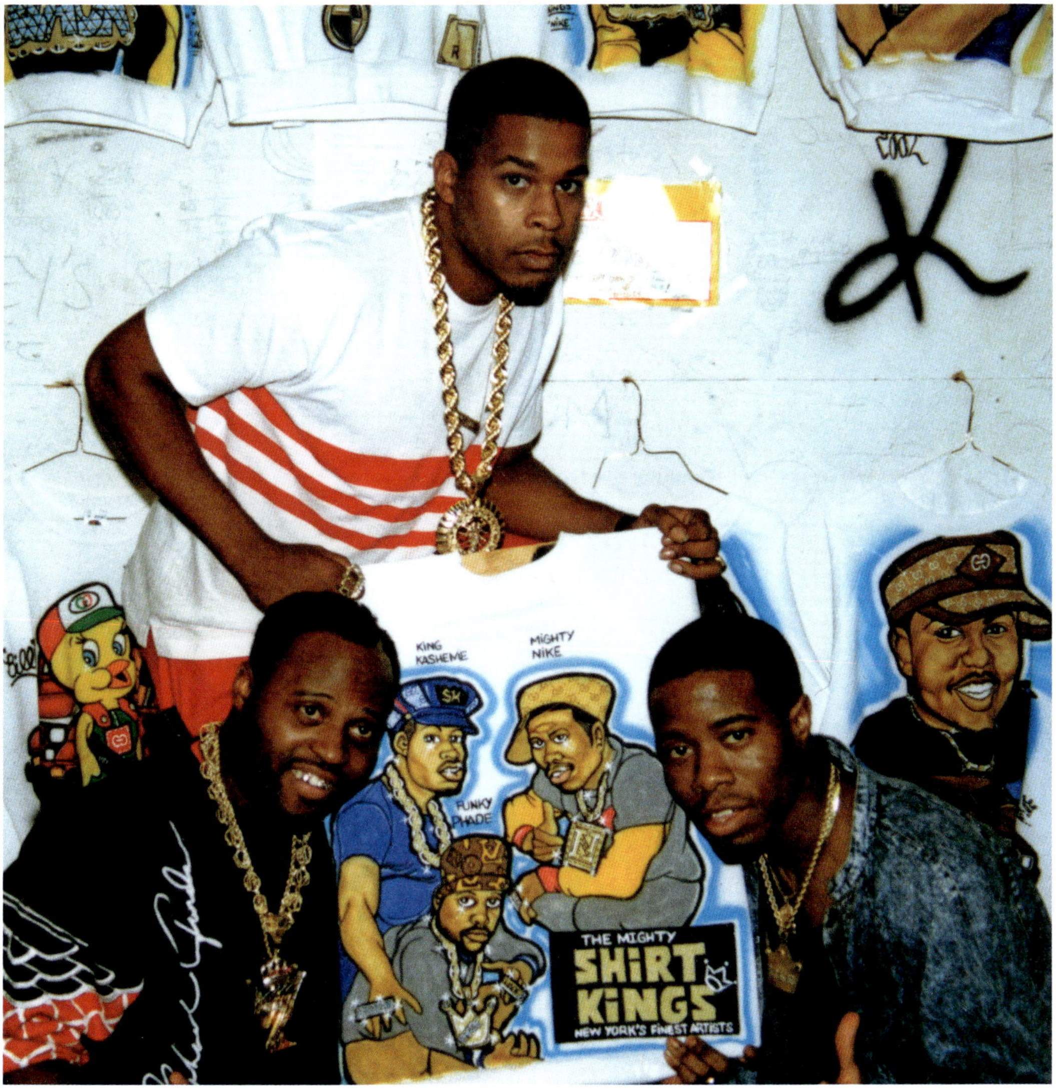

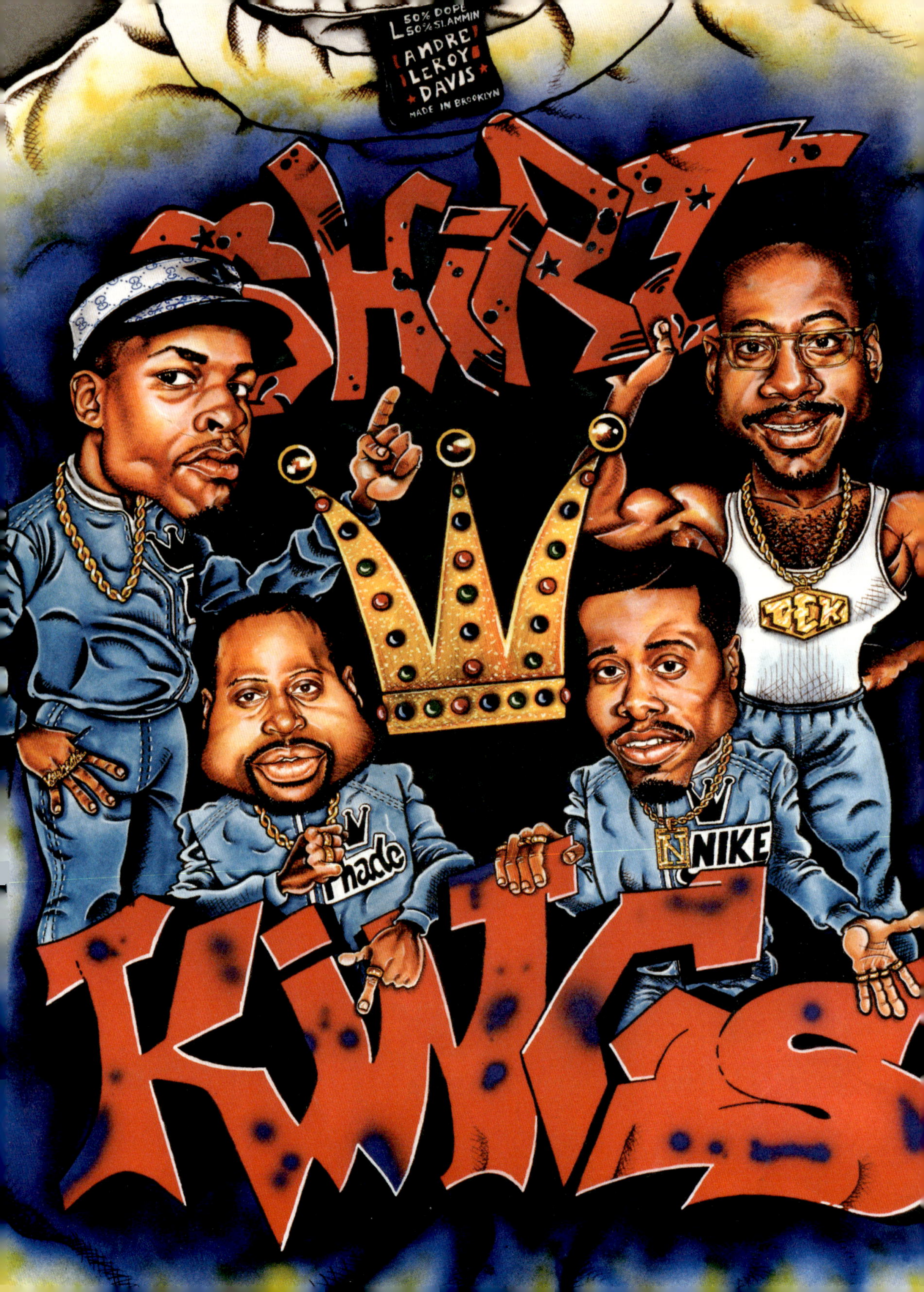
L 50% DOPE 50% SLAMMIN
ANDRE LEROY DAVIS
MADE IN BROOKLYN
Phade
NIKE

THE FIRST BLACK CLOTHING LINE STRAIGHT FROM THE STREETS

by Andre Leroy Davis (A. L. Dre)

I remember it was late 1987 when I picked up a *Right On!* magazine and flipped through the pages, stopping only when I reached the centerfold poster. The poster featured LL Cool J with his patented red Kangol and mandatory thick gold chains rocking a white long sleeve sweatshirt and a pair of denim blue jeans. Now there was nothing really special about that except that the white sweatshirt that LL Cool J was wearing was adorned by a lavishly artistic and ill detailed portrait of LL himself standing in front of a sickly painted, stylized eye popping red vehicle. It was all airbrushed and it was emblazoned with precise lettering that read, "LL Cool J, Hard as Hell". On the lower right-hand side of the illustration were smaller printed letters that identified the artist as being, "Nike, Shirt Kings".

My cousin who I hadn't seen in a minute was also an artist, and he went by the name Nike, so I decided to investigate. My godmother was called, some cousins were called and after more than a couple of months had passed I finally got the necessary information. I spoke to Nike on the phone, and a week or two later I was on the N train bound for Jamaica Queens to check out The Mighty Shirt Kings at the Coliseum Mall. When I got there my cousin, Mighty Nike, quickly introduced me to the other Kings: King Funky Phade, King Kasheme and at that time a brother named Dek was on board helping to beautify clothes in the Shirt King way. It was controlled madness. It was non-stop with mall shoppers, regular folks and prominent rappers of the time just casually dropping by to kick it or to try and get their t-shirts, jean jackets or jean pants legs airbrushed. Folks were lined up. The Shirt Kings were like rap stars. They were ghetto celebs that were in demand. The Mighty Shirt kings were the first black clothing line straight from the streets.

Having seen some of my artwork that first day when I met him at The Coliseum, Phade proposed to me an idea of an art for art trade. If I hooked up a caricature of The Mighty Shirt Kings, he'd hook me up with a custom made t-shirt or whatever I wanted in return. Shaking his hand and leaving with about ten pictures of photo references in my possession, I bid everyone else goodbye and I was out of there and didn't return for a good couple of months. The Shirt King t-shirt illustration was done in actual extra large t-shirt size. I worked on it weekly in between freelance gigs and I even decided to use an airbrush that I had sitting in a closet for the very first time, along with my normal painting procedures and techniques. I wound up bringing the completed illustration back to the mall in the summer of 1988. On that same day I remember the diabolical Biz Markie being in the house and stopping by to share a new song that he had just completed for the Shirt Kings to hear. Popping a cassette into a small box, that day became even more memorable for me as I heard the now classic *Just a Friend* for the very first time. Although I don't know exactly what happened to the original illustration and I never did get that custom-made piece from Phade, this particular illustration and the story behind it remains one of my favorite pieces of hip hop history.

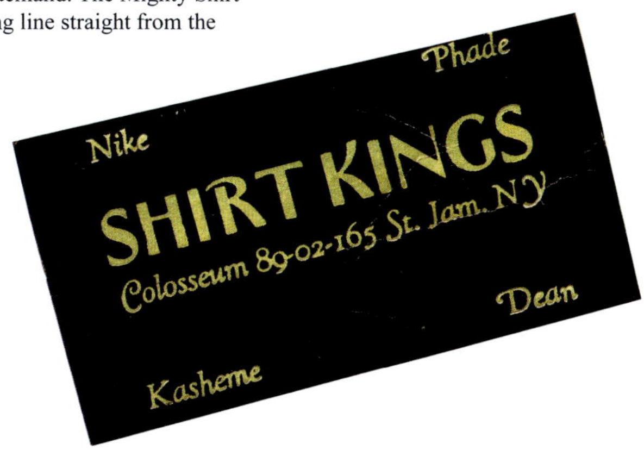

The Shirt Kings, Illustration by A.L.Dre, 1987.

HIP HOP FASHION

The fashion was about standing out and looking crisp. Aspiring to look rich and paid in order to impress the opposite sex. You had to be fresh and fly in order to be noticed. Bucket hats and Kangols were accessories that young men wore while the doorknocker earrings were the trend with the ladies. The brands to wear ranged from inexpensive (BVD) to expensive (Cazal) but everyone saved their paychecks to go shopping. The Italian luxury brands made a big splash but in a modified way via Dapper Dan's custom creations and the Shirt Kings illustrated works. MCM, Fendi, Gucci and Louis Vuitton didn't have stores in the hood out in Queens but they were represented in styles that certainly didn't come out of their Fifth Avenue stores.

The following pages are a brief snapshot of some of the people that came thru the doors of the Jamaica Coliseum out in Jamaica, Queens, New York City to see the Shirt Kings and at the same time possibly buy some gold teeth or chains or sneakers, all readily available along the avenue. Buying a Shirt Kings shirt or hoody was a major statement and those that put their money up gladly posed for photos.

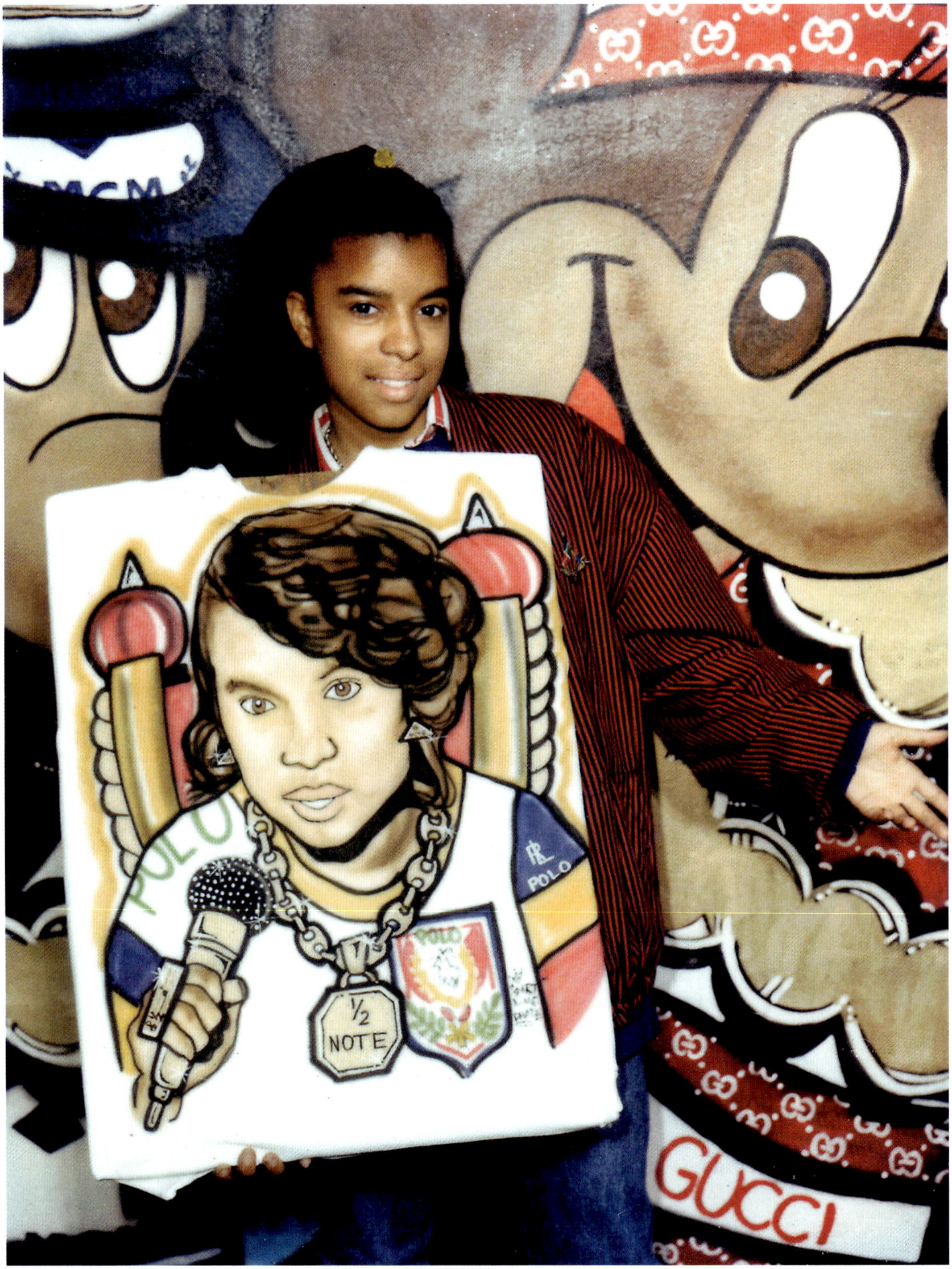

This page: Half Note, Jamaica Coliseum, 1987. **Opposite page:** Nike's Gucci Burger design, Jamaica Coliseum, 1987.

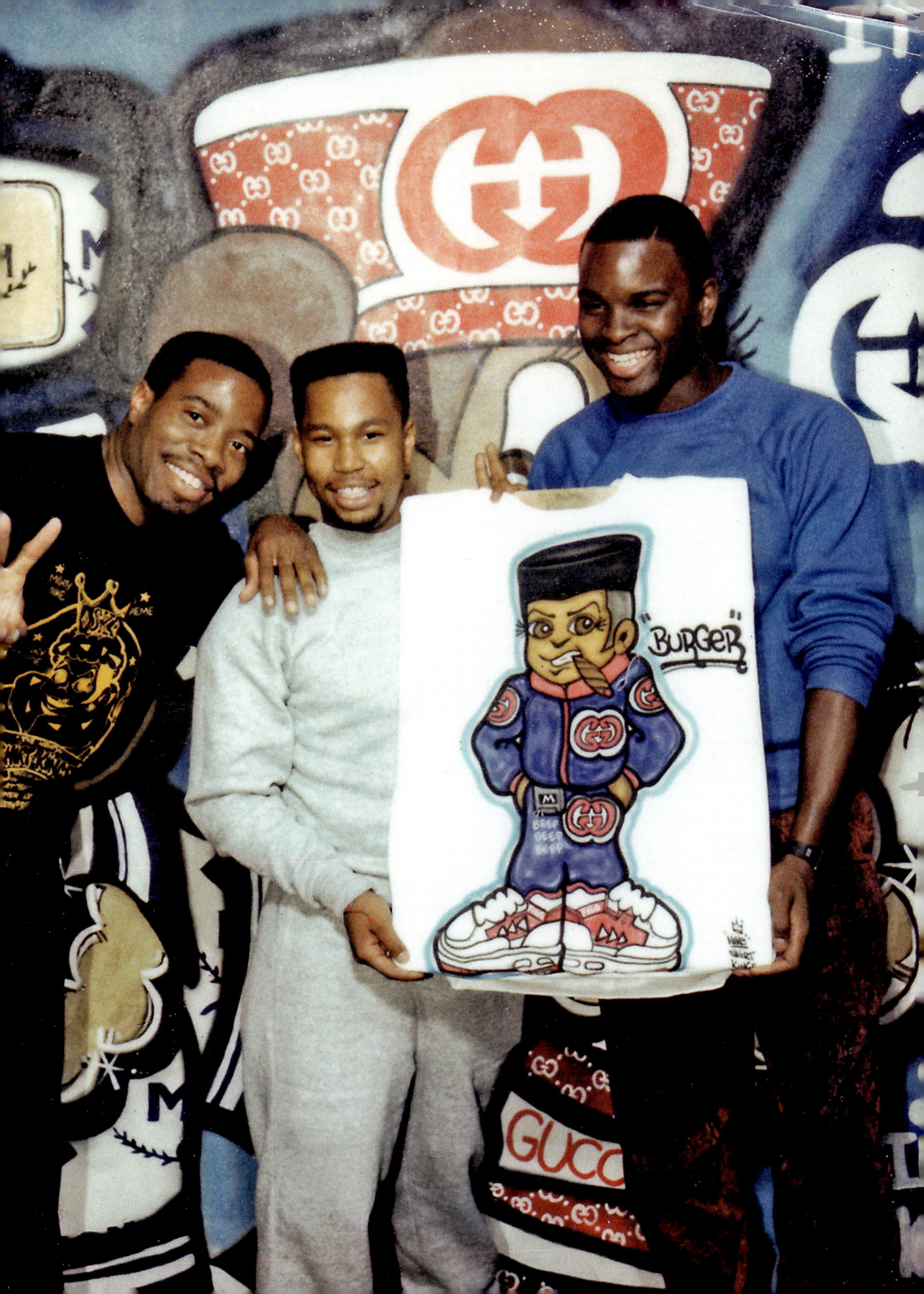
"BURGER"
BEEP BEEP BEEP

"The Shirt Kings have been the bomb since day one; since the days in the Coliseum in Queens and the first airbrushed jackets and banners I ever saw. They brought that texture of the hot tagging onto stuff for all the hot artists that I can remember in the game. Long live hip hop and long live the Shirt Kings."
Special K / Awesome 2

Jazz O from Long Island, Jamaica Coliseum, 1987.

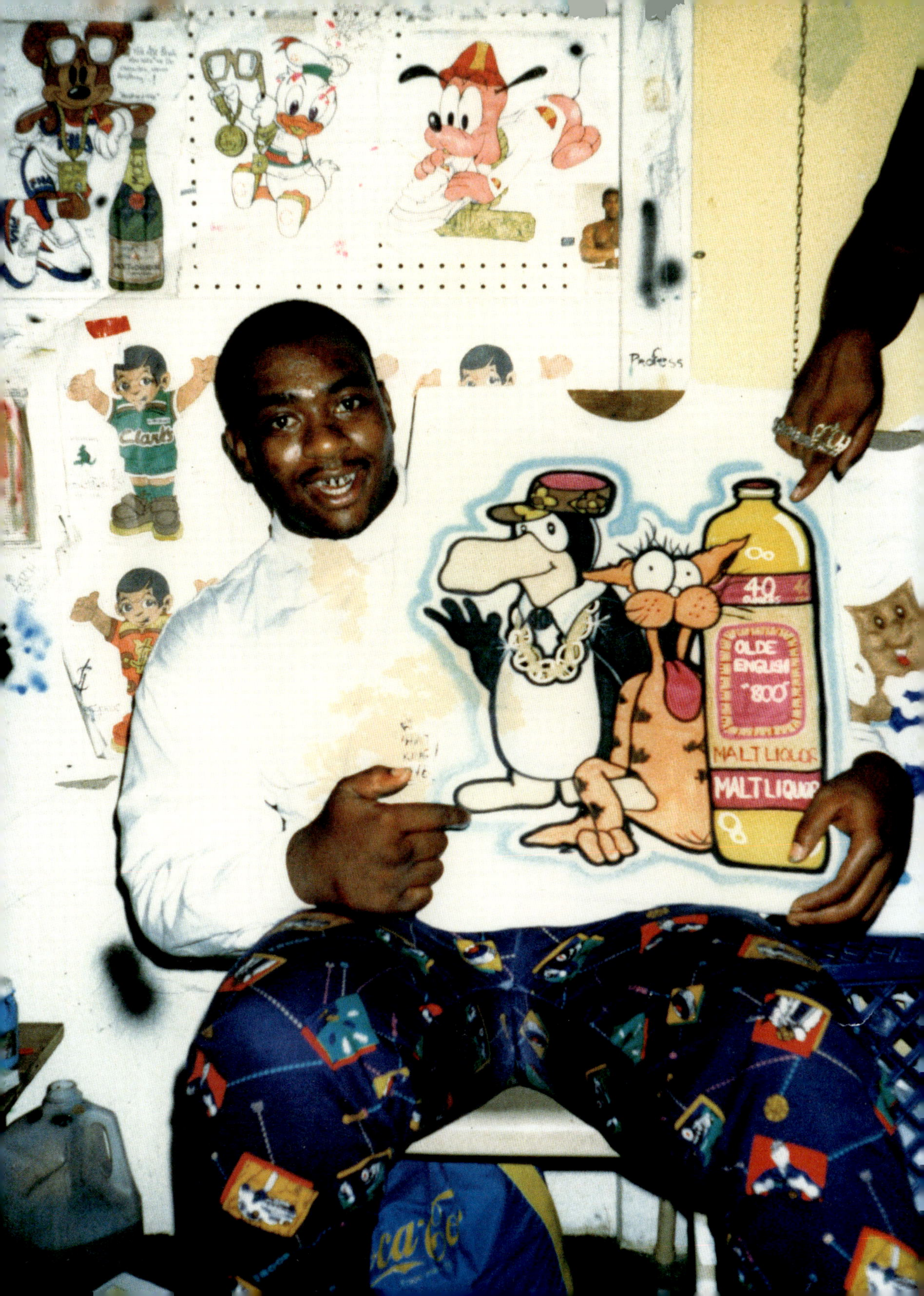
40
OLDE ENGLISH "800"
MALT LIQUOR
MALT LIQUOR

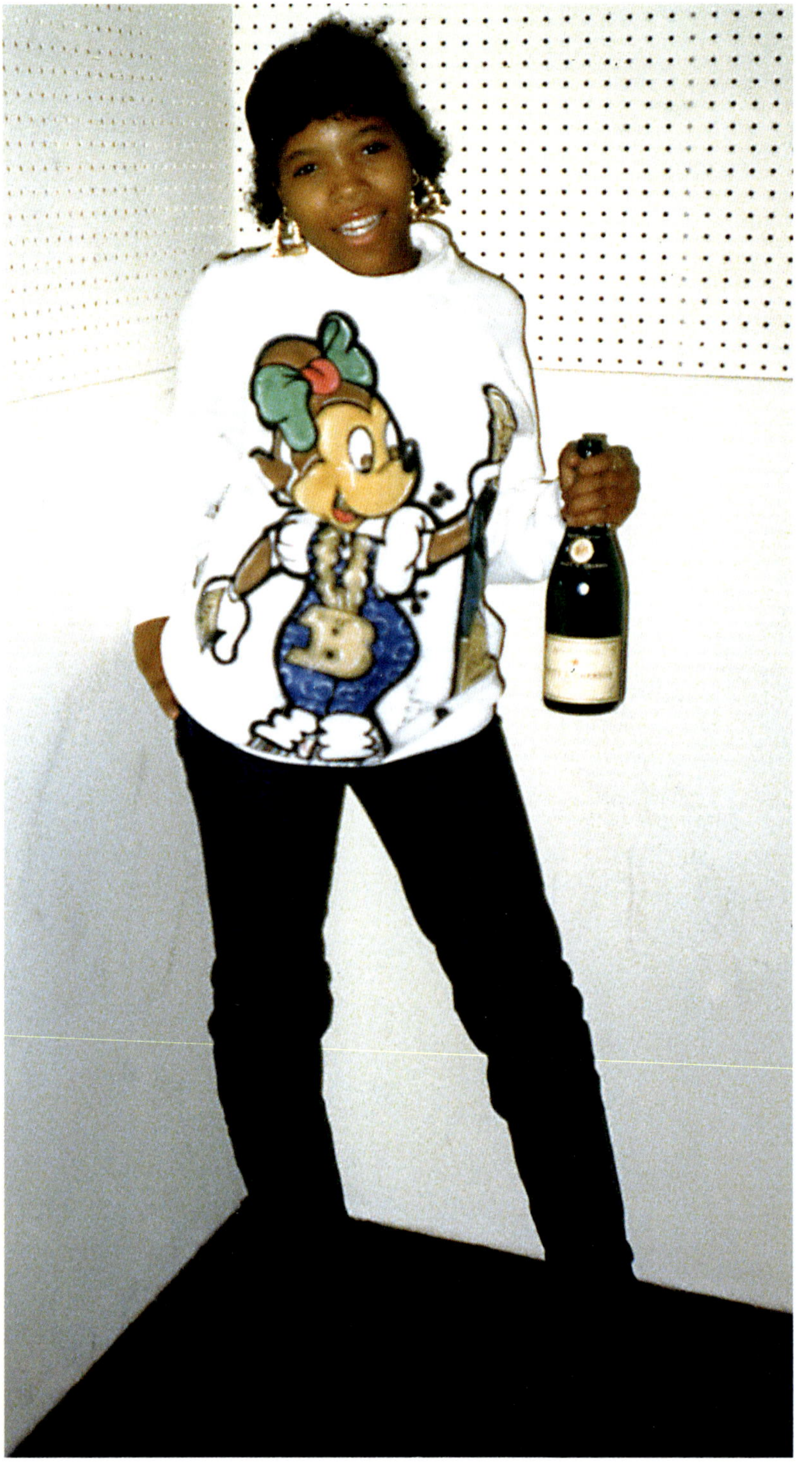

A customer with champagne wishes, Jamaica Coliseum, 1986.

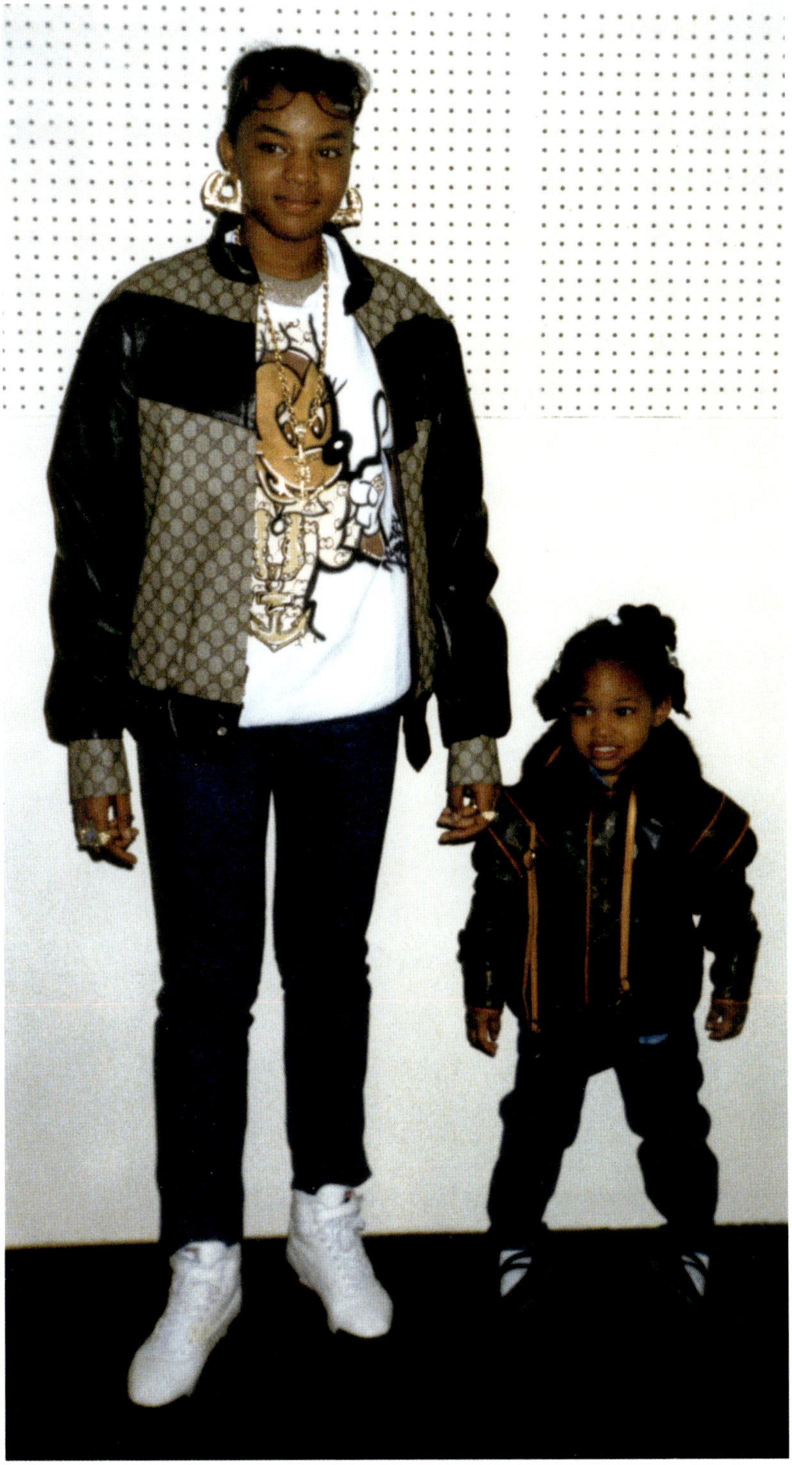

Tasja from South Side Jamaica, Queens, a proud customer wearing Dapper Dan and Shirt Kings, 1986.

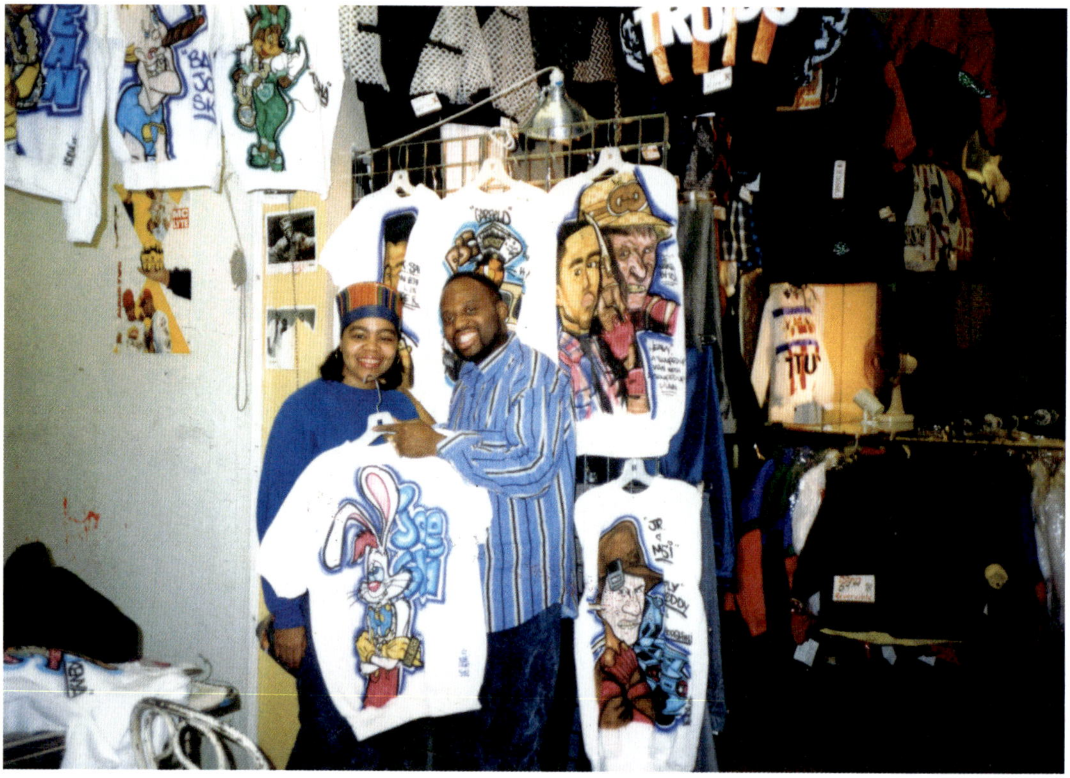

Above: Phade and a customer at the Shirt Kings booth**,** Jamaica Coliseum, 1987.
Opposite: Tamar from Rochdale Village, Jamaica Coliseum, 1987.

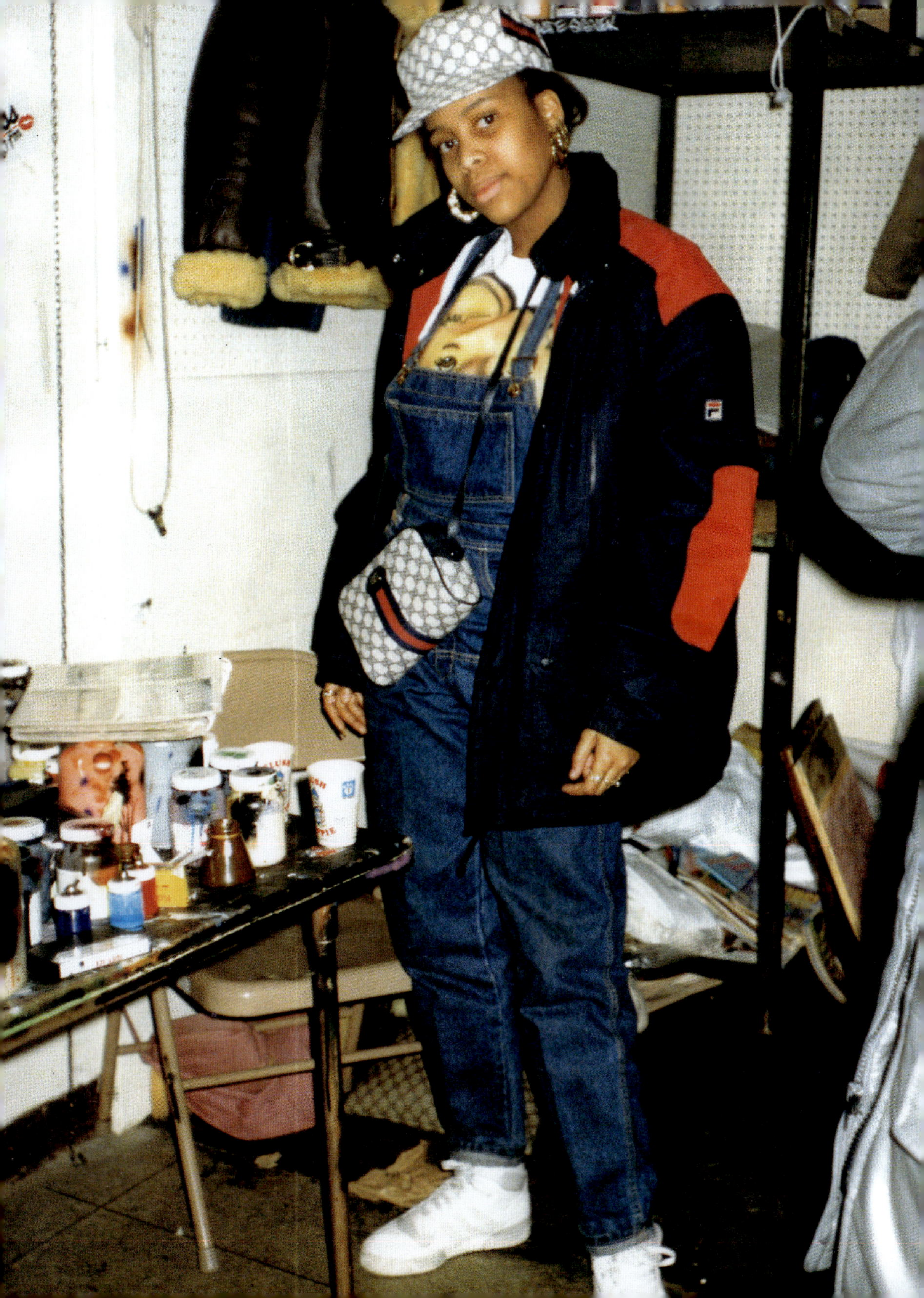

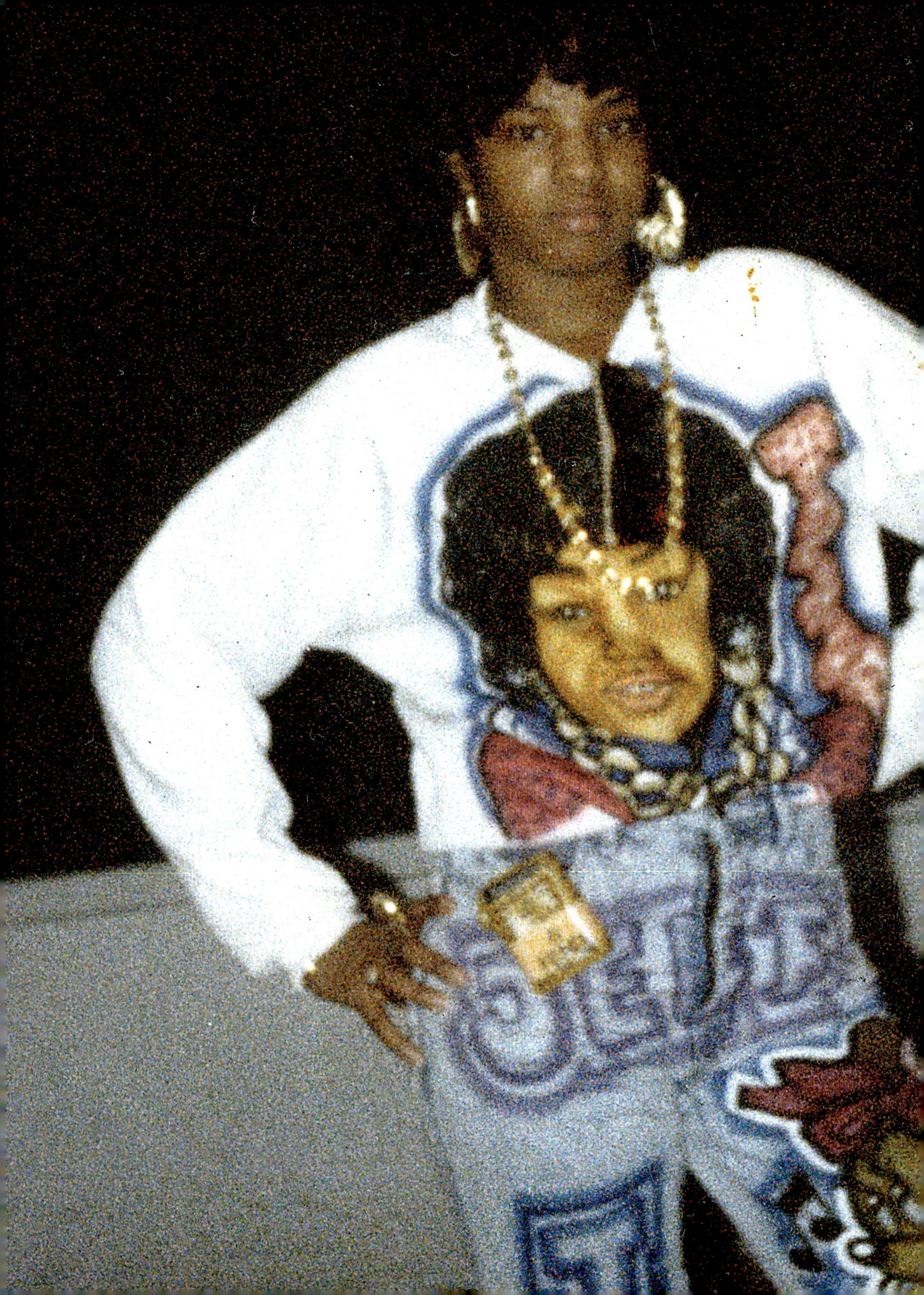

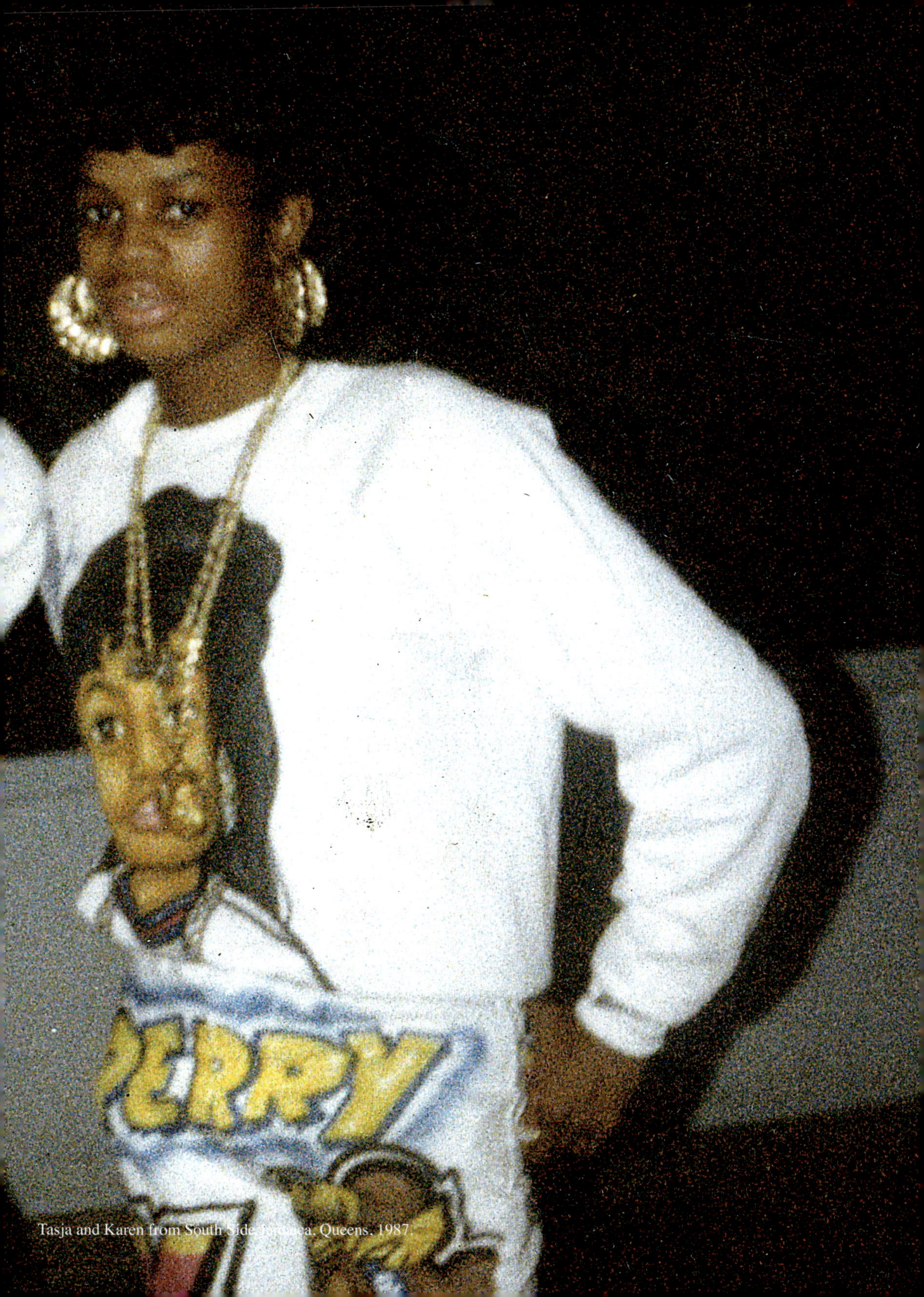

Tasja and Karen from South Side Jamaica, Queens, 1987.

"Before the commercial success of the hip hop clothing industry, before the commodification of the culture and before the phenomenon of the industrialized monotone hip hop uniform there was Ed 'Shirt King Phade' Sacasa. Ed comes from the days of do-it-yourself shine when imagination and flavor spoke volumes about your style and finesse. The man is a straight pioneer, paving the way for the hip hop designer."

Devious Doze TC5

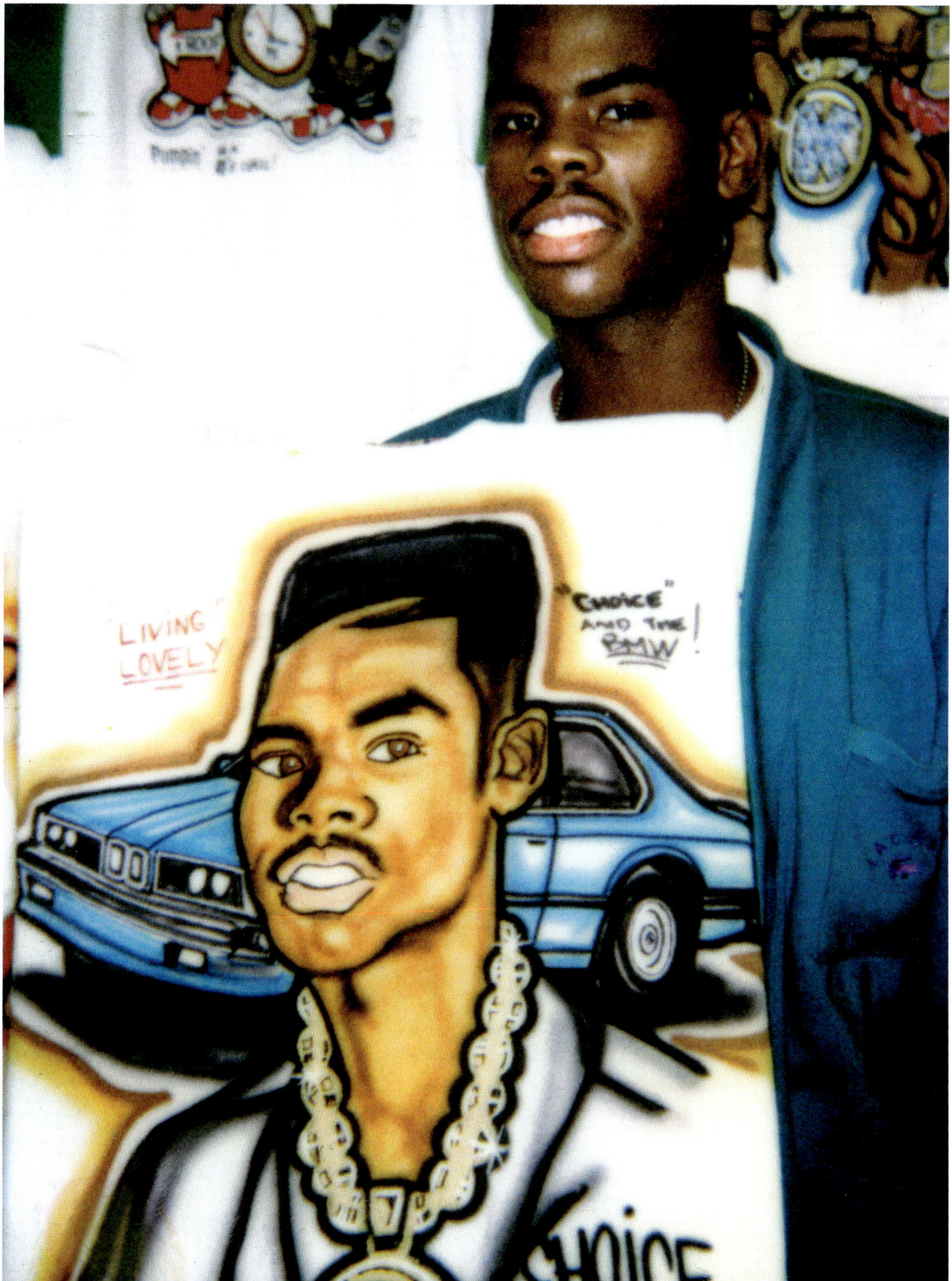

Choice, Jamaica Coliseum, 1987.

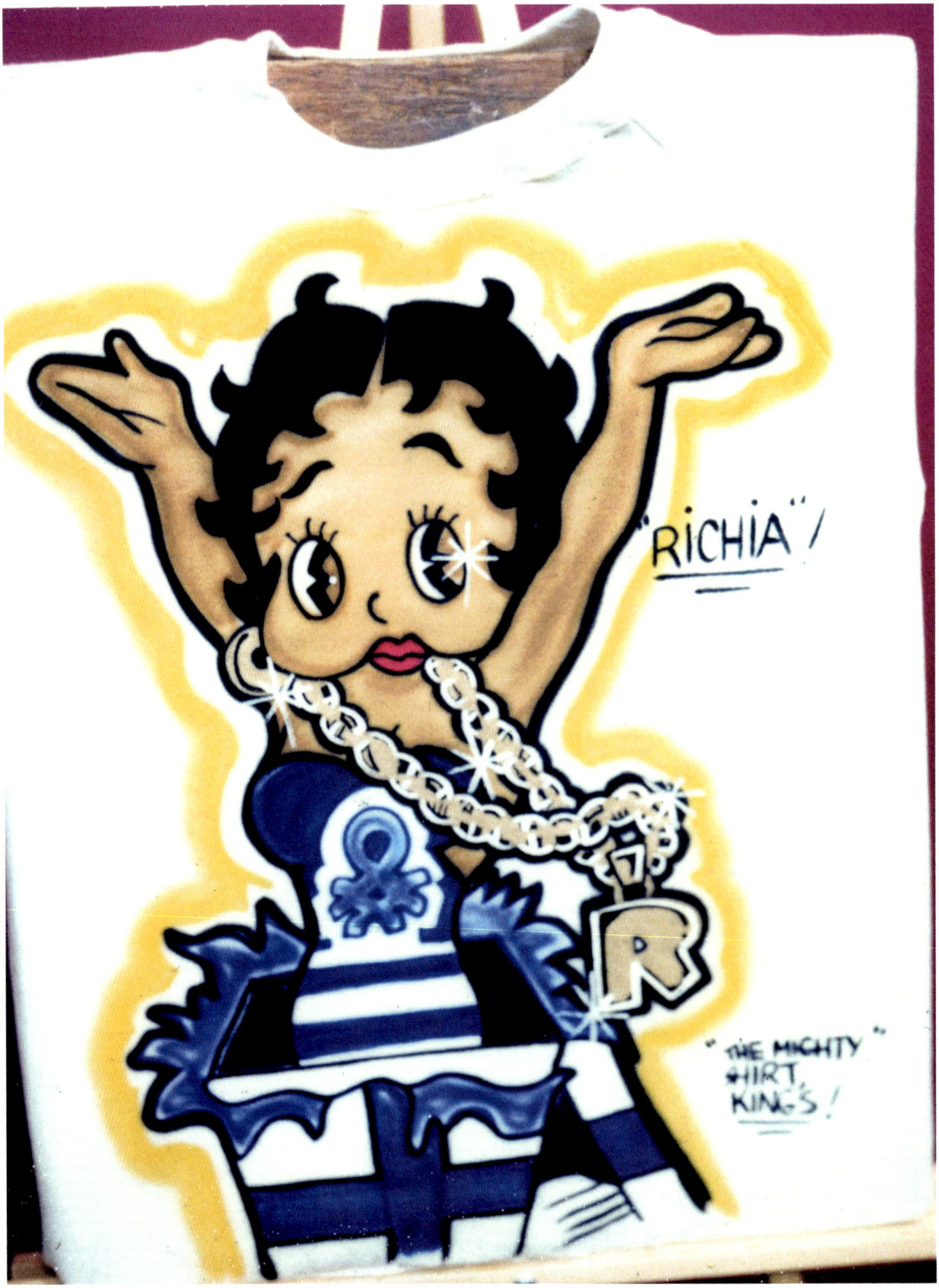

Betty Boop Benneton for Richia, 1987.

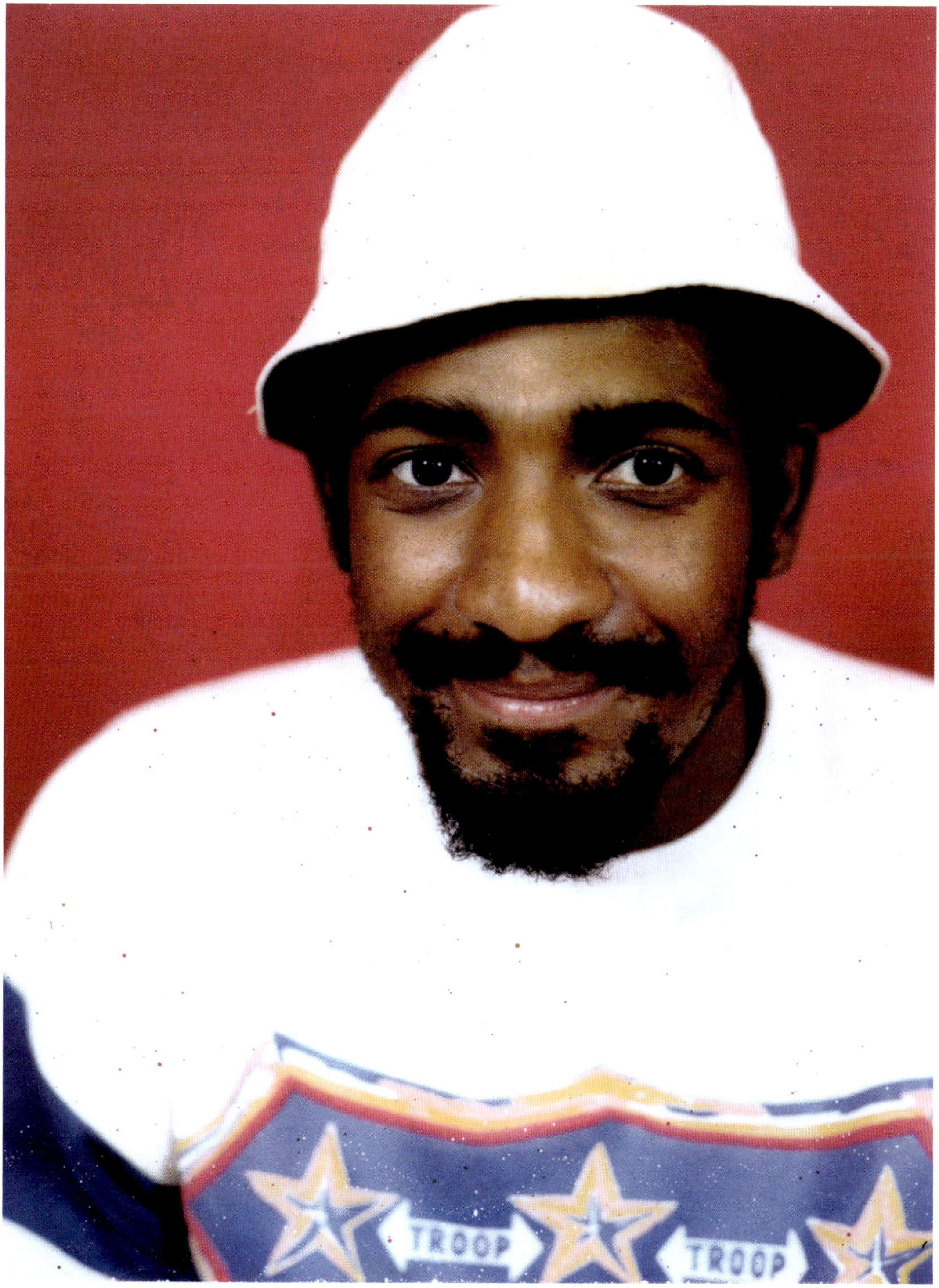

Donna's husband, Jamaica Coliseum, 1986.

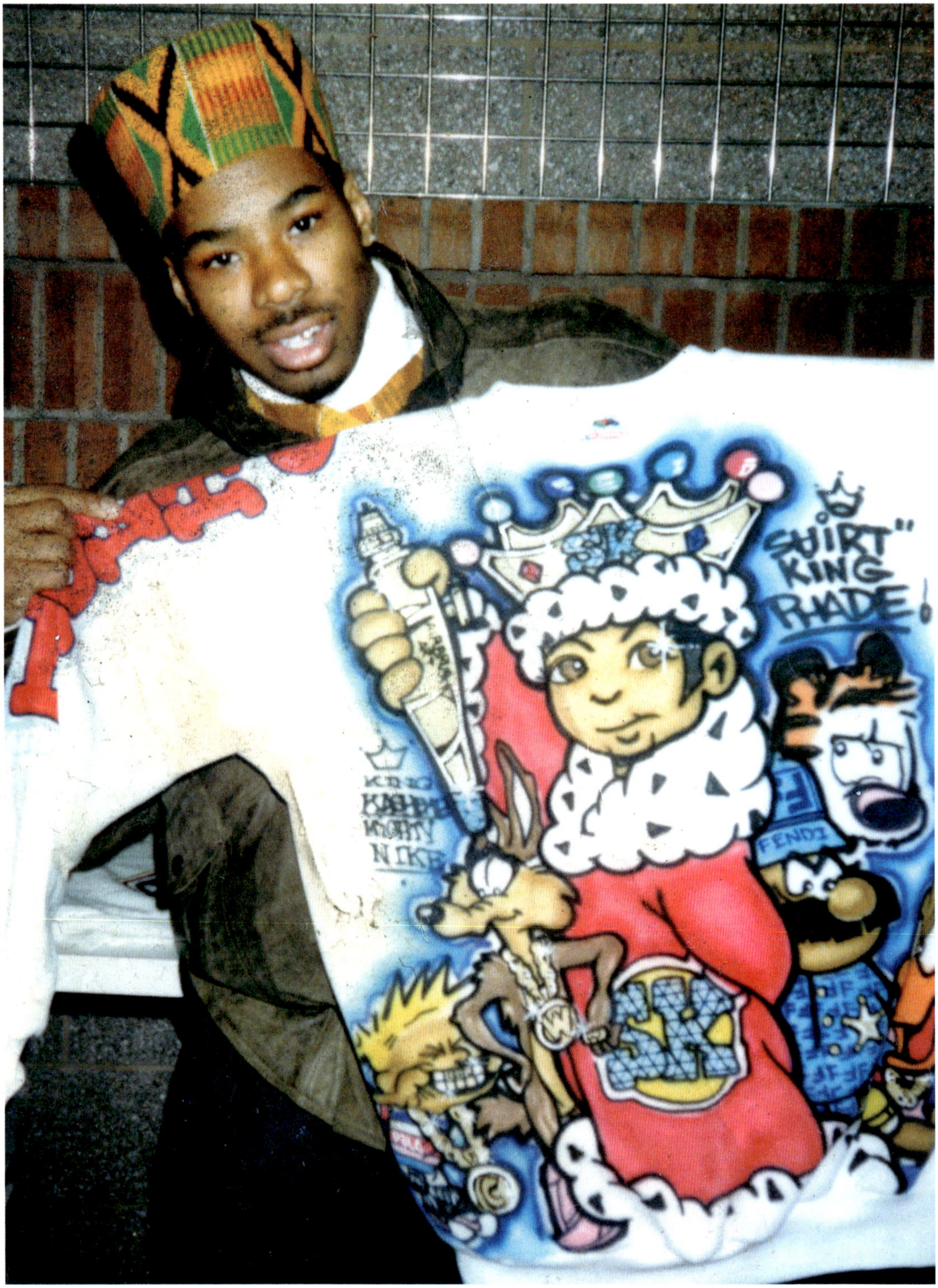

This page: G-Wiz, Mart 125, 1989. **Right:** Prince Messiah, Jamaica Coliseum, 1987.

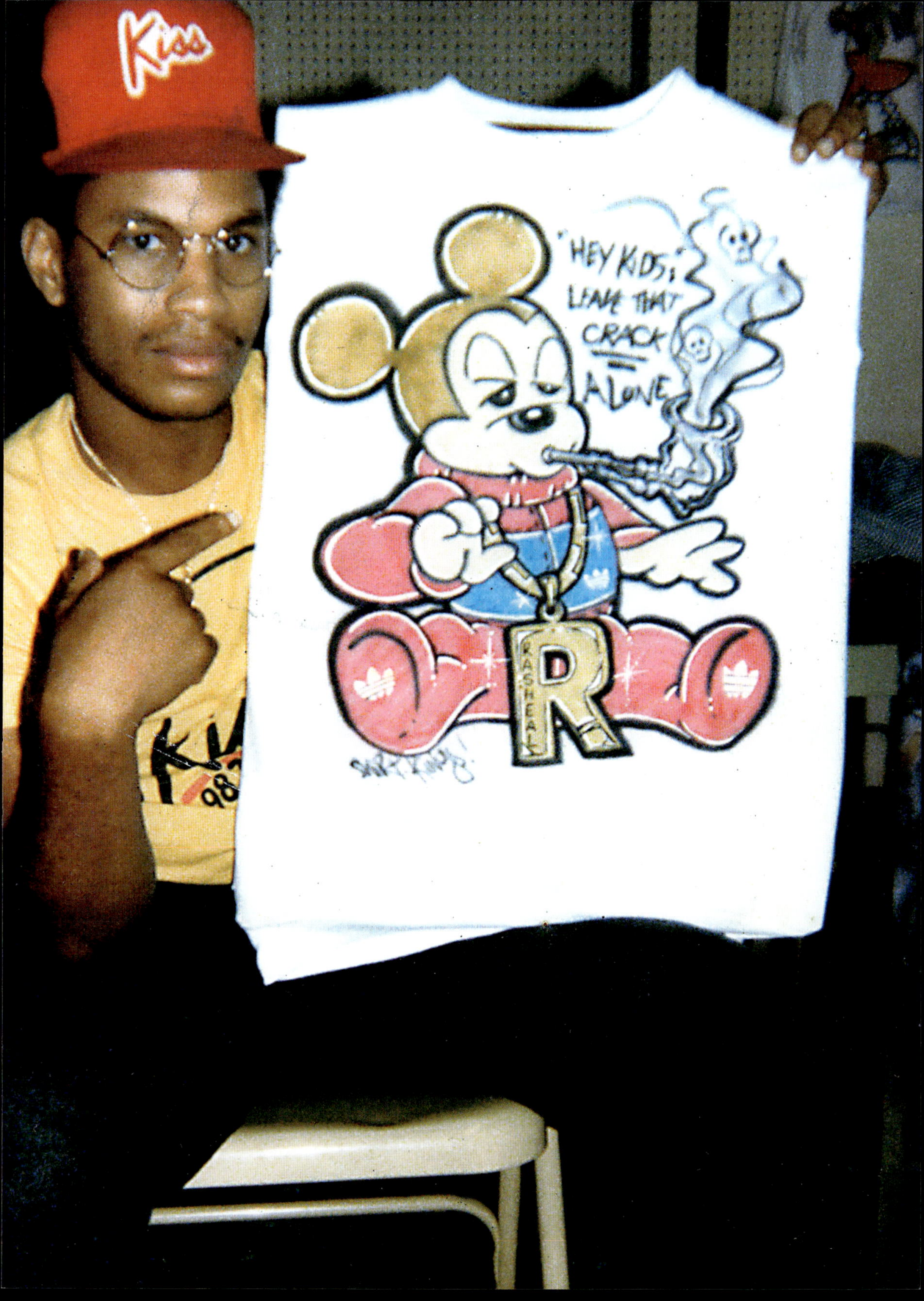
Kiss
"HEY KIDS, LEAVE THAT CRACK ALONE"
R
RASHEAL

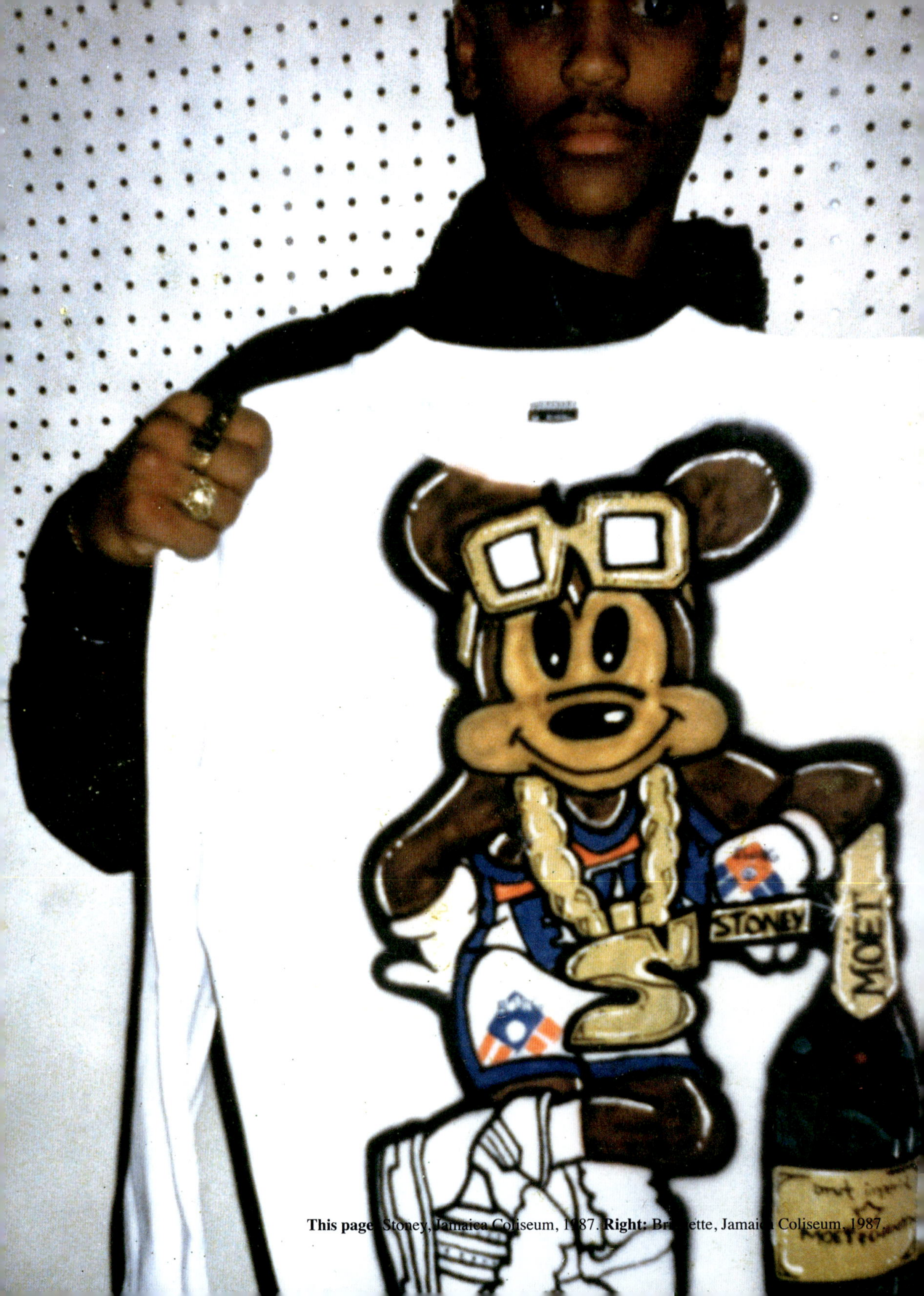

This page: Stoney, Jamaica Coliseum, 1987. **Right:** Brigette, Jamaica Coliseum, 1987.

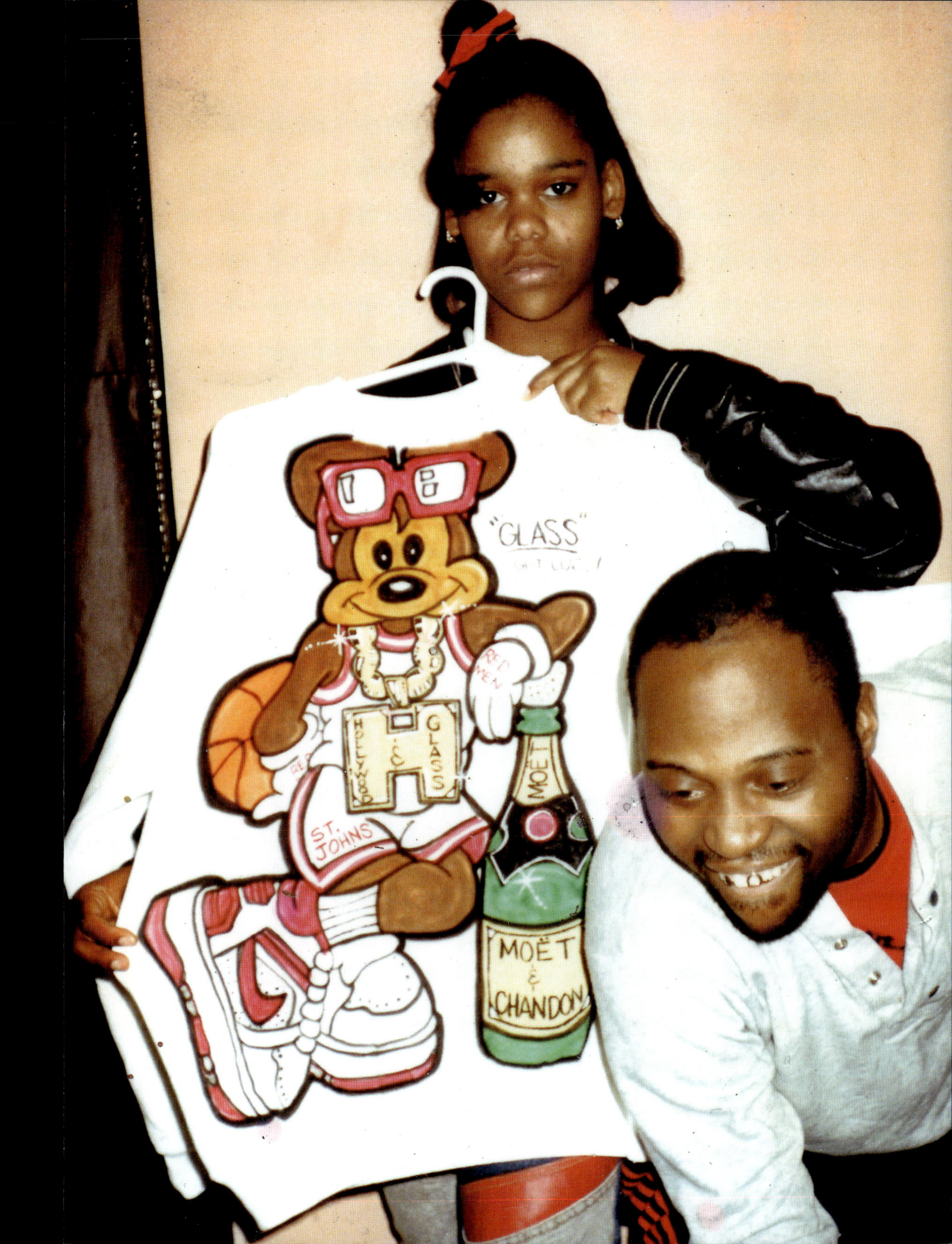
"GLASS"
HOLLYWOOD
GLASS
ST. JOHNS
MOËT
MOËT & CHANDON

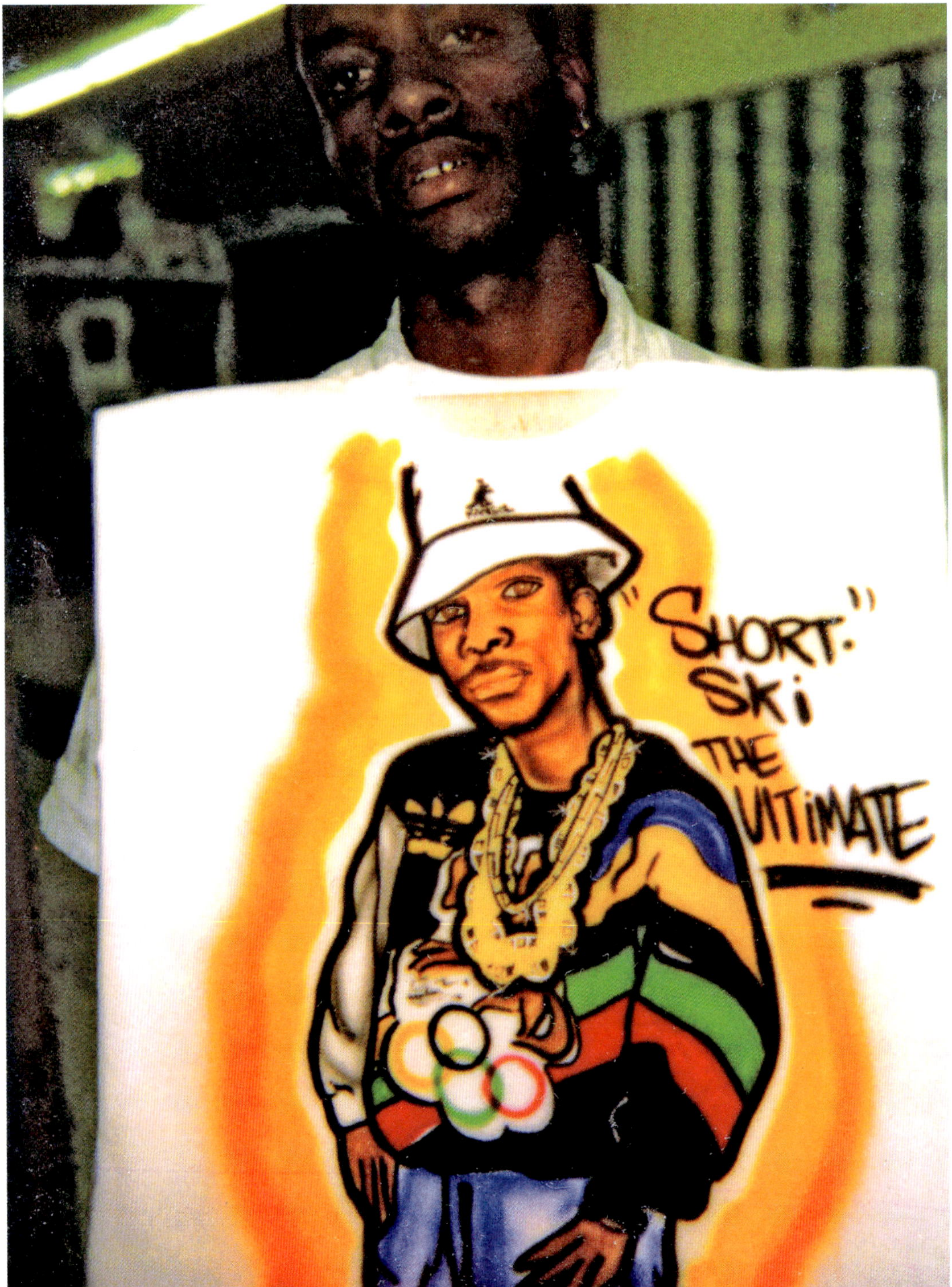

Short Ski, Miami, 1988.

"The Shirt Kings represented a time of art brought to life in hip hop — making something out of nothing."
MC Lyte

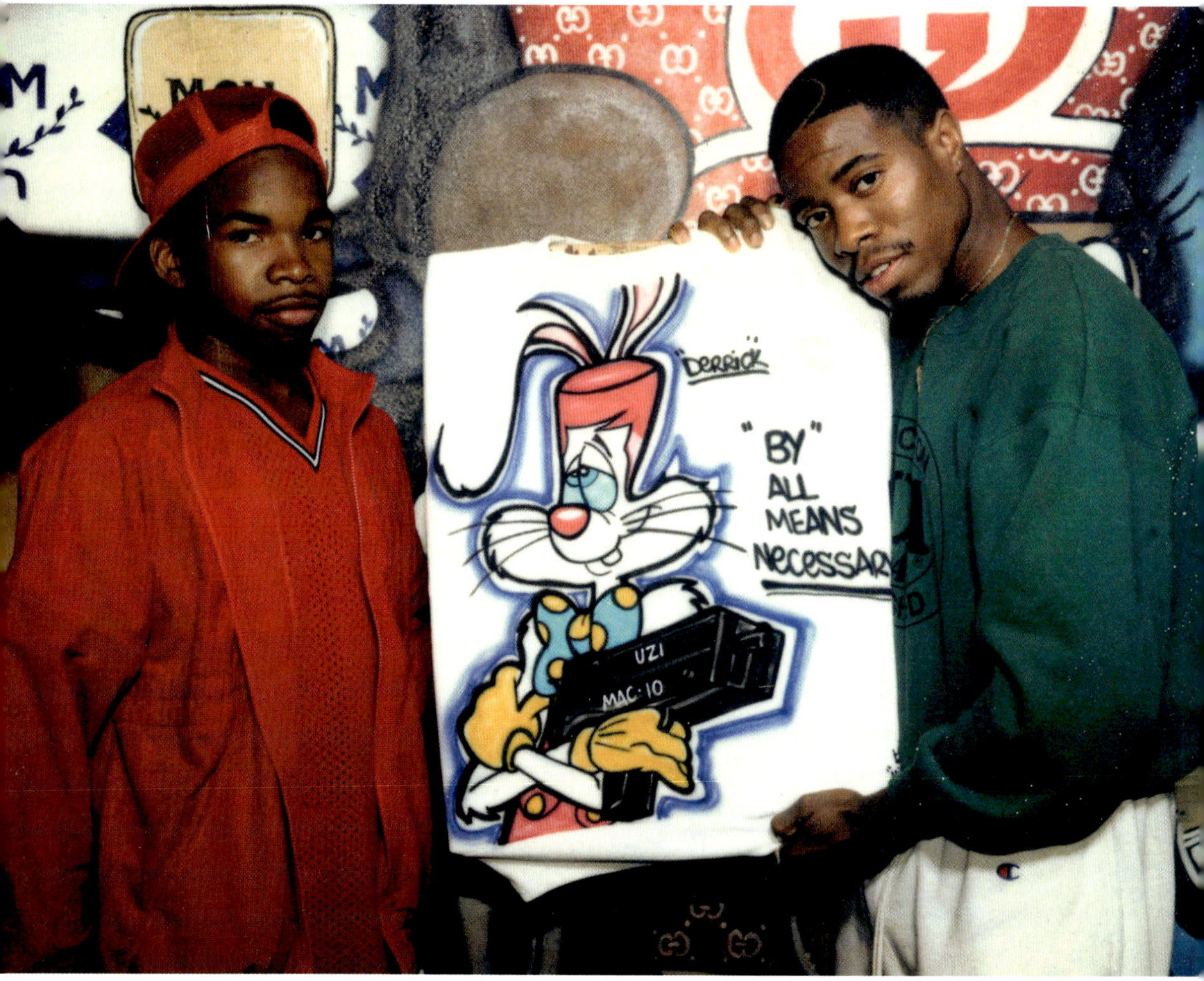

Derrick's Roger Rabbit shirt by Nike, Jamaica Coliseum, 1987.

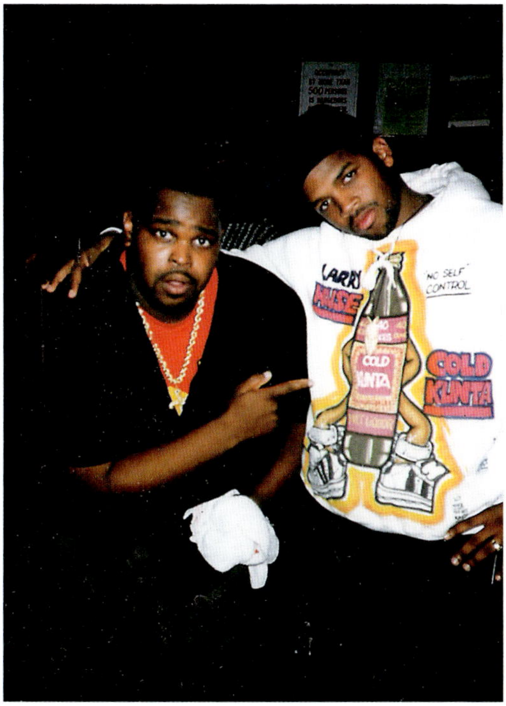

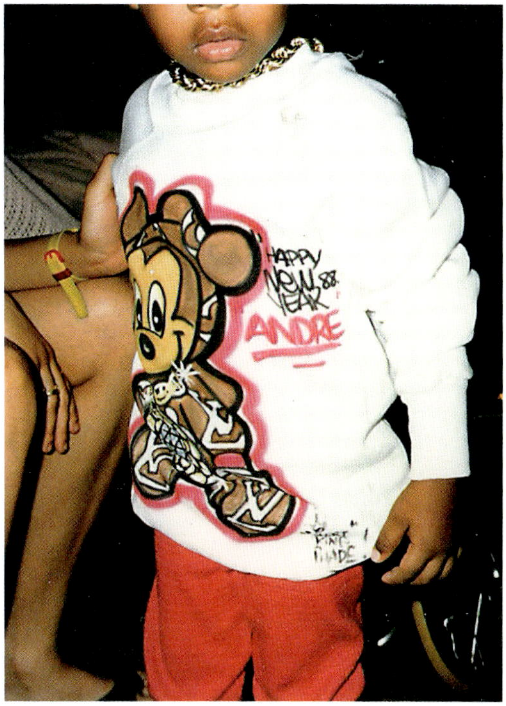

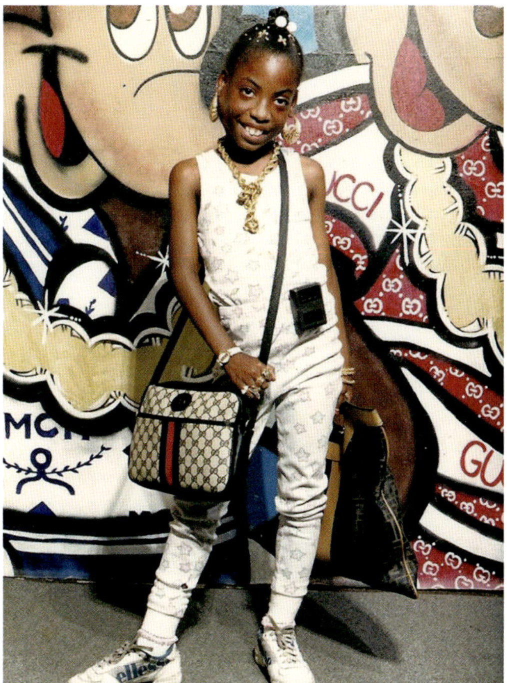

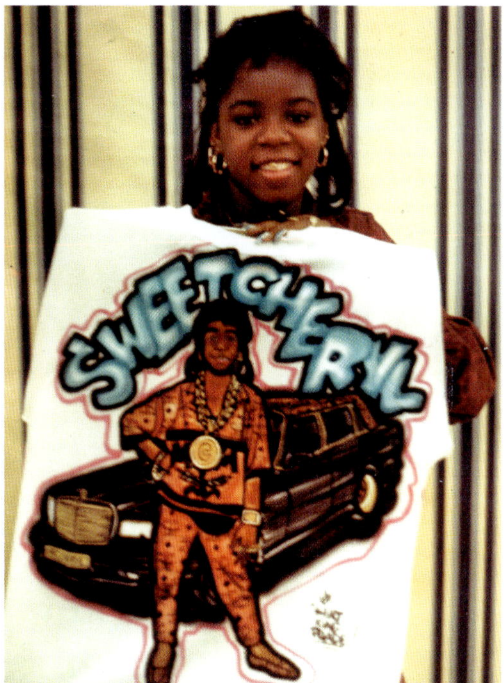

Clockwise from top left: Cold Kunta in Queens, Andre in the Bronx, Cheryl in Miami, and Aisha at the Coliseum, 1987-1988.

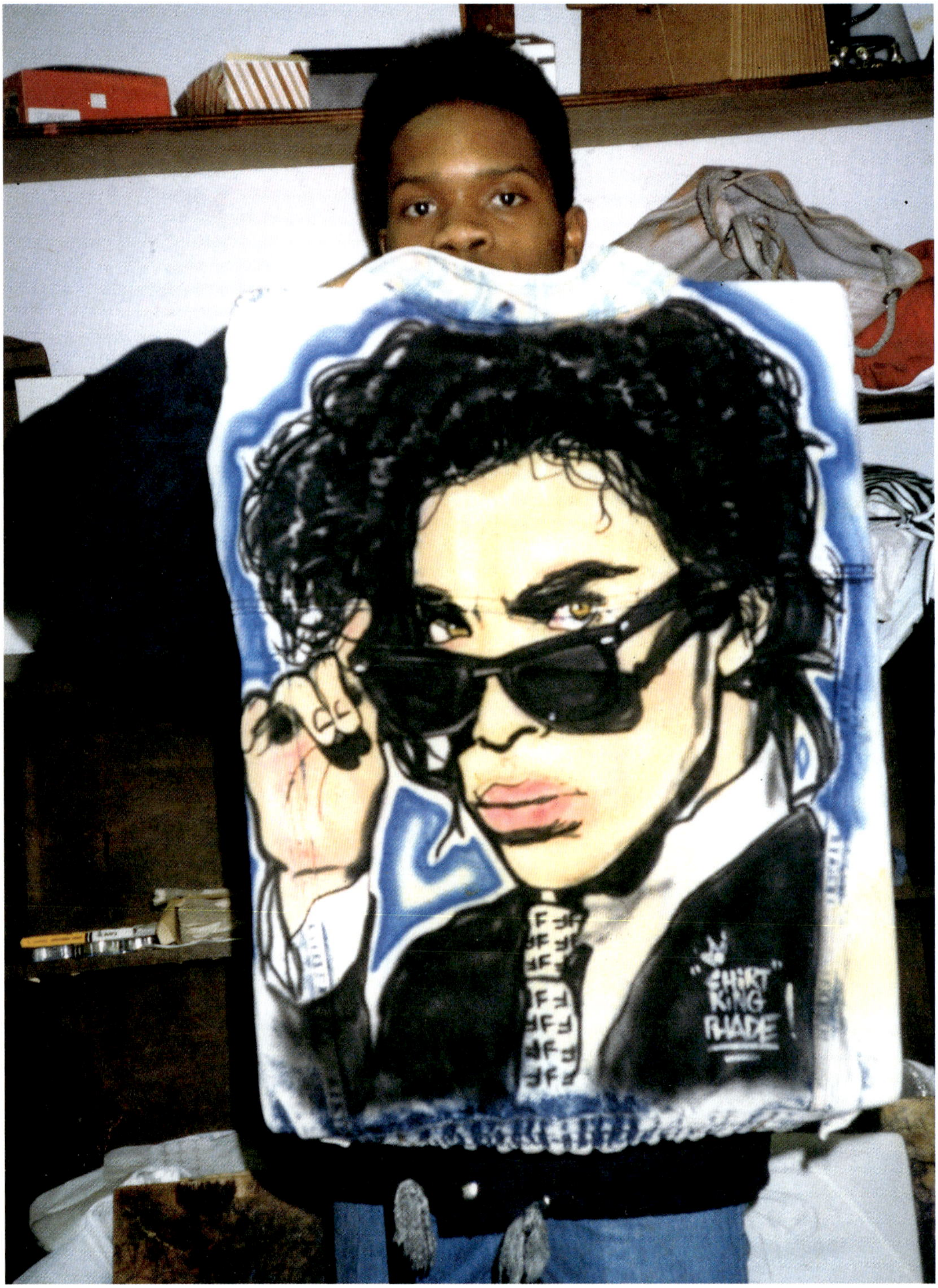

Derrick with his Prince jacket, Jamaica Coliseum, 1989.

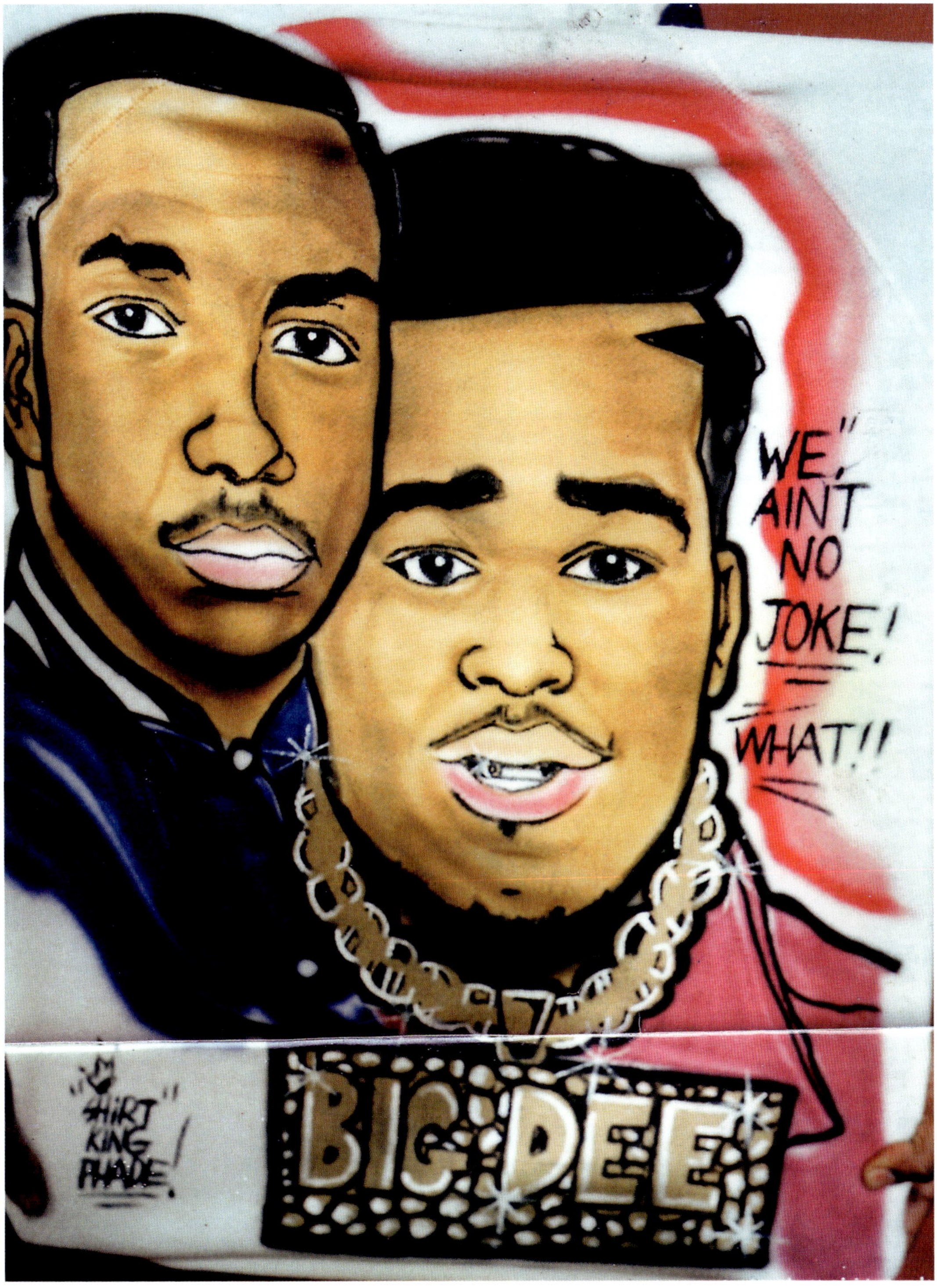

Big Dee, Jamaica Coliseum, 1987.

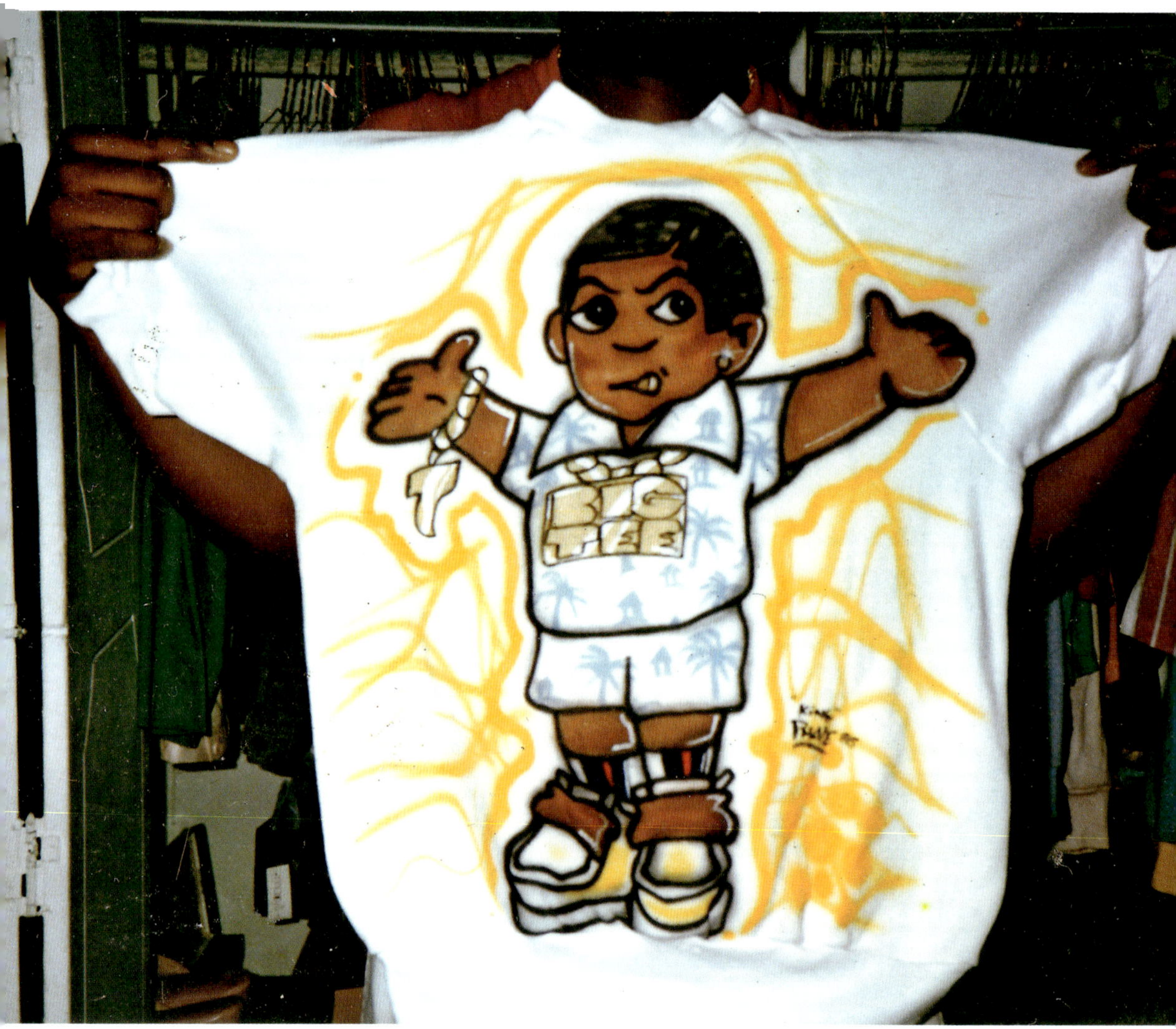

Big Tee, the Bronx, 1989.

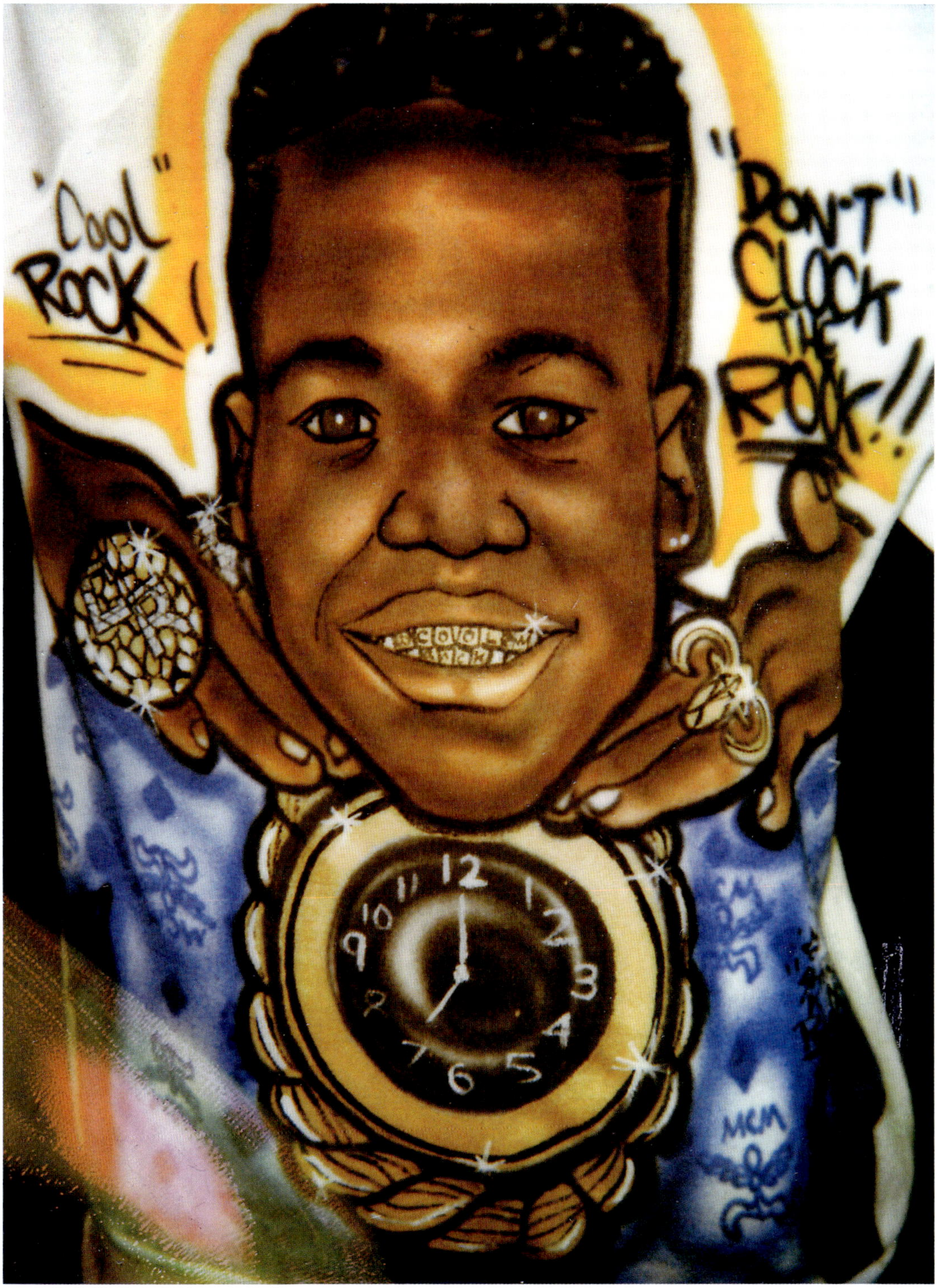

Cool Rock, Miami, 1988.

"As far as peaking my interest and me saying 'oh that's fly, that's cool, that's unique', the Shirt Kings were definitely real influential. I remember all the photos, I used to love to come to the booth and see the shirts they were getting made, the sweat hoods, the sneakers, and all the different things they were doing."
LL Cool J

Opposite page: Shirt King Phade at work, Jamaica Coliseum, 1987.

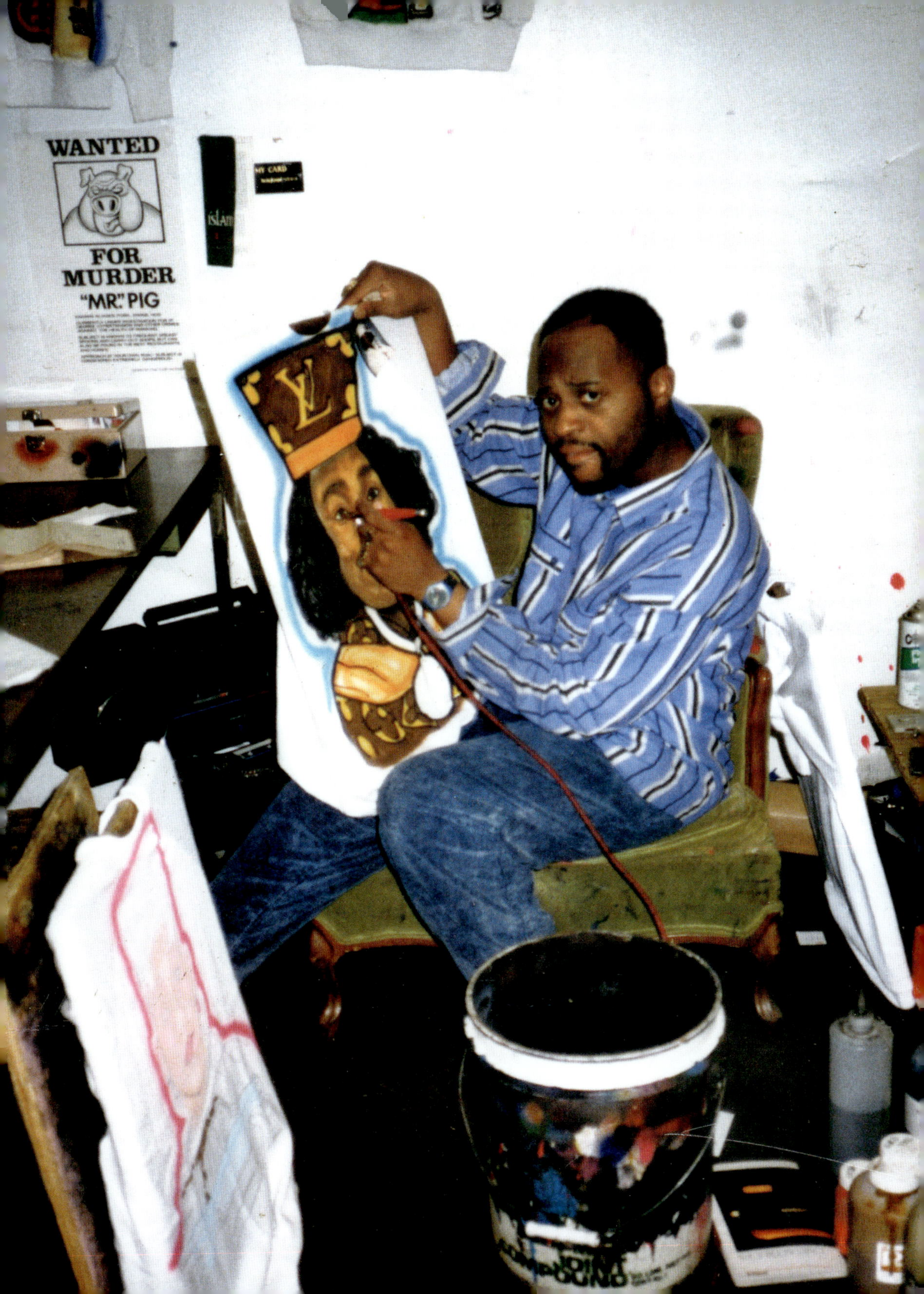
WANTED
FOR
MURDER
"MR." PIG

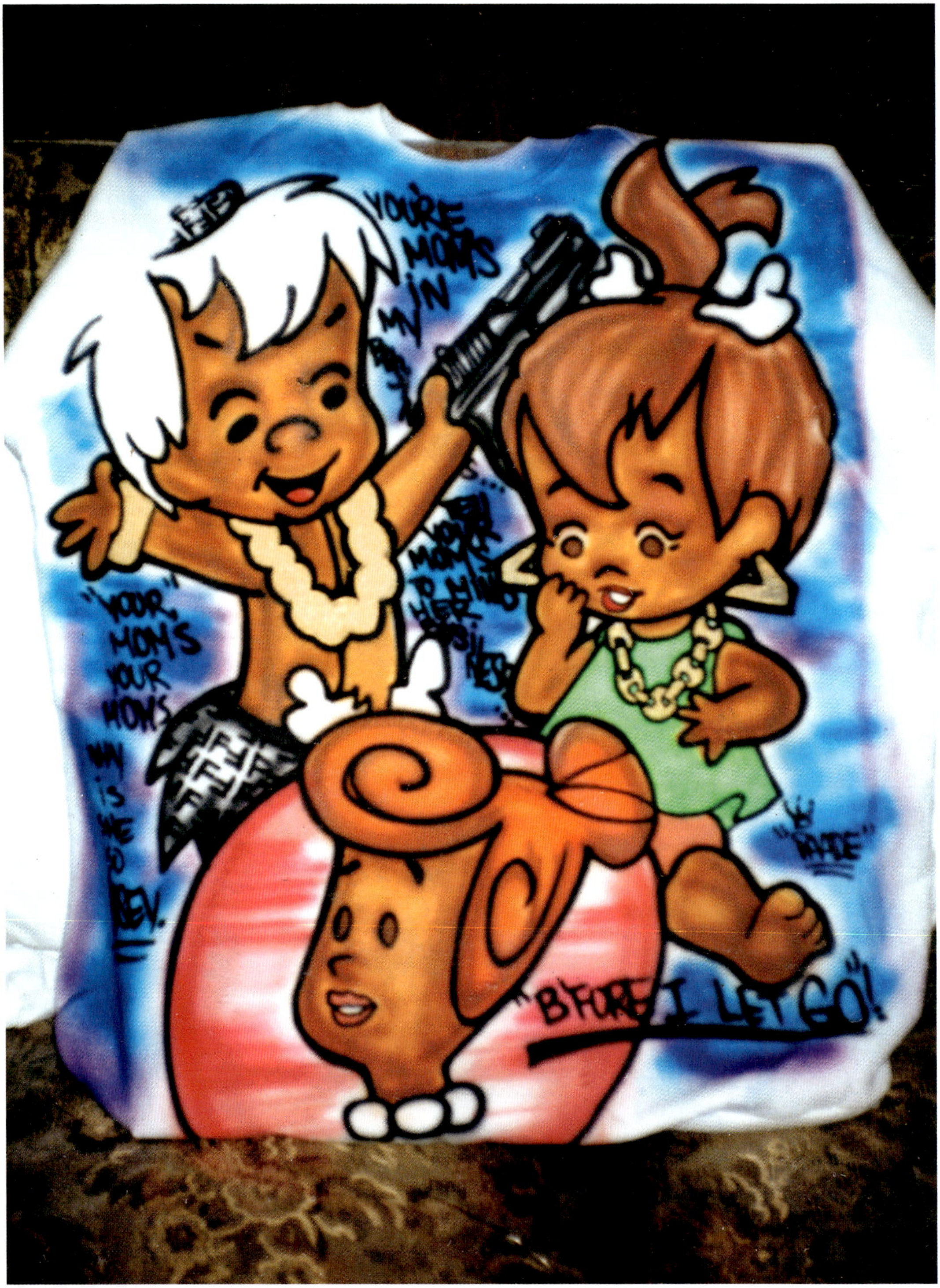

K-Solo meets the Flinstones, the Bronx, 1990.

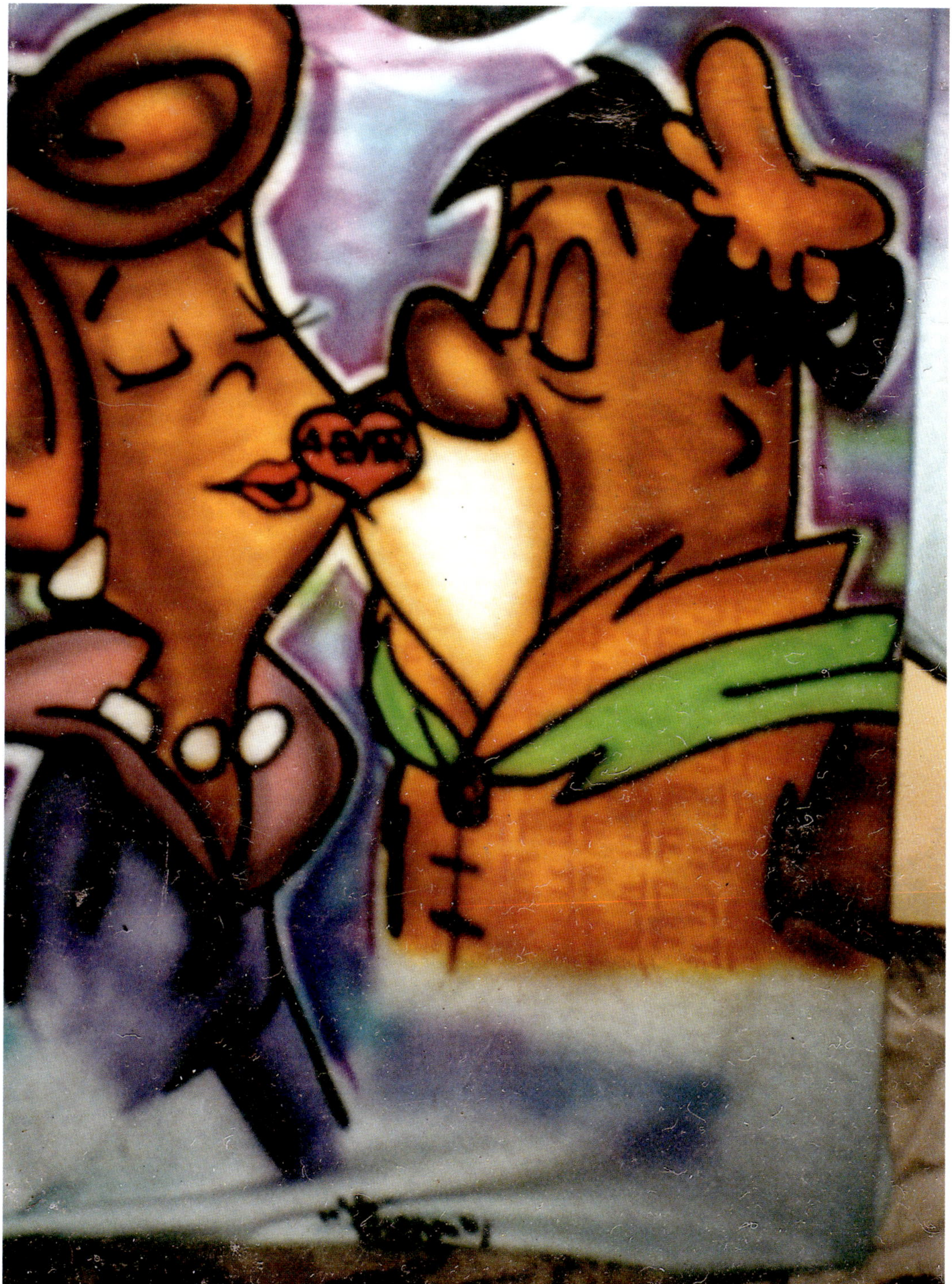

Wilma and Fendi Fred, Baltimore, 1990.

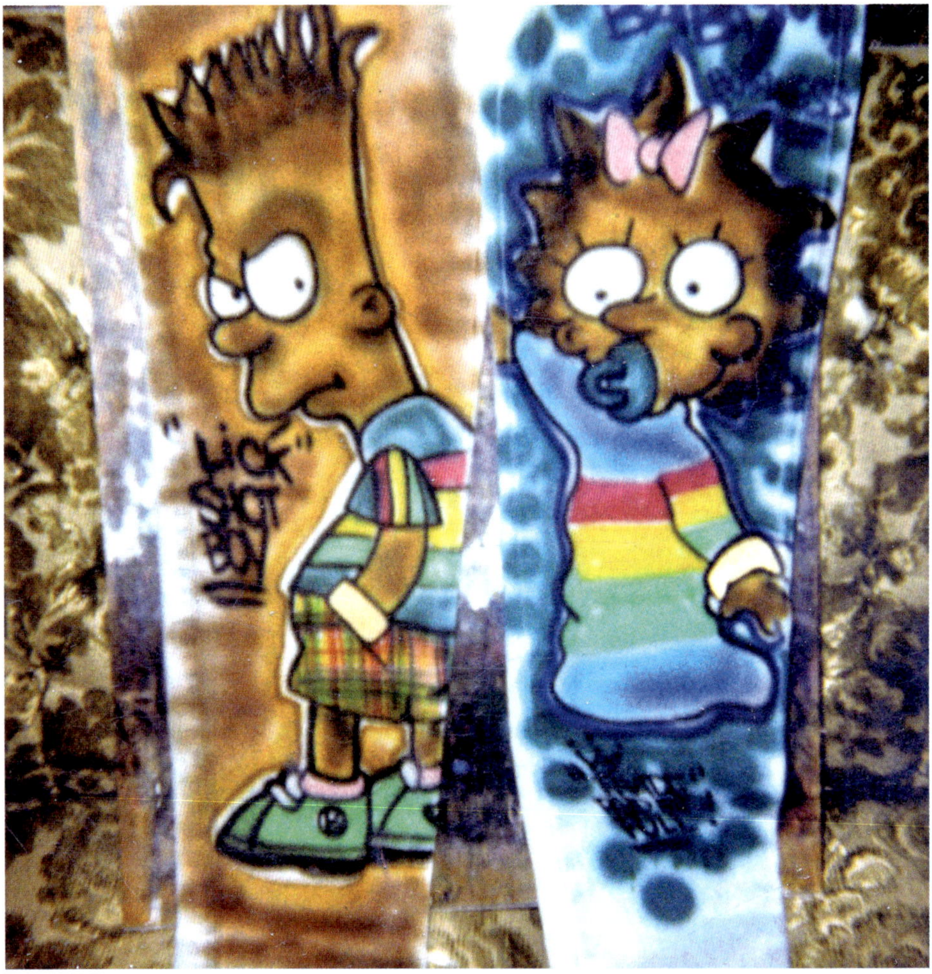

The Jamaican Simpsons for Bigga Pong, the Bronx, 1990.

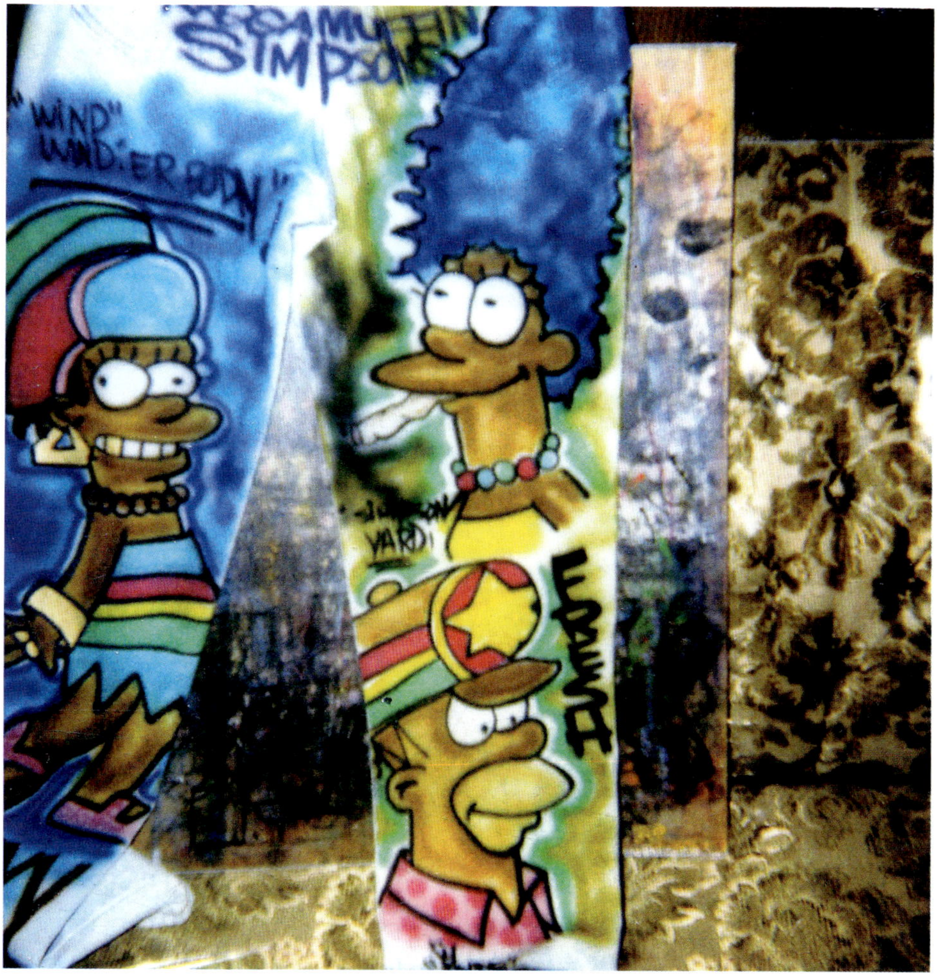

The Jamaican Simpsons for Bigga Pong, the Bronx, 1990.

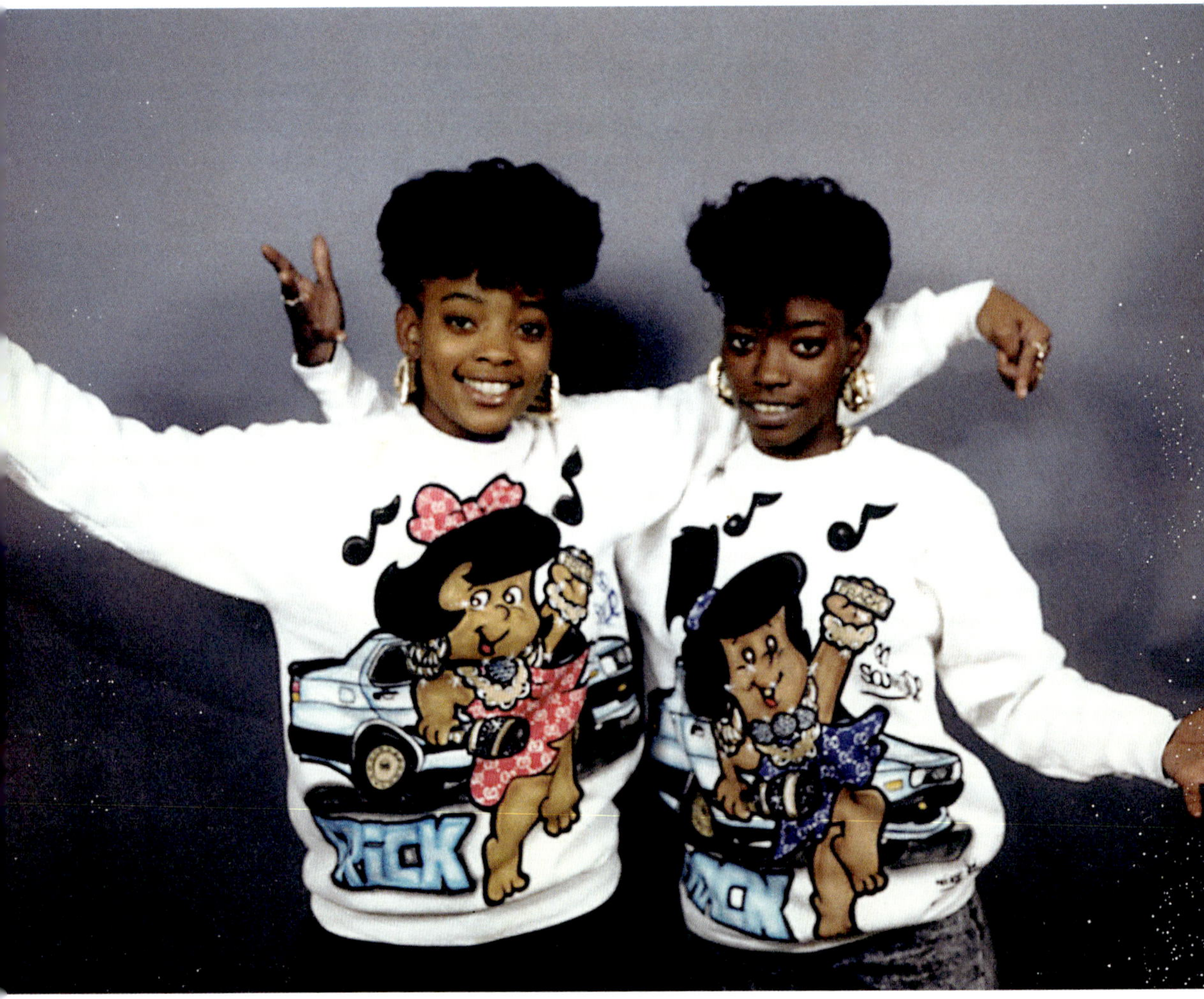

Frick and Frack, Jamaica Coliseum, 1987.

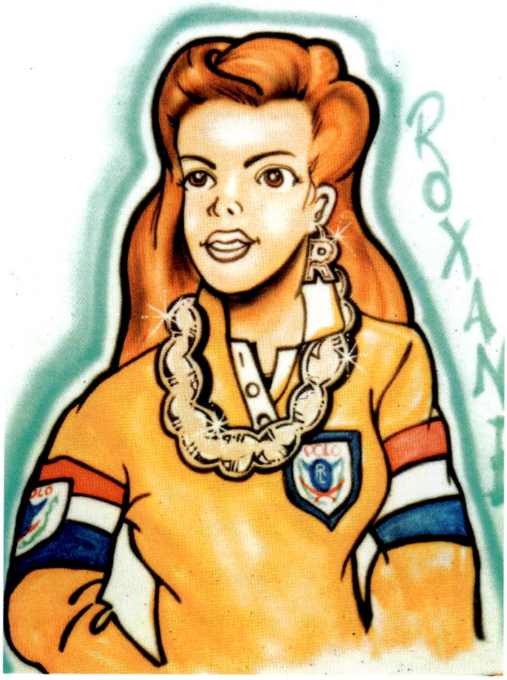

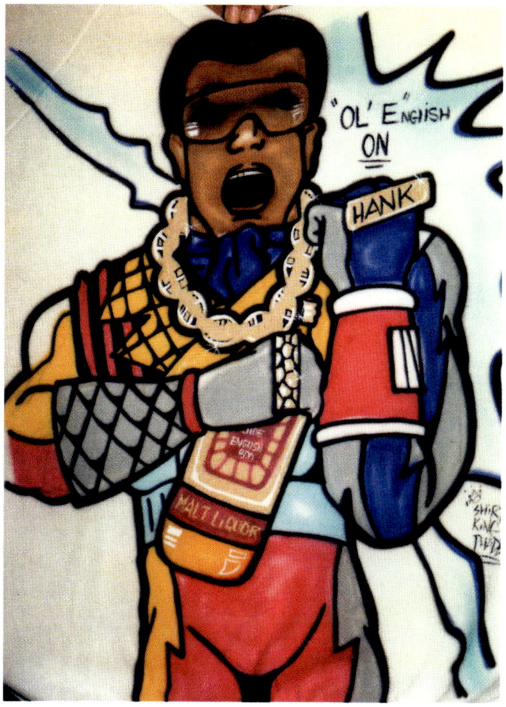

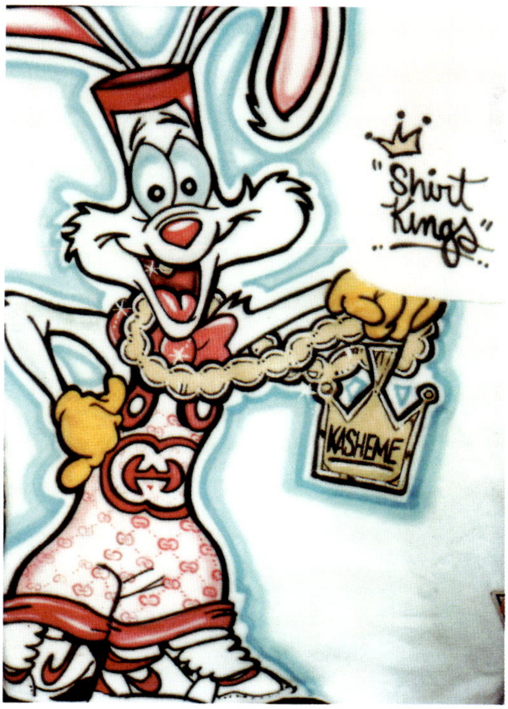

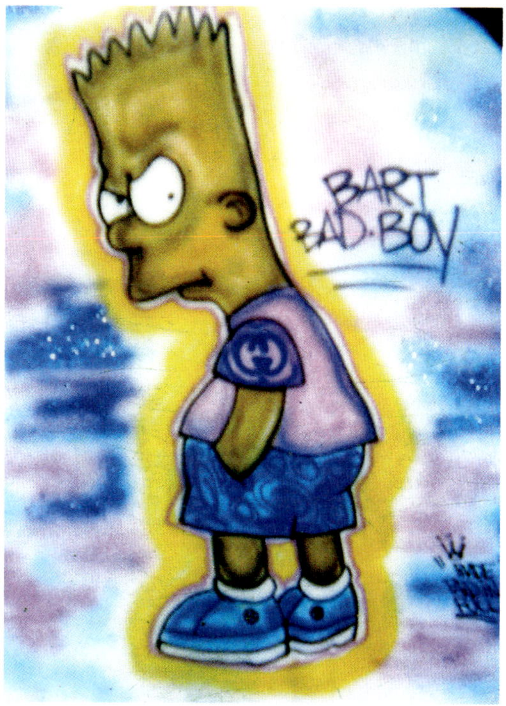

Clockwise from top left: Roxanne by Kasheme, Bionic 6 by Phade, Bart by Phade, Roger Rabbit by Kasheme, 1987-1990.

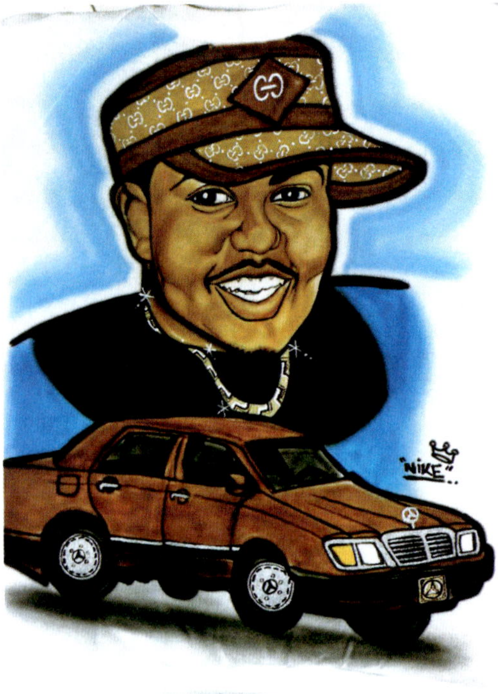

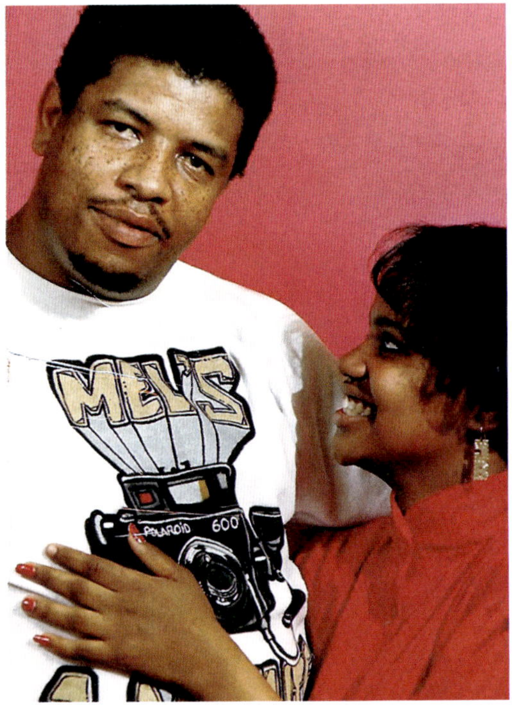

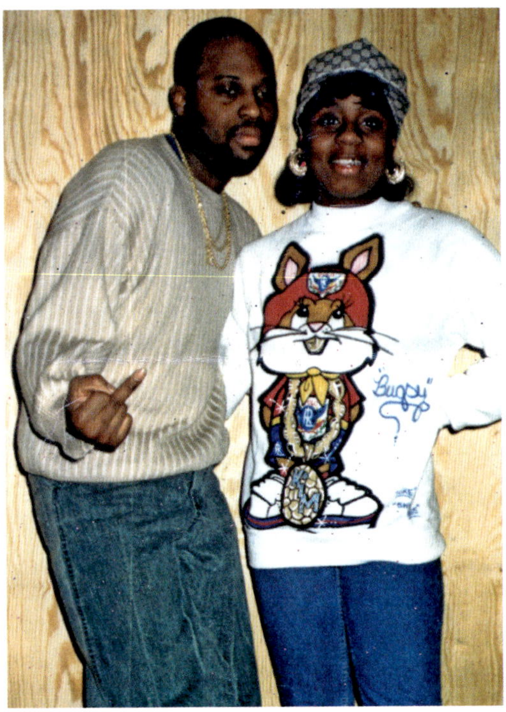

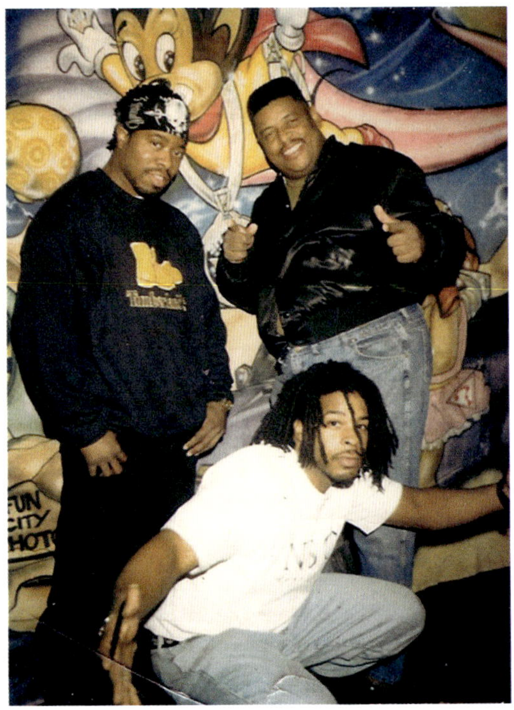

Clockwise from top left: Nike design, 1989. Mel and Janette, 1988. Mel and the crew, 1992. Phade and his Bugsy design, 1987.

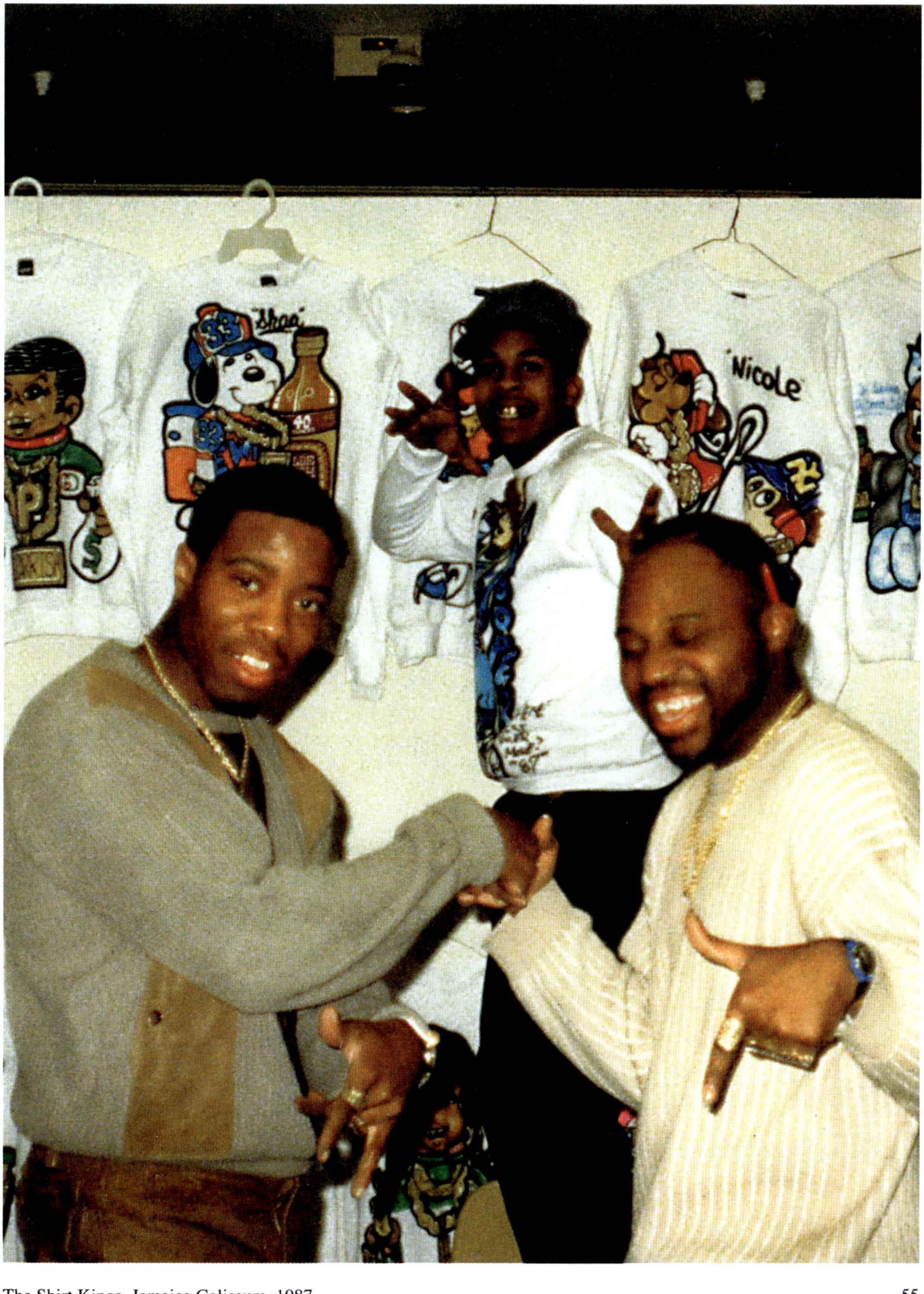

The Shirt Kings, Jamaica Coliseum, 1987.

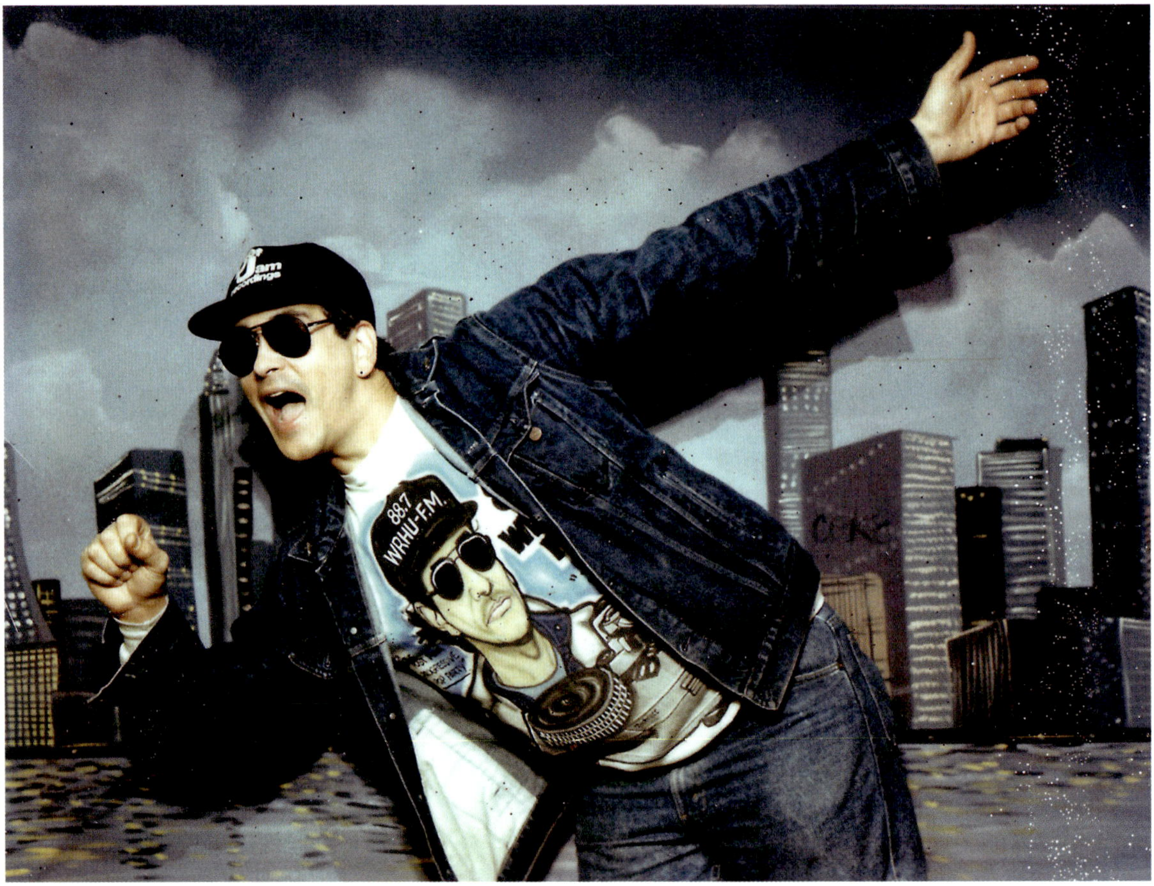

Above: Radio jock Jeff Foss, Jamaica Coliseum, 1987.

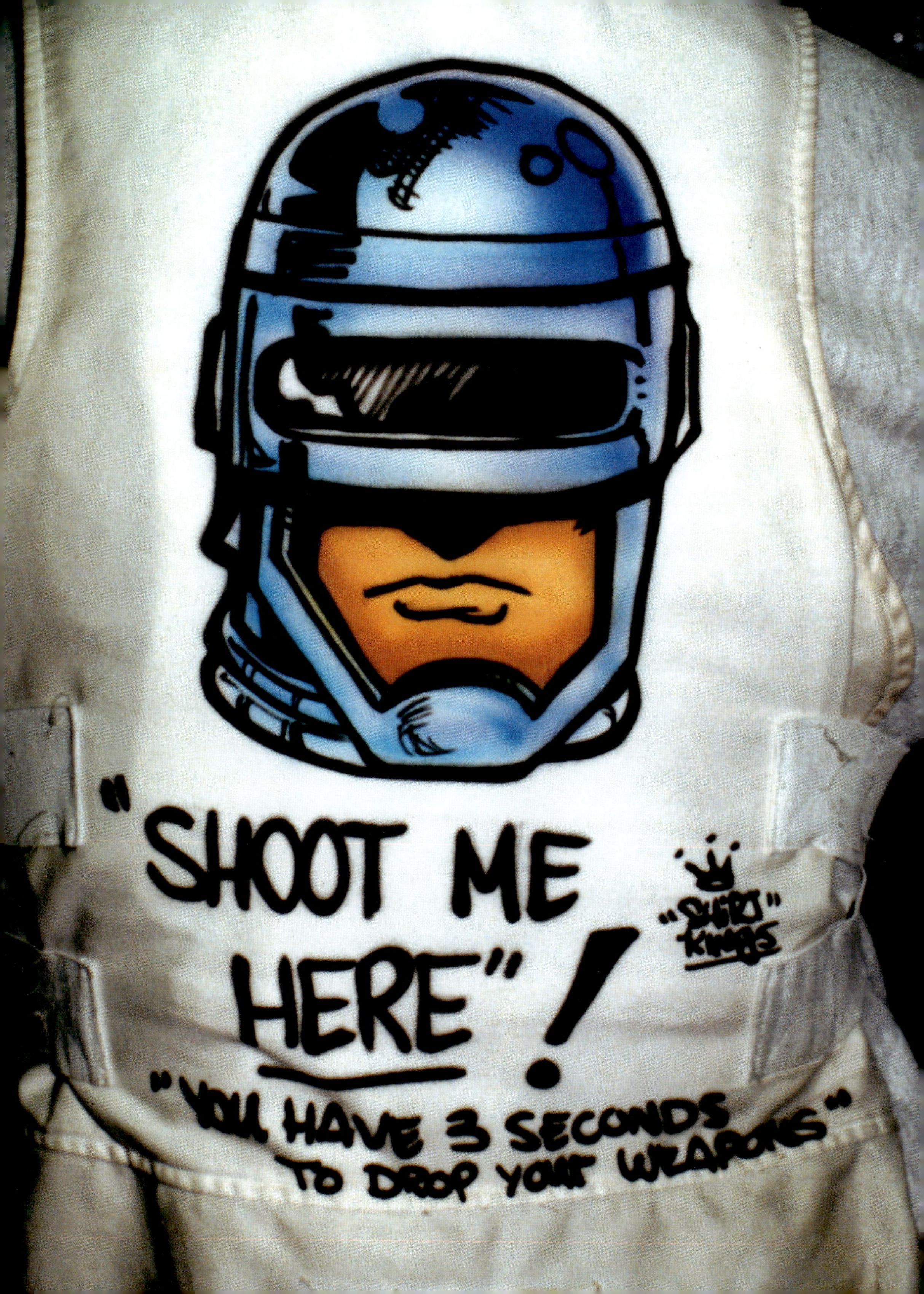
"SHOOT ME HERE"!
"YOU HAVE 3 SECONDS TO DROP YOUR WEAPONS"
"SHIRT" KINGS

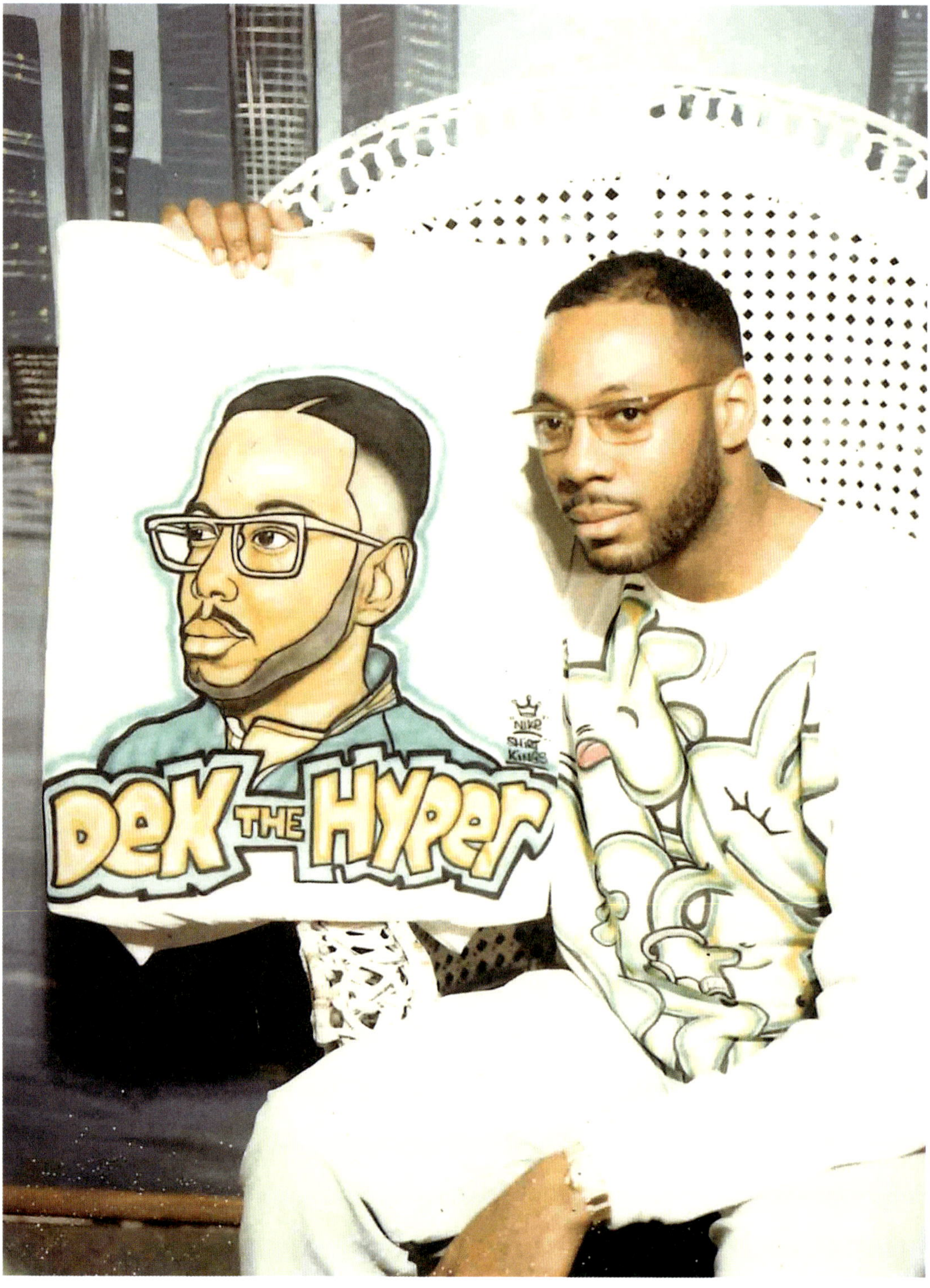

Lance Dekie aka Shirt King Dek, Dek TBC CIA TNT, East New York, Brooklyn, 1989/90.

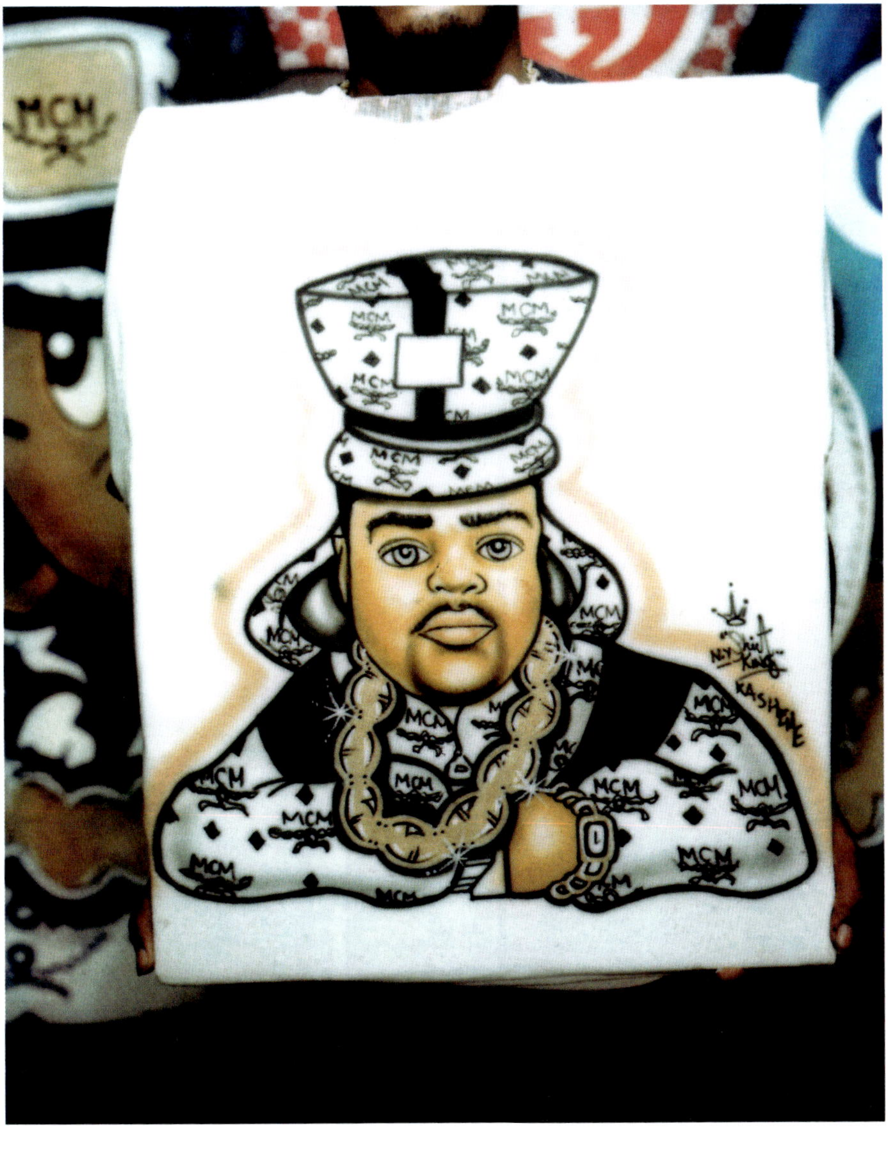

Shirt for Shaheem Reid by Kasheme, Jamaica Coliseum, 1987.

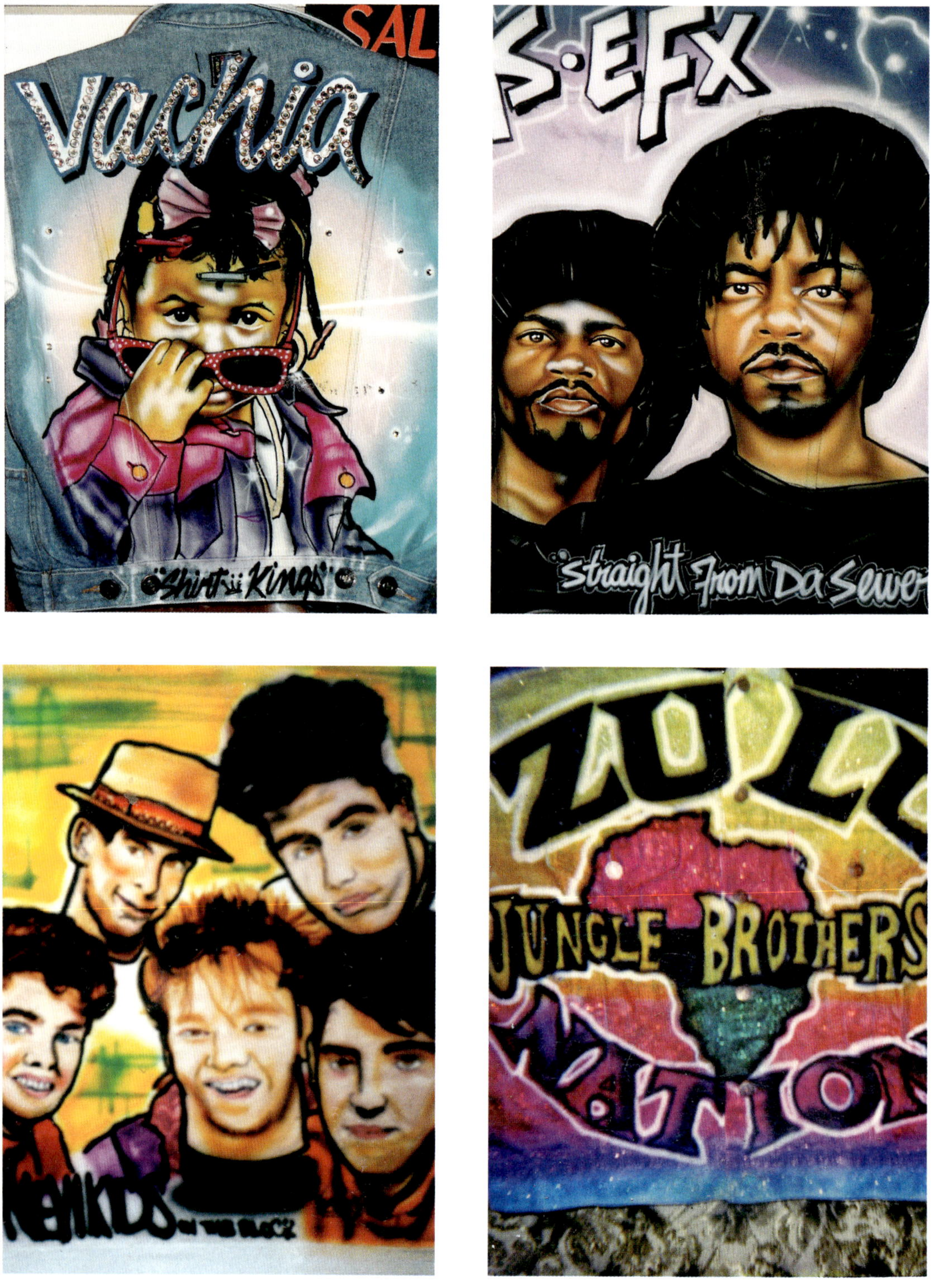

A selection of Shirt Kings art, 1990s.

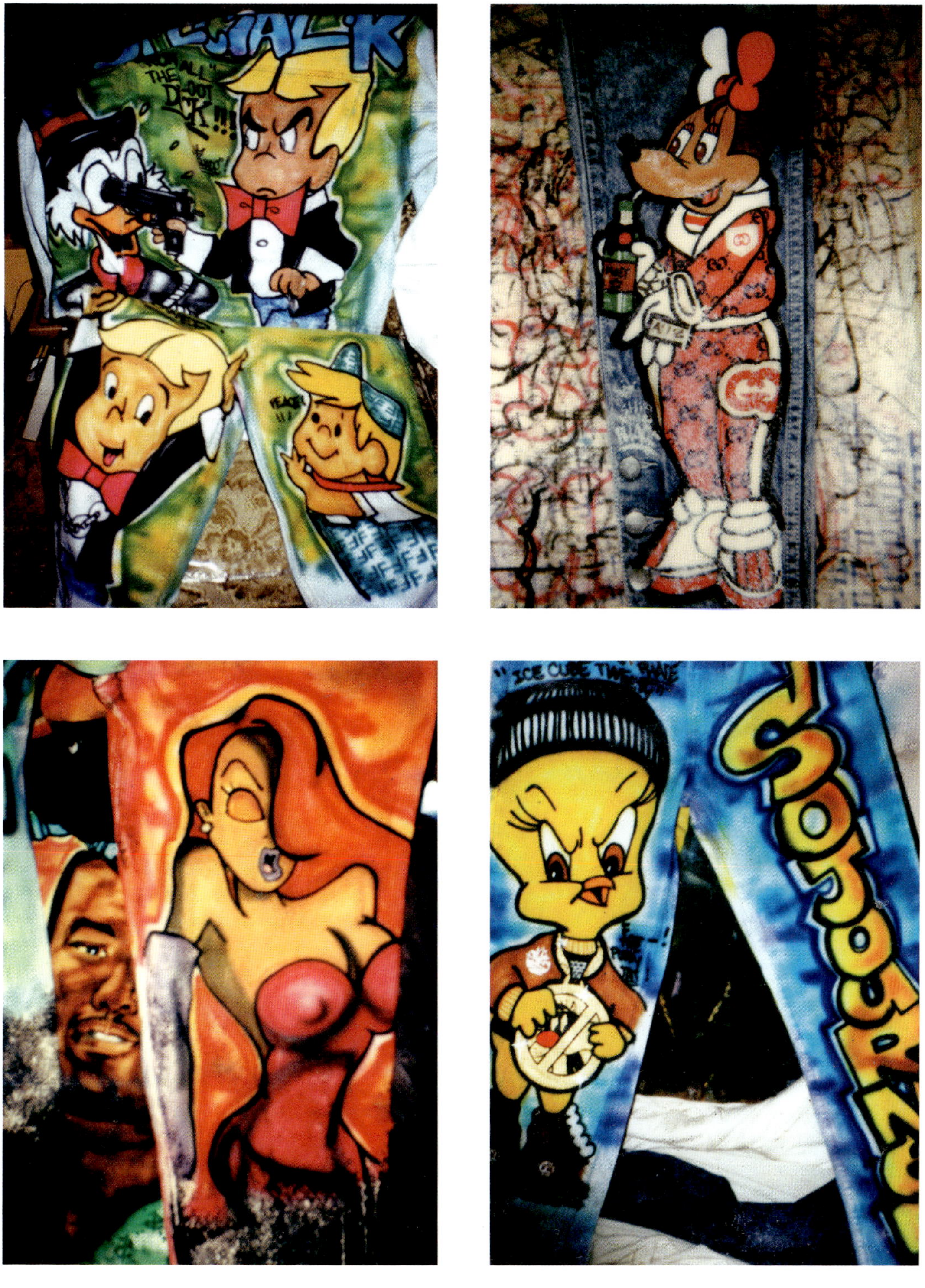

A selection of Shirt Kings art, 1990s.

"I had a sweatshirt made from the Shirt Kings back in the days. It was a shirt with the Decepticons logo since I was down with that gang. I got my ass kicked for having it out in Albee Square Mall. At the game room in the mall cats called me out and said, 'hey, are you one of those Transformer dudes?' I said 'yeah', and they fucked me up and tried to throw me in a dumpster. Thanks for the shirt buddy!"
Sean Price

Phade strikes a pose, Jamaica Coliseum, 1987.

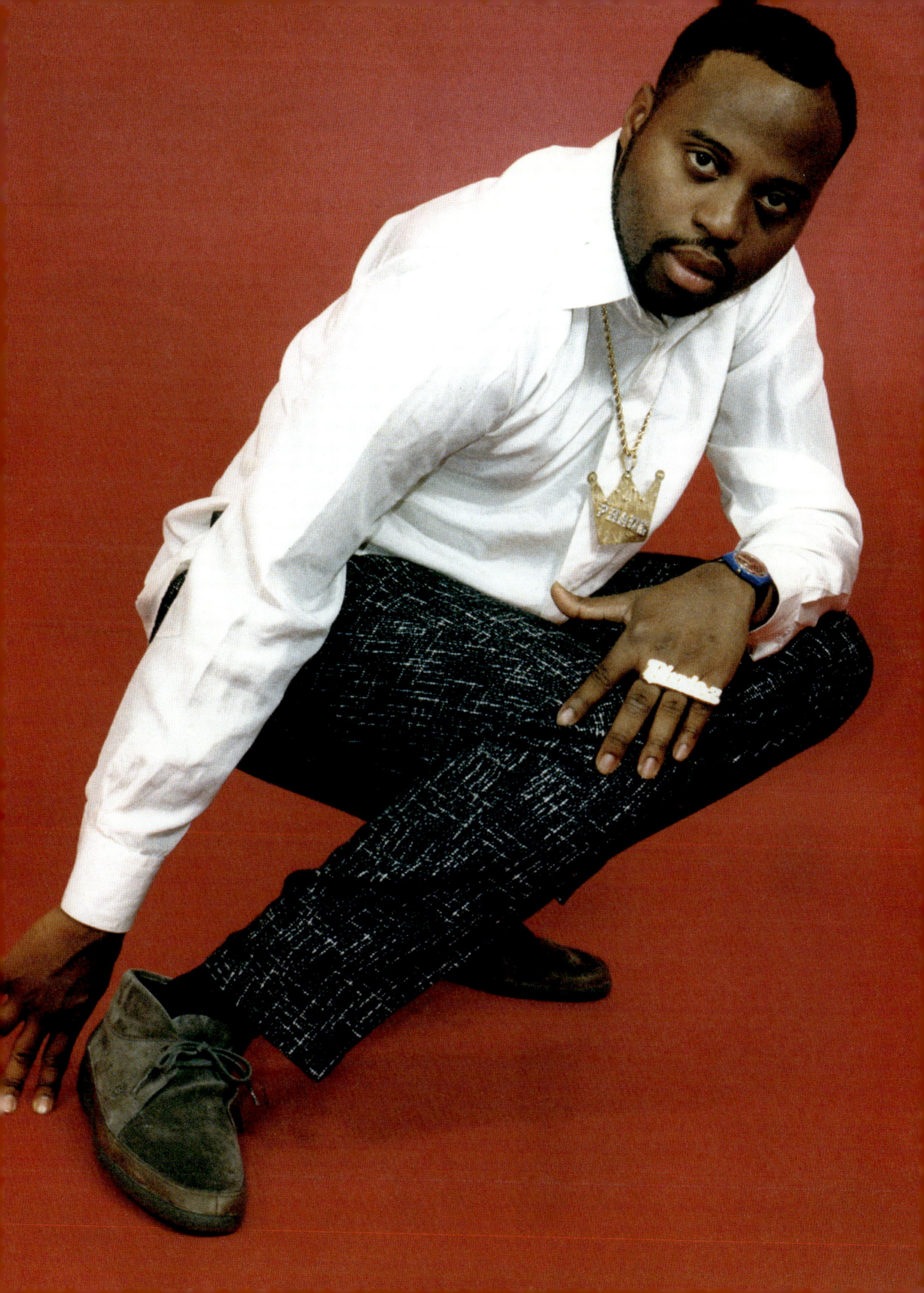

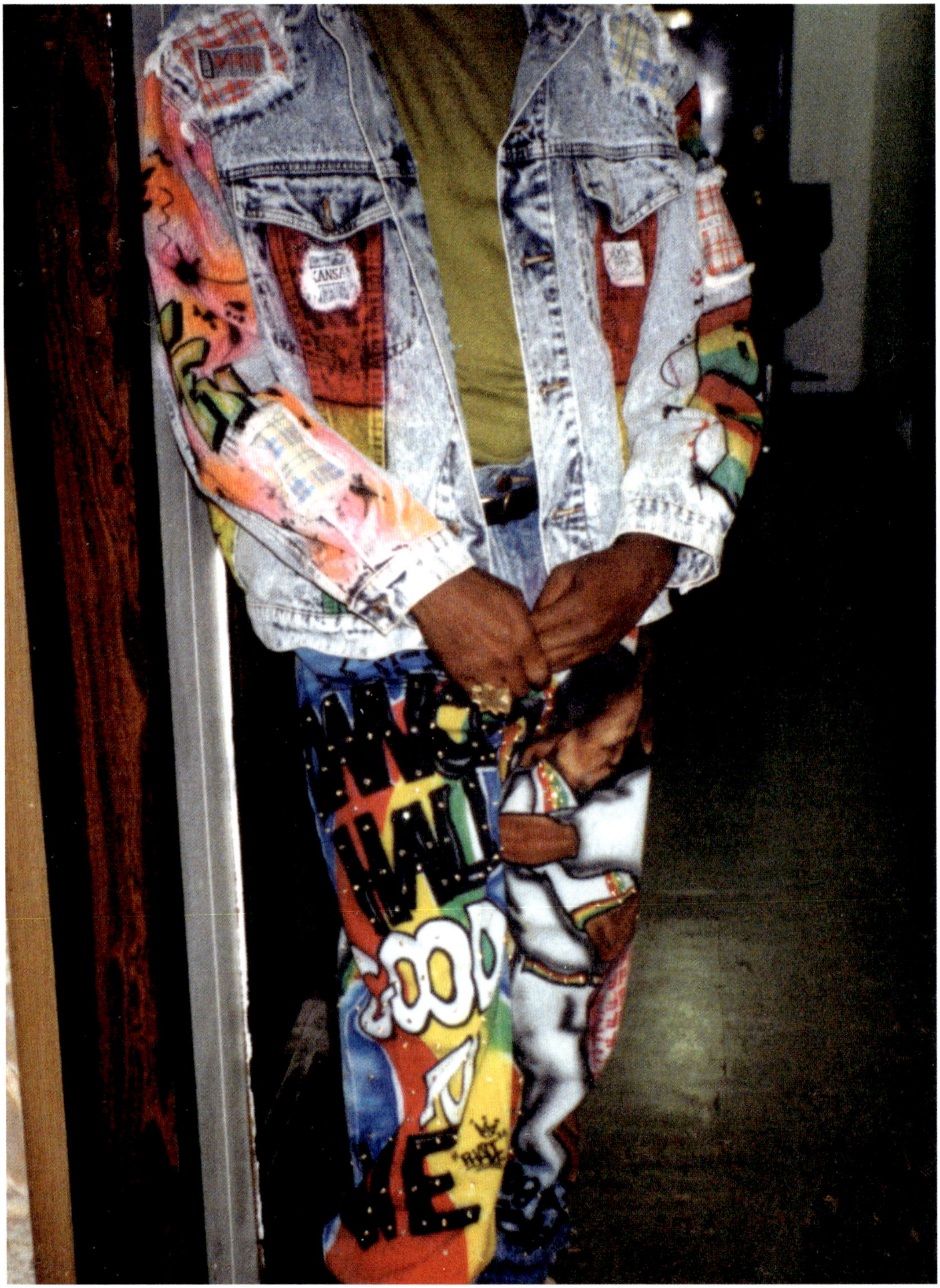

Papa San on the set of his video for *Dancehall Good to We*, Brooklyn, 1991.

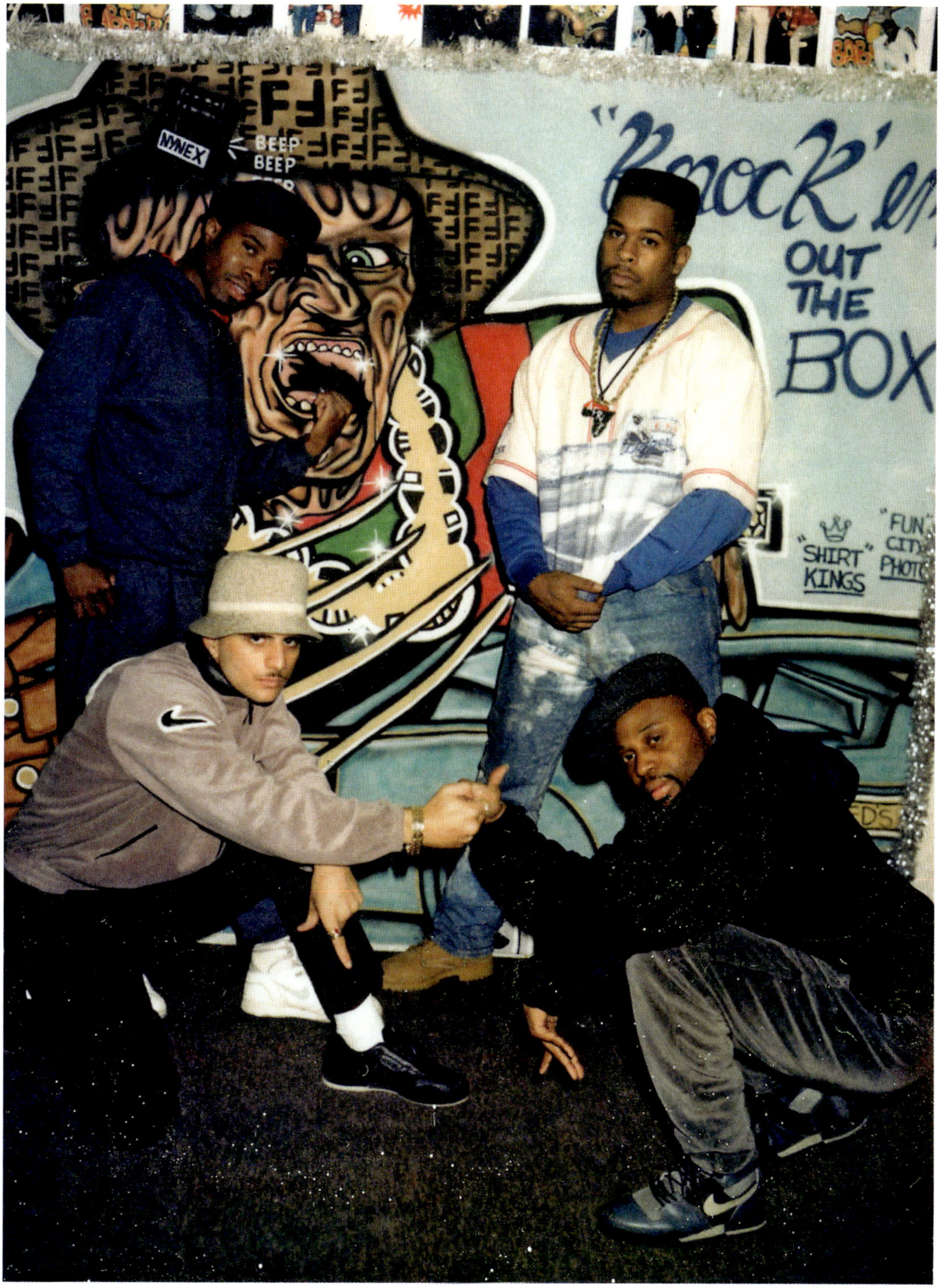

Noel from Miami with the Shirt Kings crew, Jamaica Coliseum, 1989.

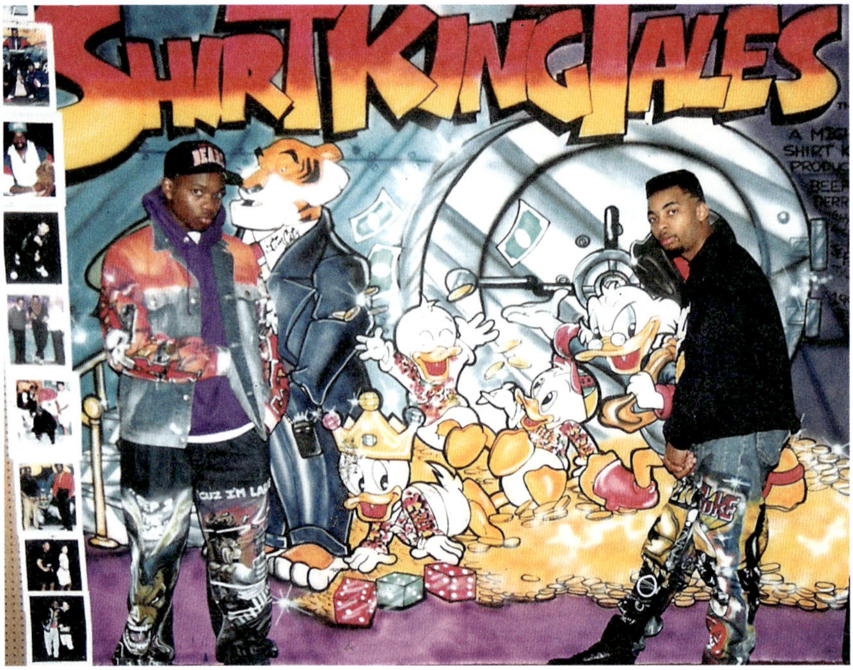

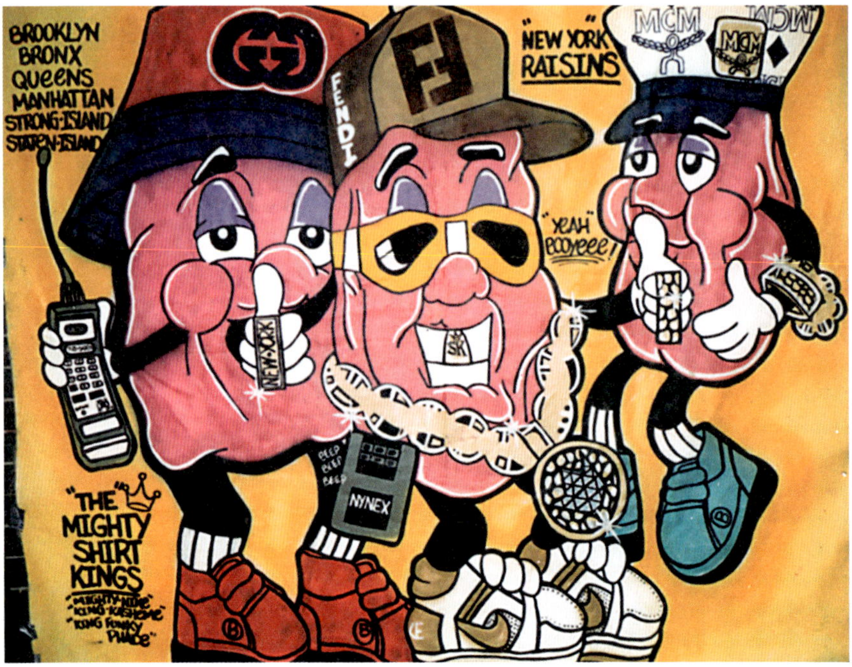

Top: Derrick and Sike, Jamaica Coliseum, 1993. **Below:** The New York Raisins, 1987.

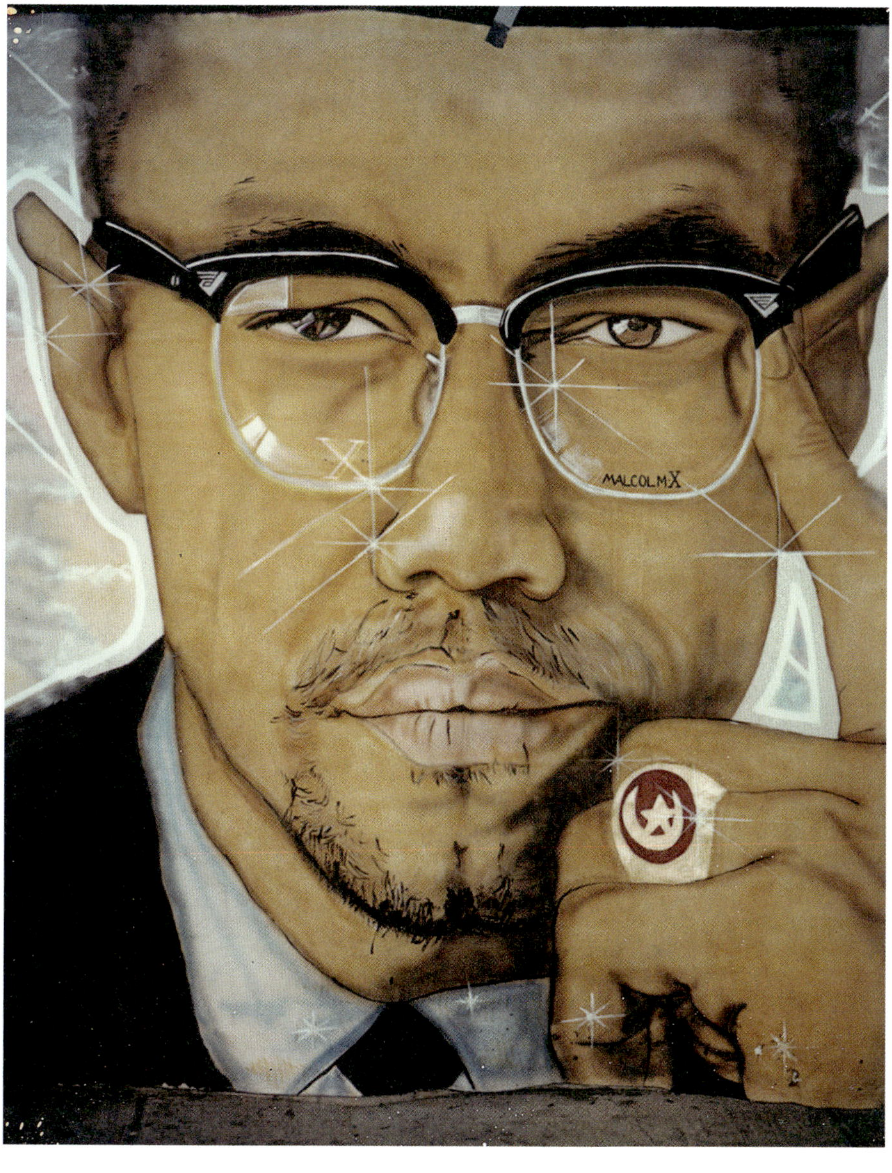

By Any Means Necessary! Malcolm X portrait by Phade, 125th Street, 1990/91.

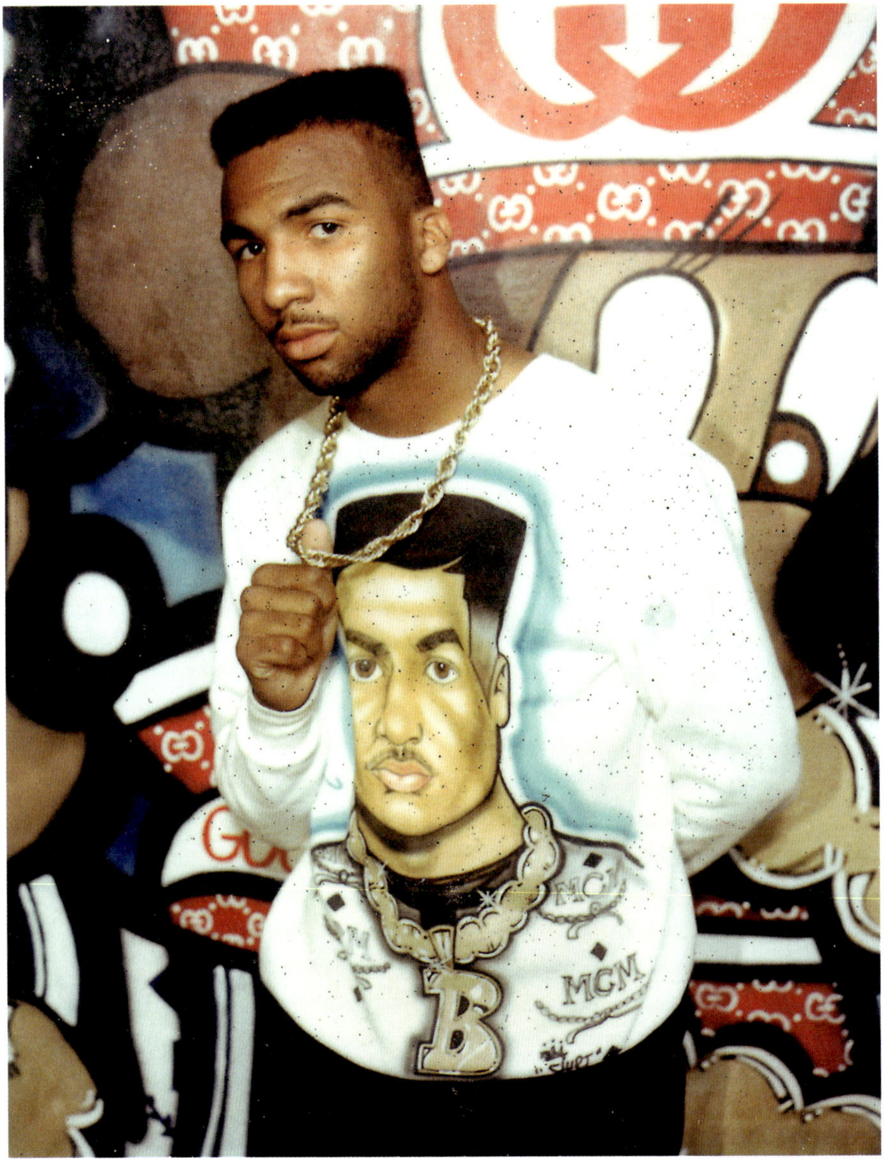

Bernard Alexander, Jamaica Coliseum, 1987.

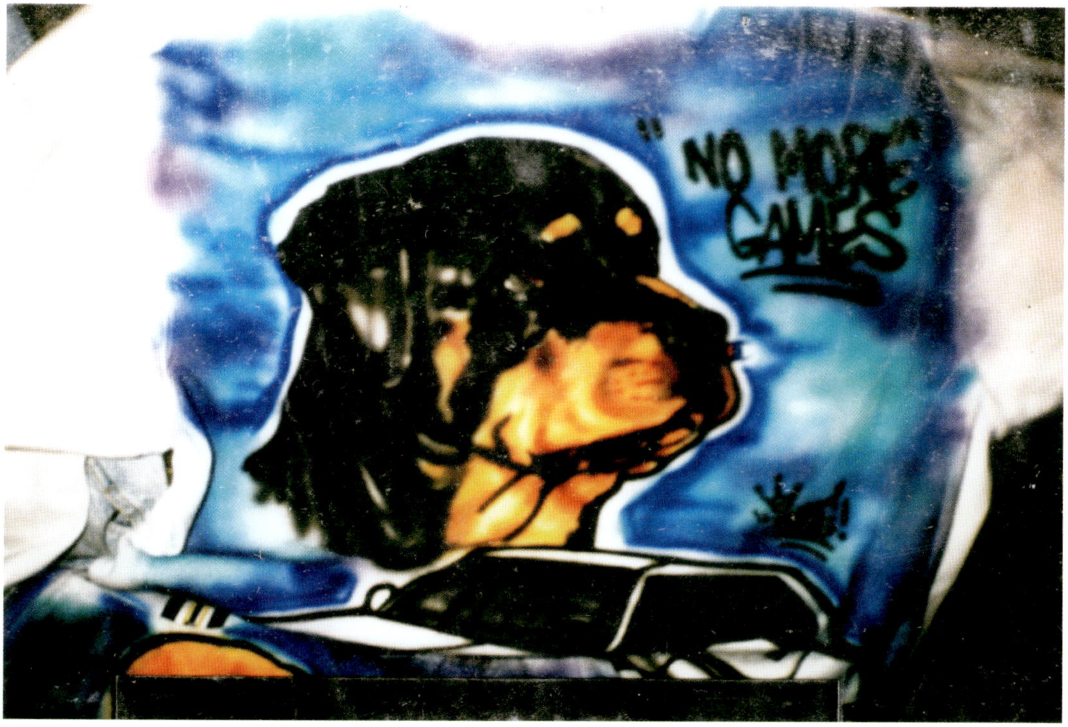

No more games, Jamaica Coliseum, 1987.

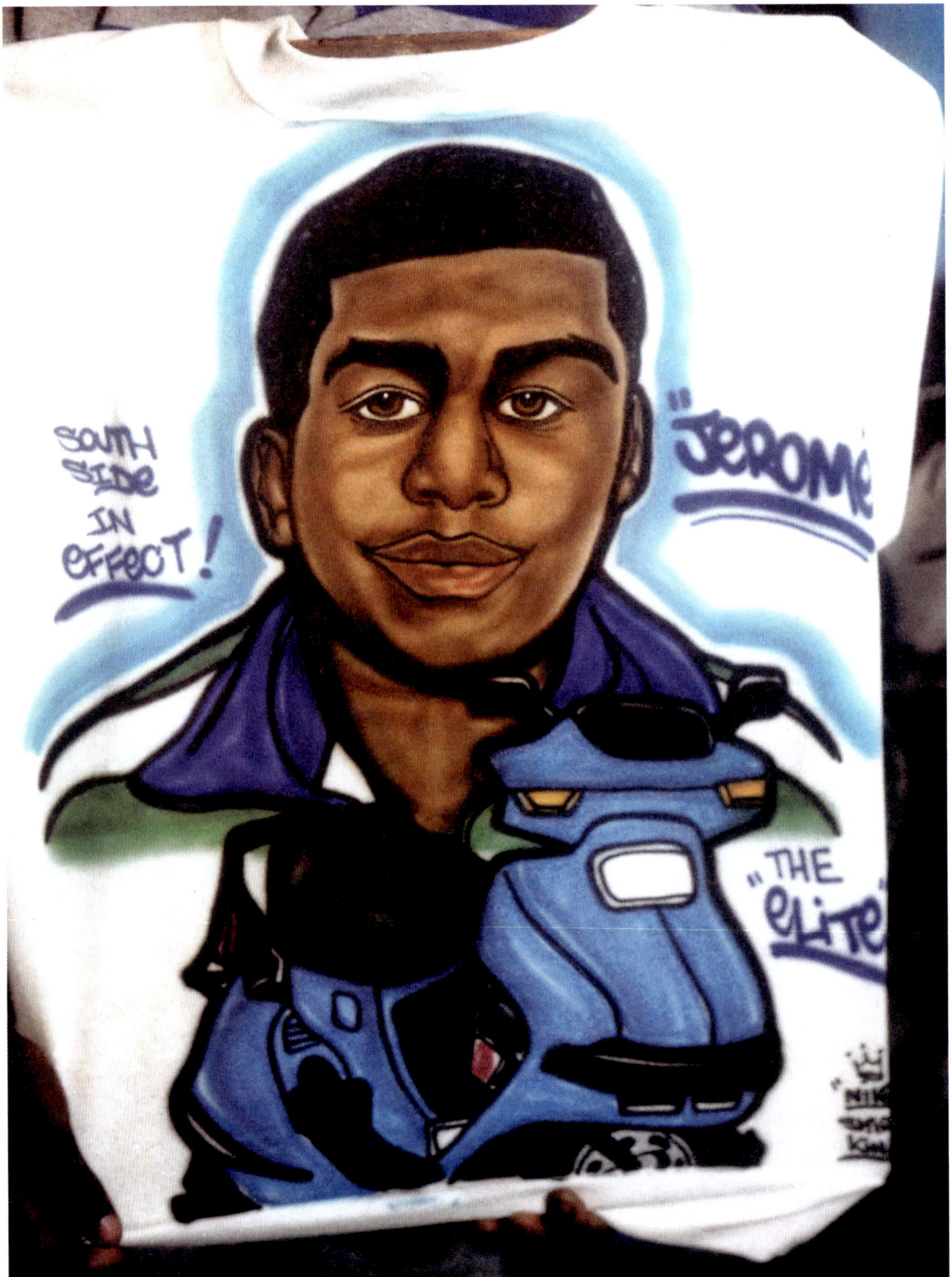

Jerome, Jamaica Coliseum, 1987.

"I loved to hear Red Alert shout out the famous Shirt Kings on the radio back in the days. If you had a shirt from the Shirt Kings, you were automatically down by law! They had the freshest graffiti artwork going on any clothing. They had the crazy classic b-boy style that all others tried to imitate. I'm proud they representin' Queens to the fullest."
DJ Wiz / Kid and Play

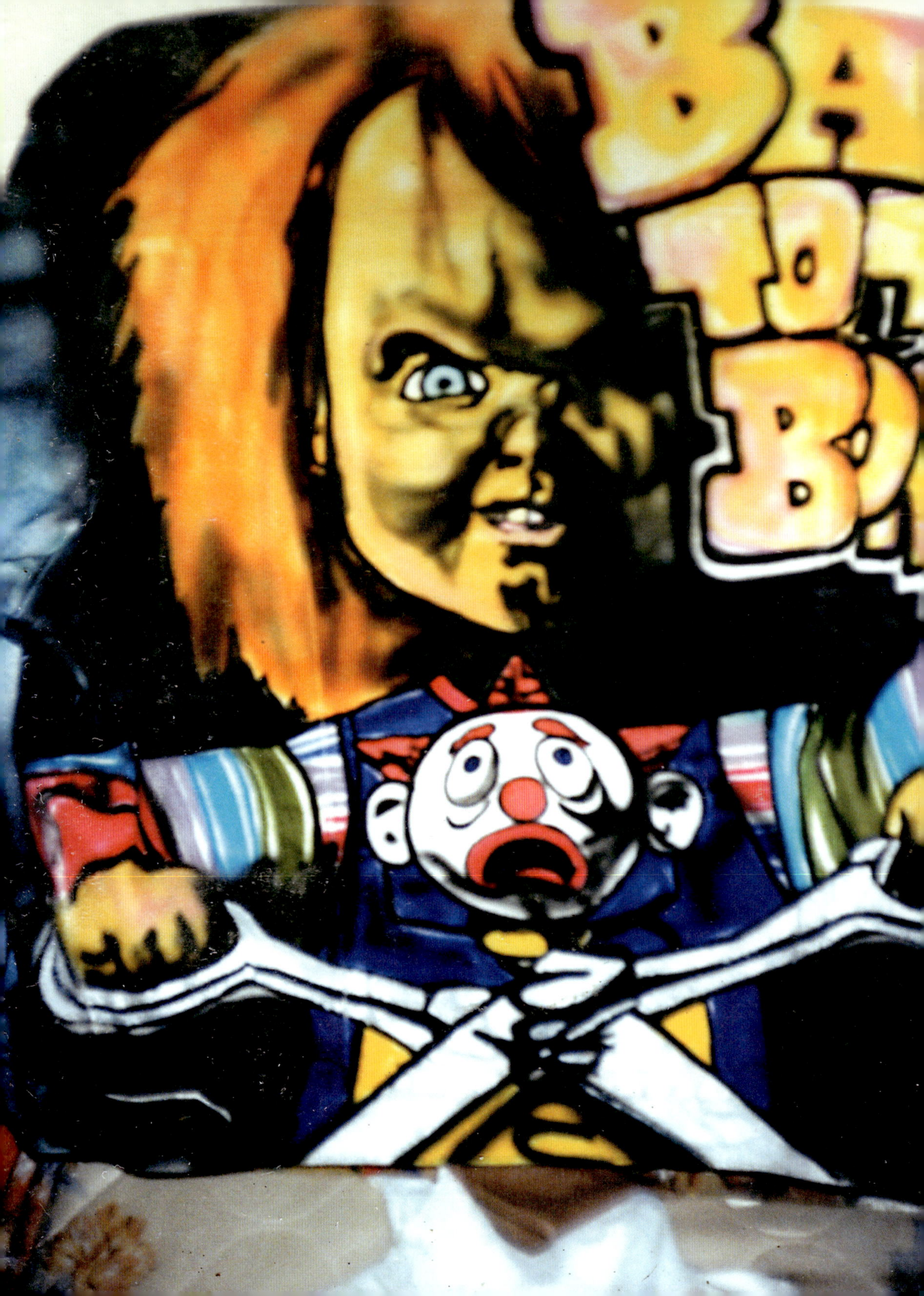

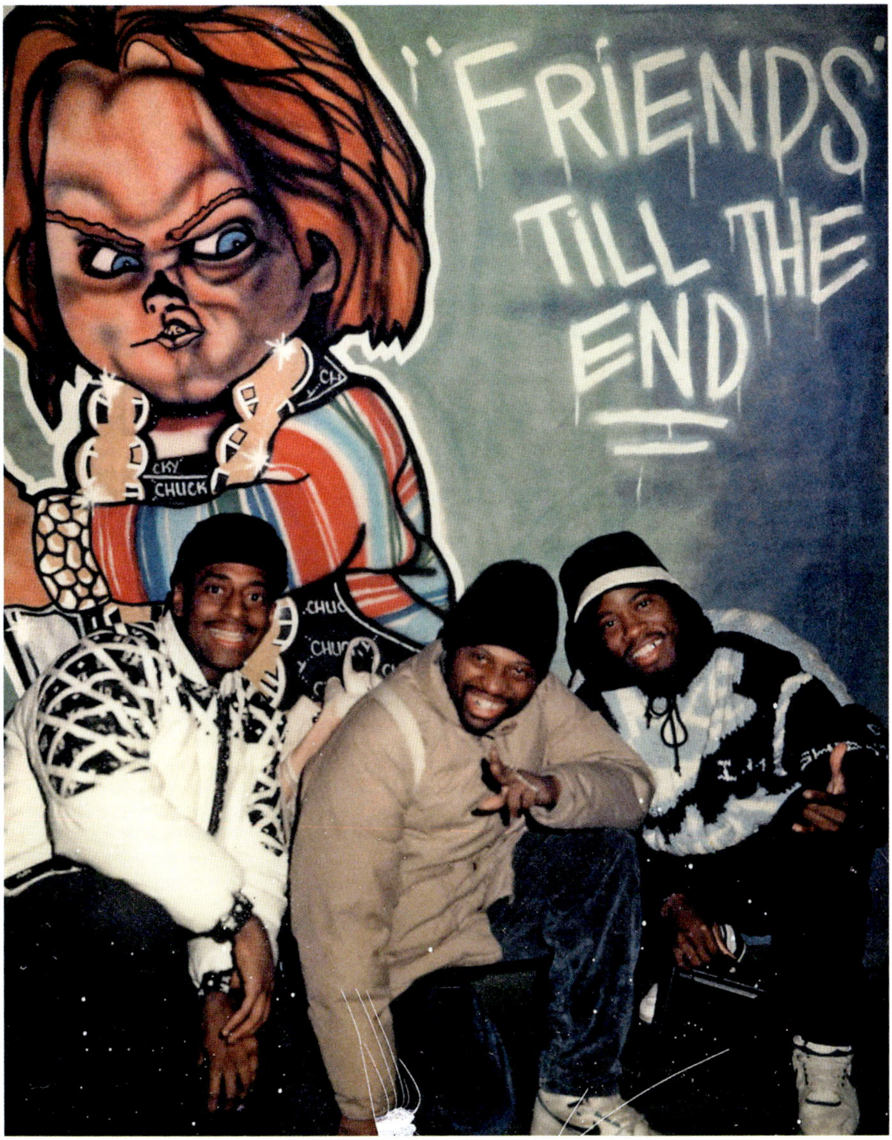

Opposite page: Bad to the bone Chucky jacket, Baltimore, 1991.
Above: Barry of the Shabazz Brothers with Phade and Nike, Harlem, 1989.

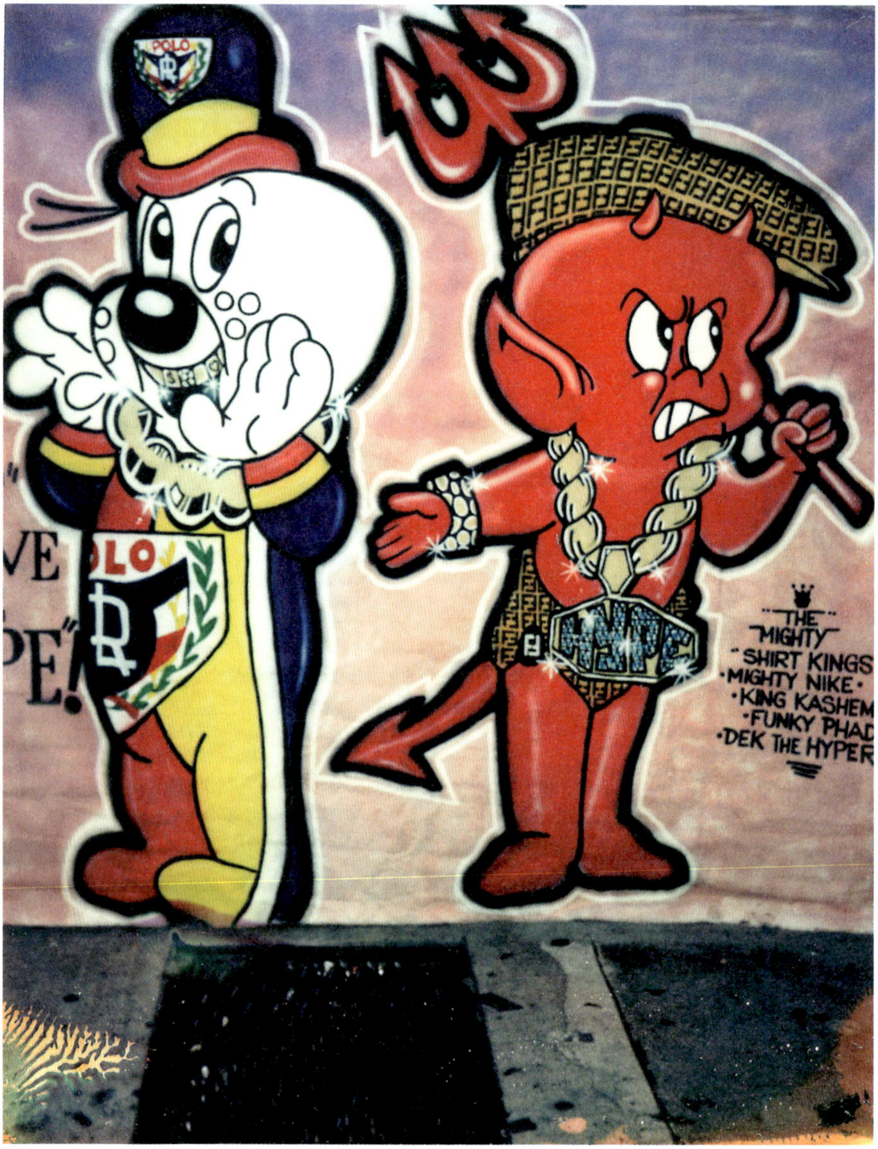

Don’t believe the hype, Jamaica Avenue, 1988.

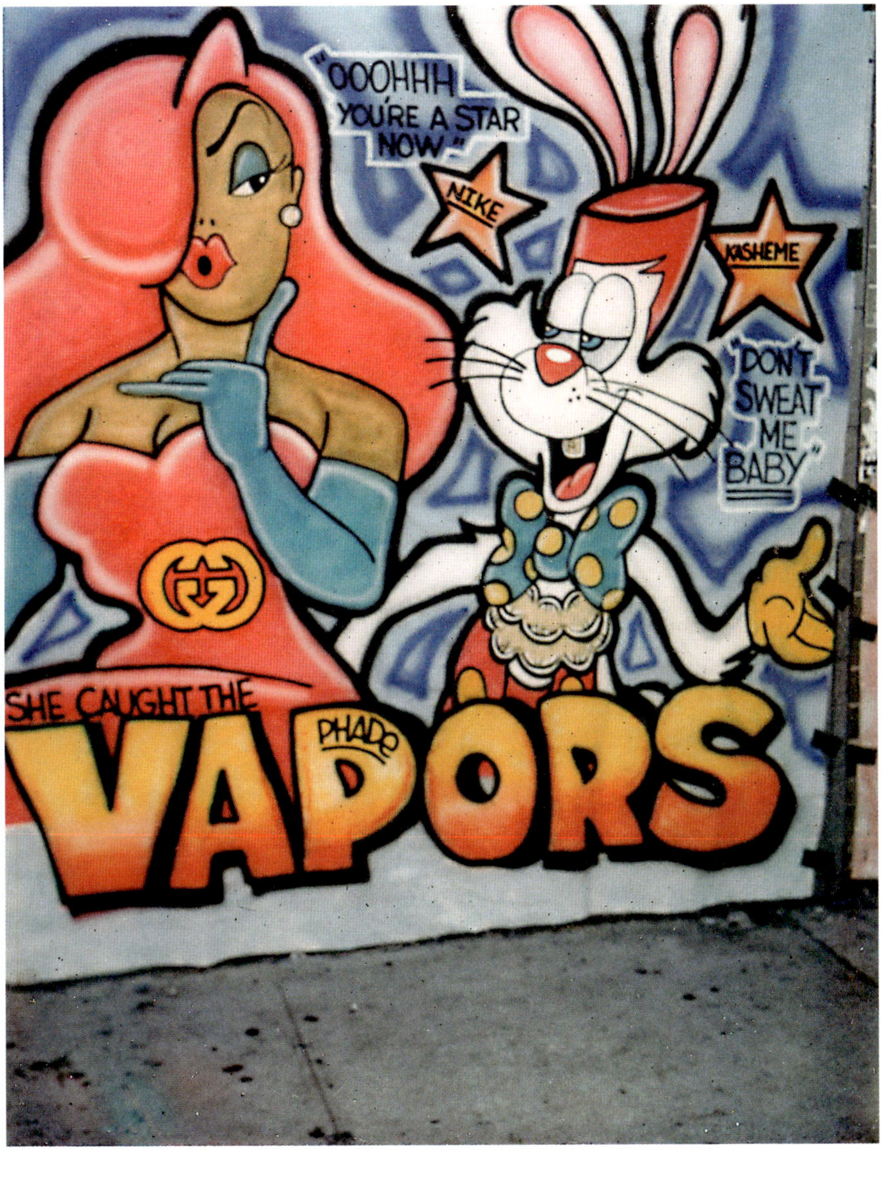

The Vapors, Jamaica Avenue, 1988.

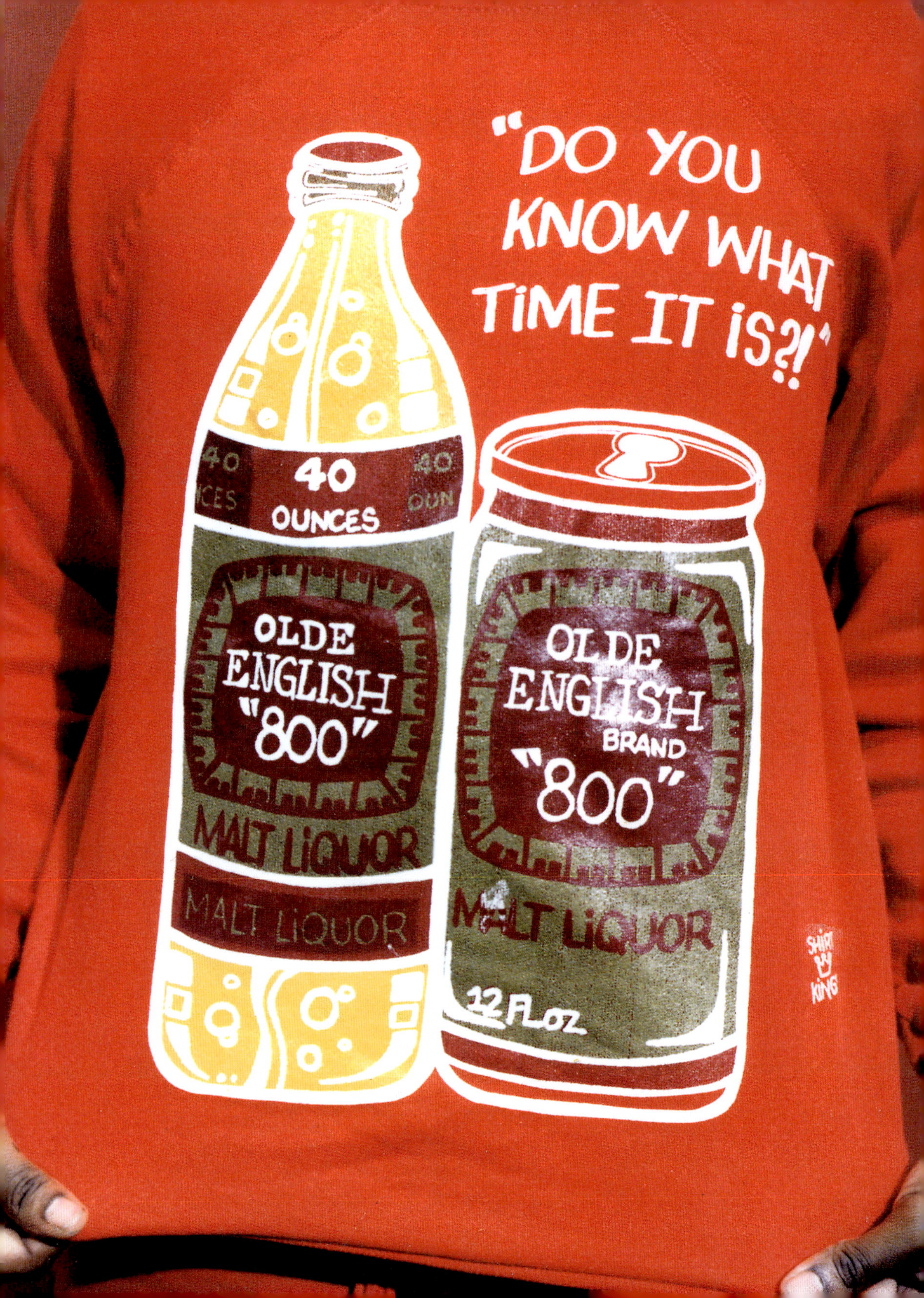
"DO YOU KNOW WHAT TIME IT IS?!"
40
OUNCES
OLDE ENGLISH "800"
MALT LIQUOR
MALT LIQUOR
OLDE ENGLISH BRAND "800"
MALT LIQUOR
12 FLoz

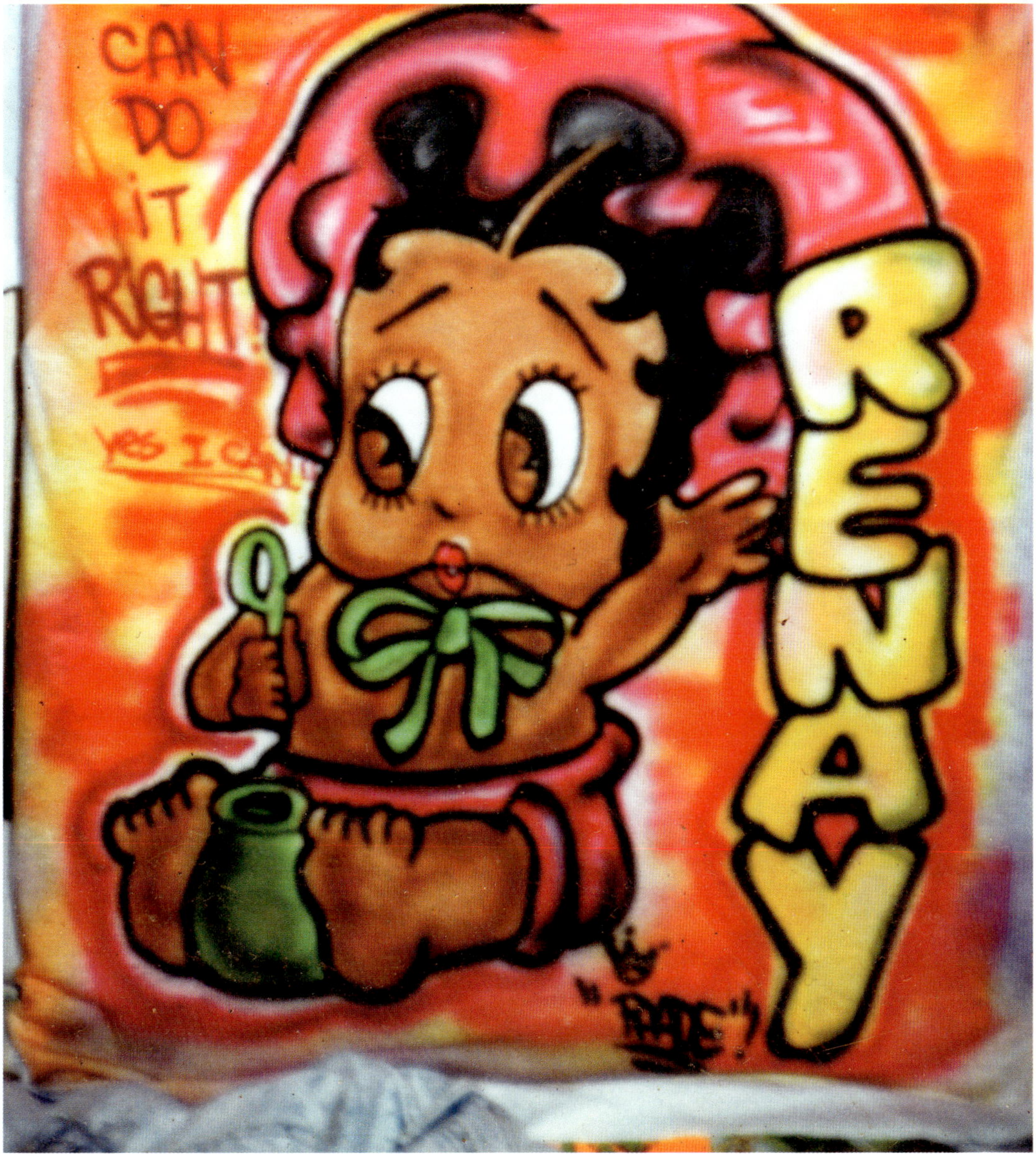

Opposite page: Inspired by Kool Moe Dee and Old English 800, 1987. **This page:** Renay design by Phade, 1987.

“Back in the days the whole Shirt King’s style was the way the streets was. It was the best clothes you could get. You would bring a regular sweatshirt to these brothers and they would transform your whole look into a superstar immediately and you would look like your outfit cost a million. That’s real! I never could get my ends up to get me a Shirt Kings joint, but I would borrow my homeboy’s Shirt Kings joint.

Shirt Kings joints had the colors, all the stuff that everyone is doing now. It had a Dapper Dan kind of feeling cause they could put anything on your shirt. Gucci’s new book is mentioning Dapper Dan now. They [Gucci] didn’t mention it back then, even though he was pushing their whole thing forward. So were the Shirt Kings, they were pushing everybody forward. If Polo wasn’t doing the right thing, if they didn’t fit right, if the design was a little bit off, Shirt Kings would do your shirt over, put your Polo on there and make it right!

They helped Ralph Lauren, Gucci, Louis Vuitton and MCM. These big multi-million dollar brands wouldn’t be in our community if it wasn’t for brothers like the Shirt Kings. Plus, the joint was out in Queens, so you know all the who’s who would have on Shirt Kings. It just wasn’t rap celebrities, it was like street celebrities that had them on. You and your girl could have the same joints. They even did x-rated joints, they did the rhinestones, the Teddy Riley look, you know what I mean? They had it all covered, from the hood celebrities all the way to the biggest of the big.”
Nas

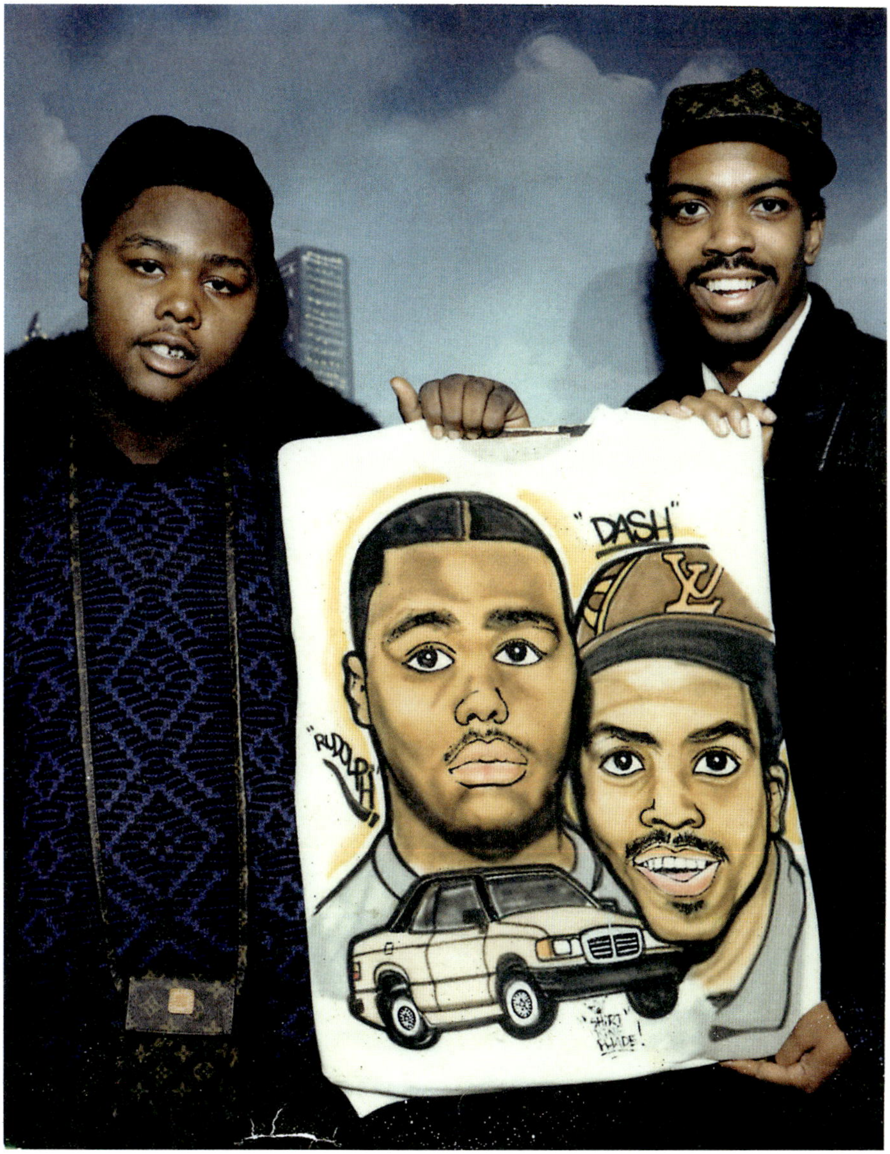

Rudolph and Dash, Jamaica Coliseum, 1987.

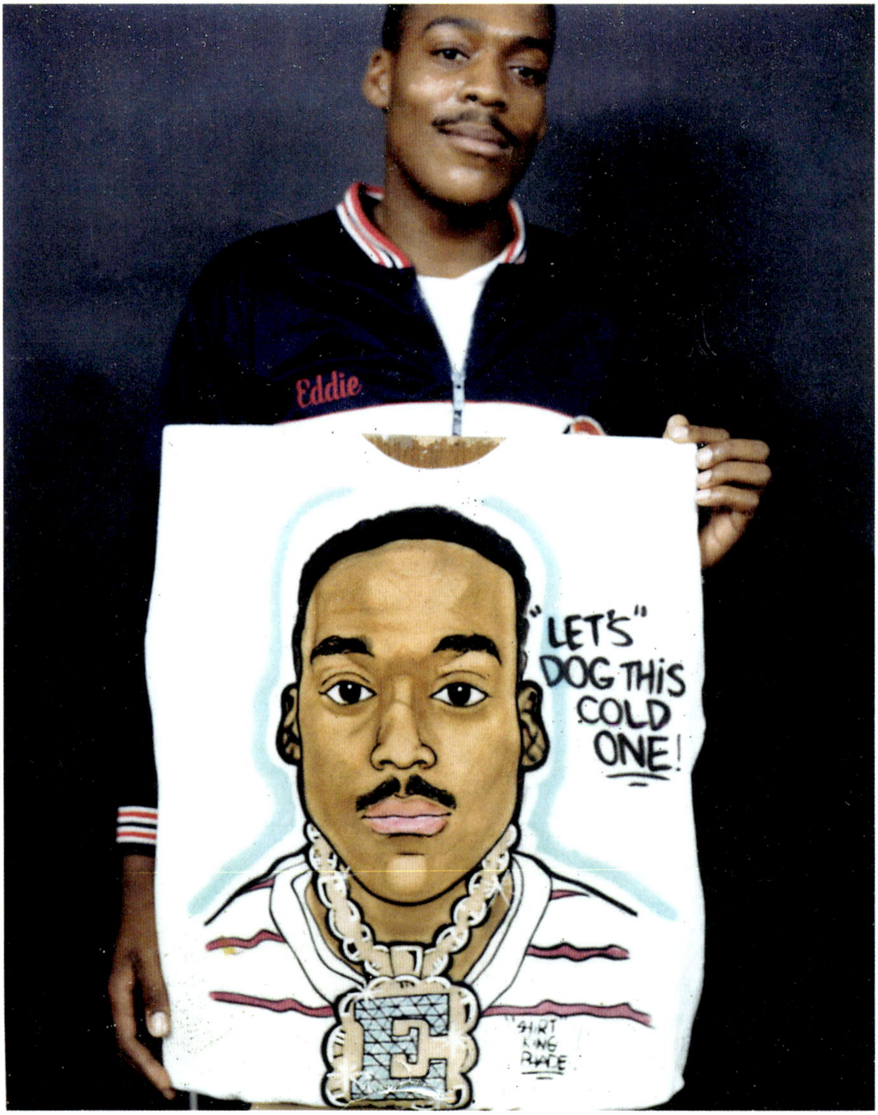

Ed, Jamaica Coliseum, 1987.

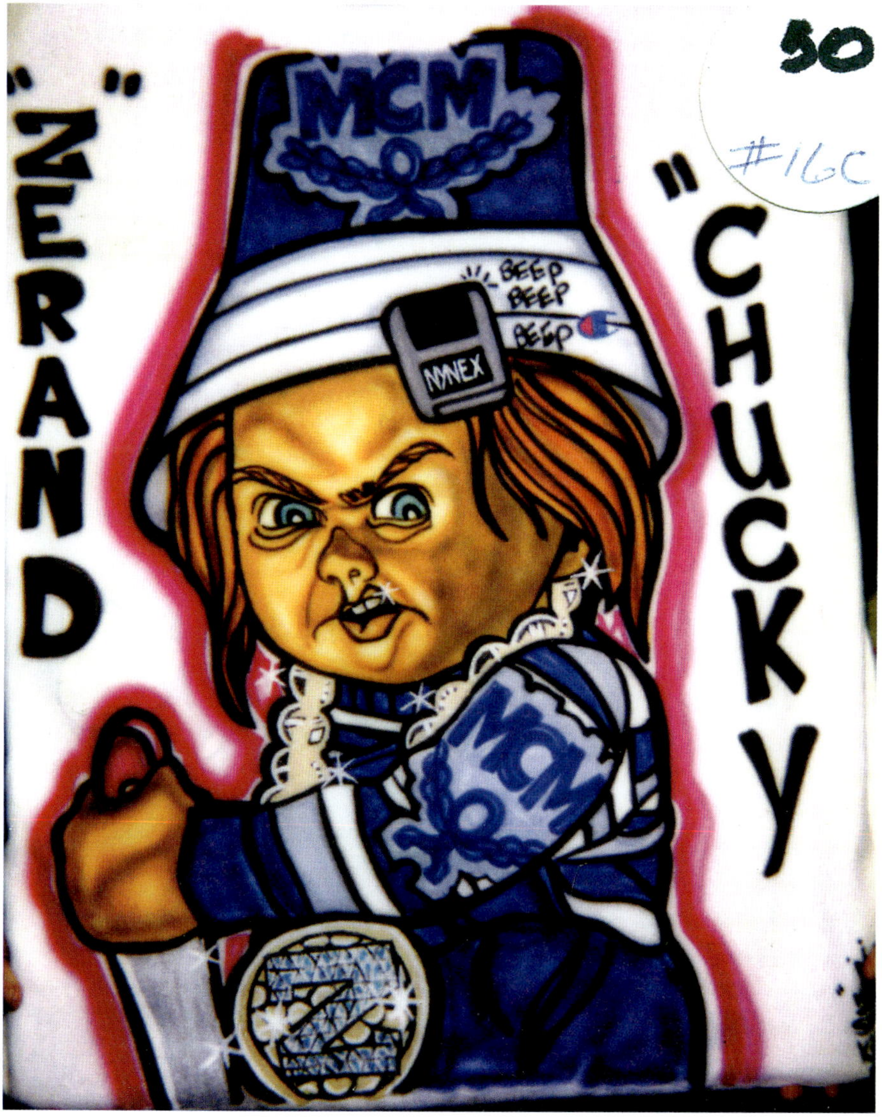

Chucky, Jamaica Coliseum, 1990.

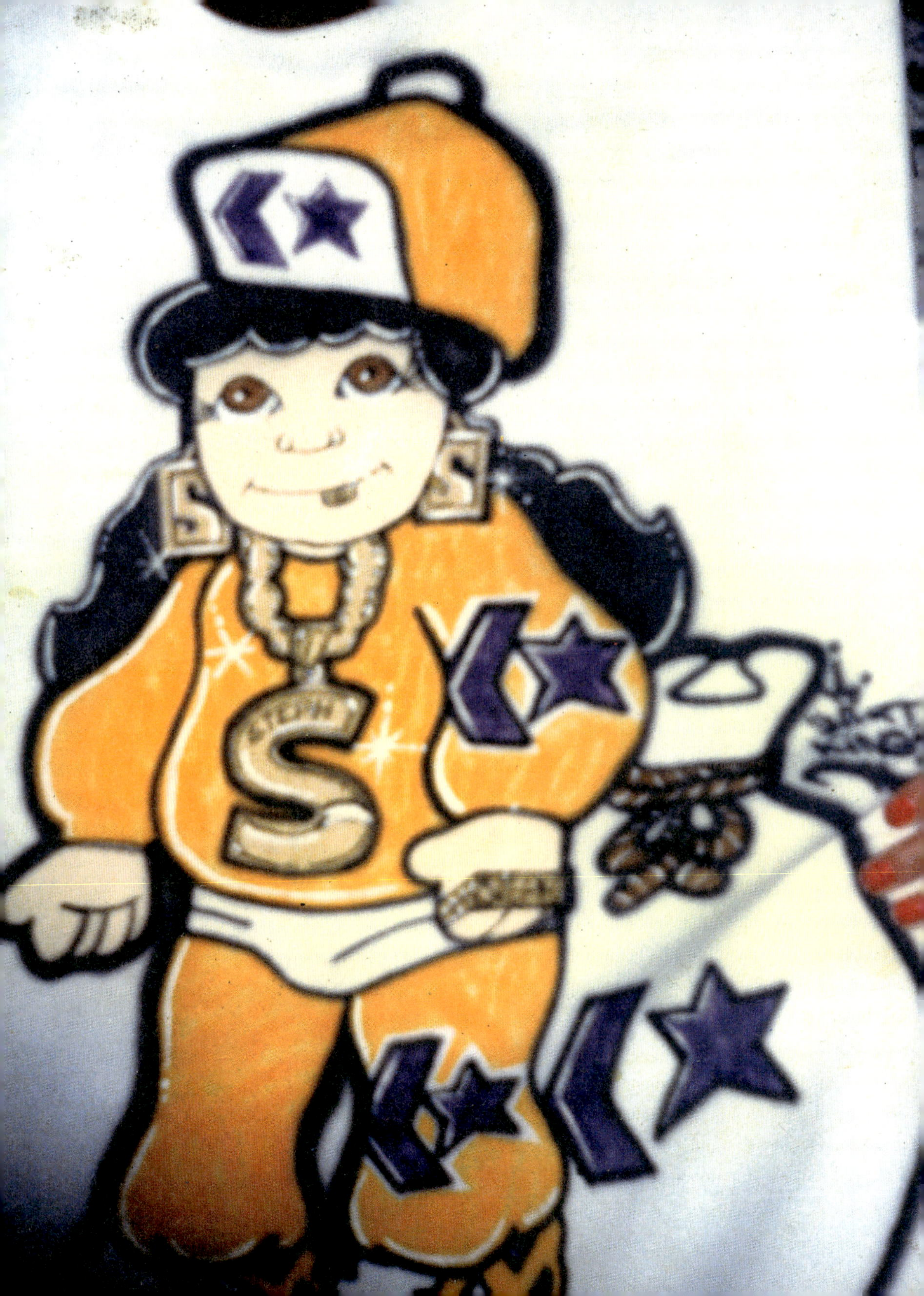

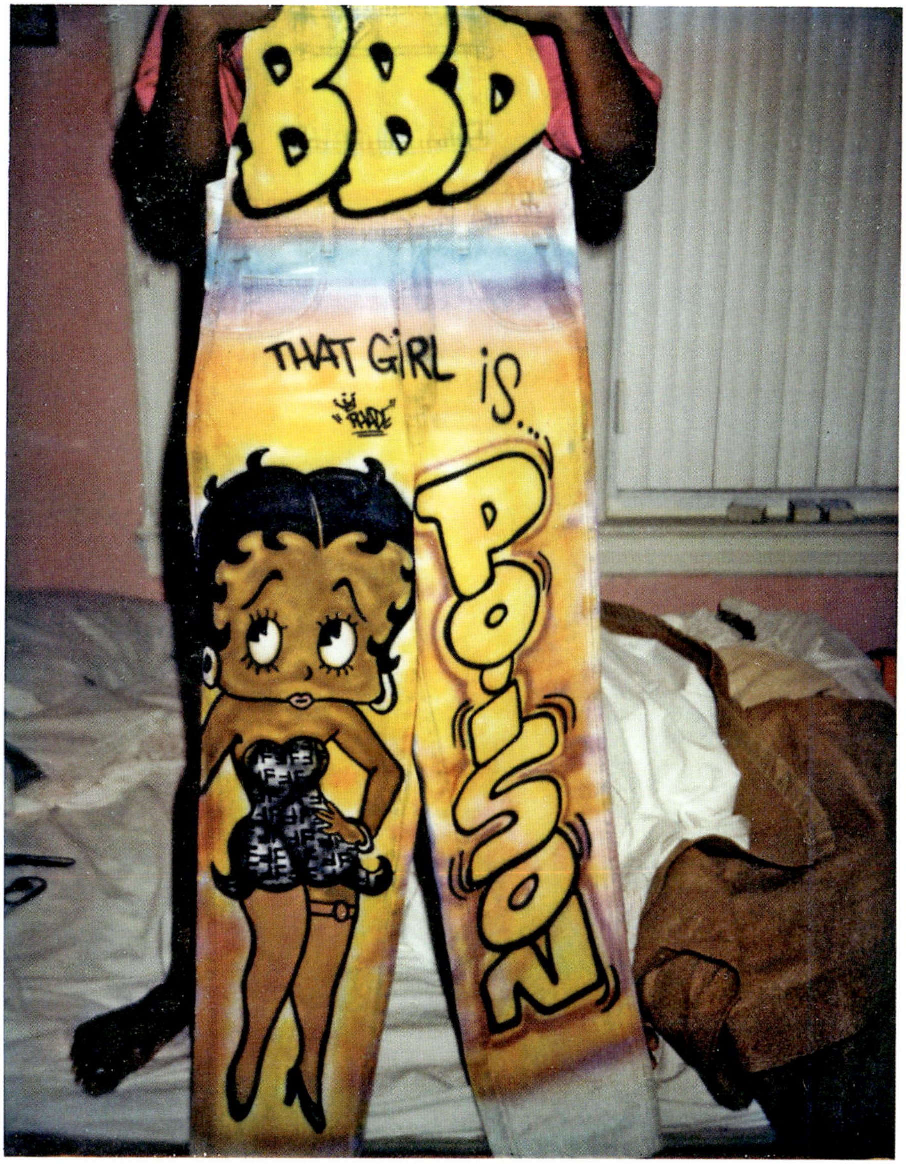

Opposite page: Cabbage Patch Converse, Jamaica Coliseum, 1986. **This page**: Poison, the Bronx, 1990.

HIP HOP ICONS

In the late 80s as rap music went worldwide the talent was for the most part home grown New Yorkers. The Shirt Kings were there to witness and dress these young talents and help create signature looks that became the trend nationwide. It was a time when many of today's most respected and well known rappers were young and still part of the hip hop movement. They were still going to clubs and just getting established. In those days, graffiti writers, b-boys, deejays, and emcees stood on a level playing field, all taking note of who was making noise in the streets. It was during this time that the Shirt Kings were making their presence known and were celebrities in their own right.

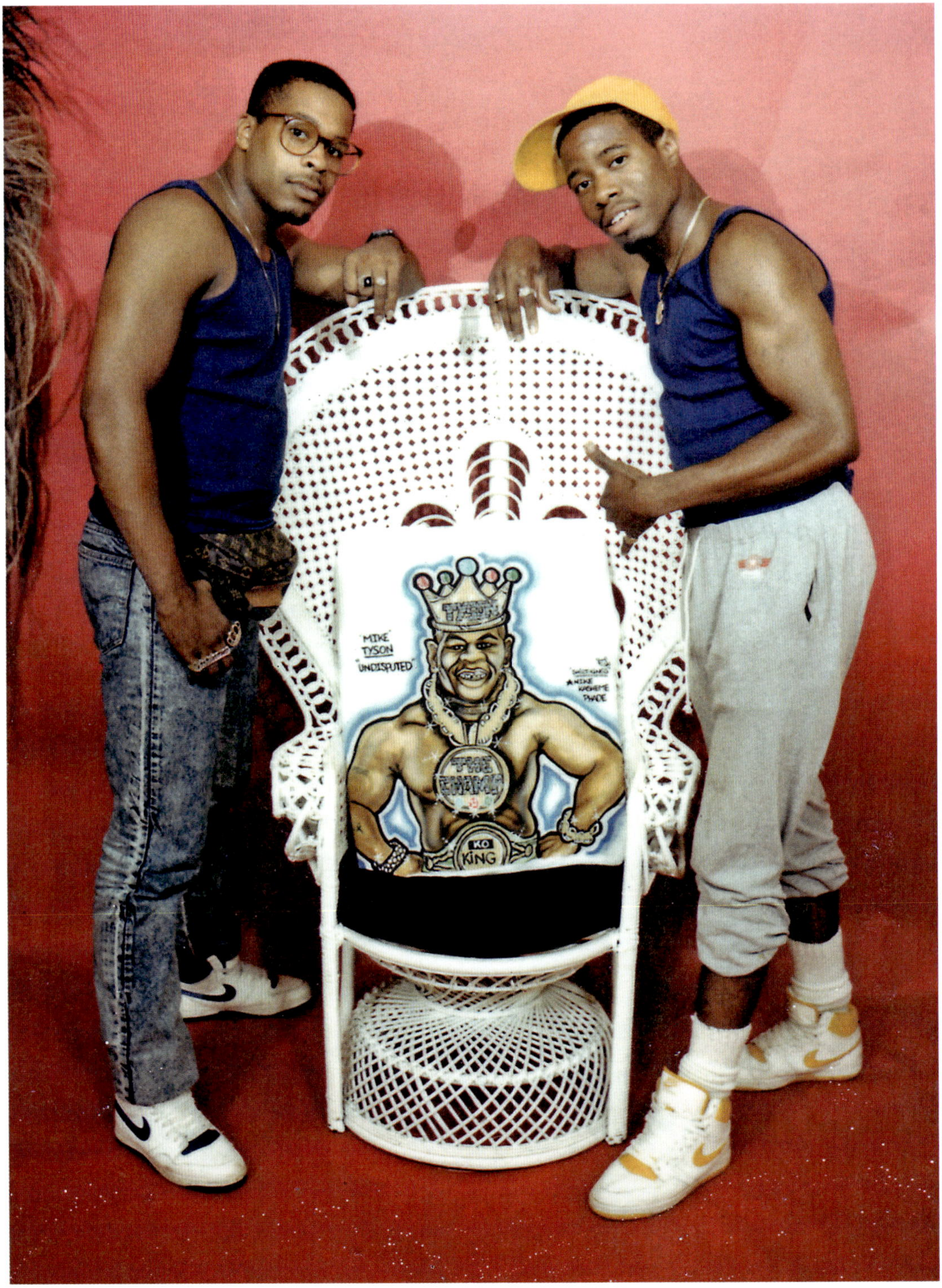

Melle Mel's Tyson shirt, Jamaica Coliseum, 1987.

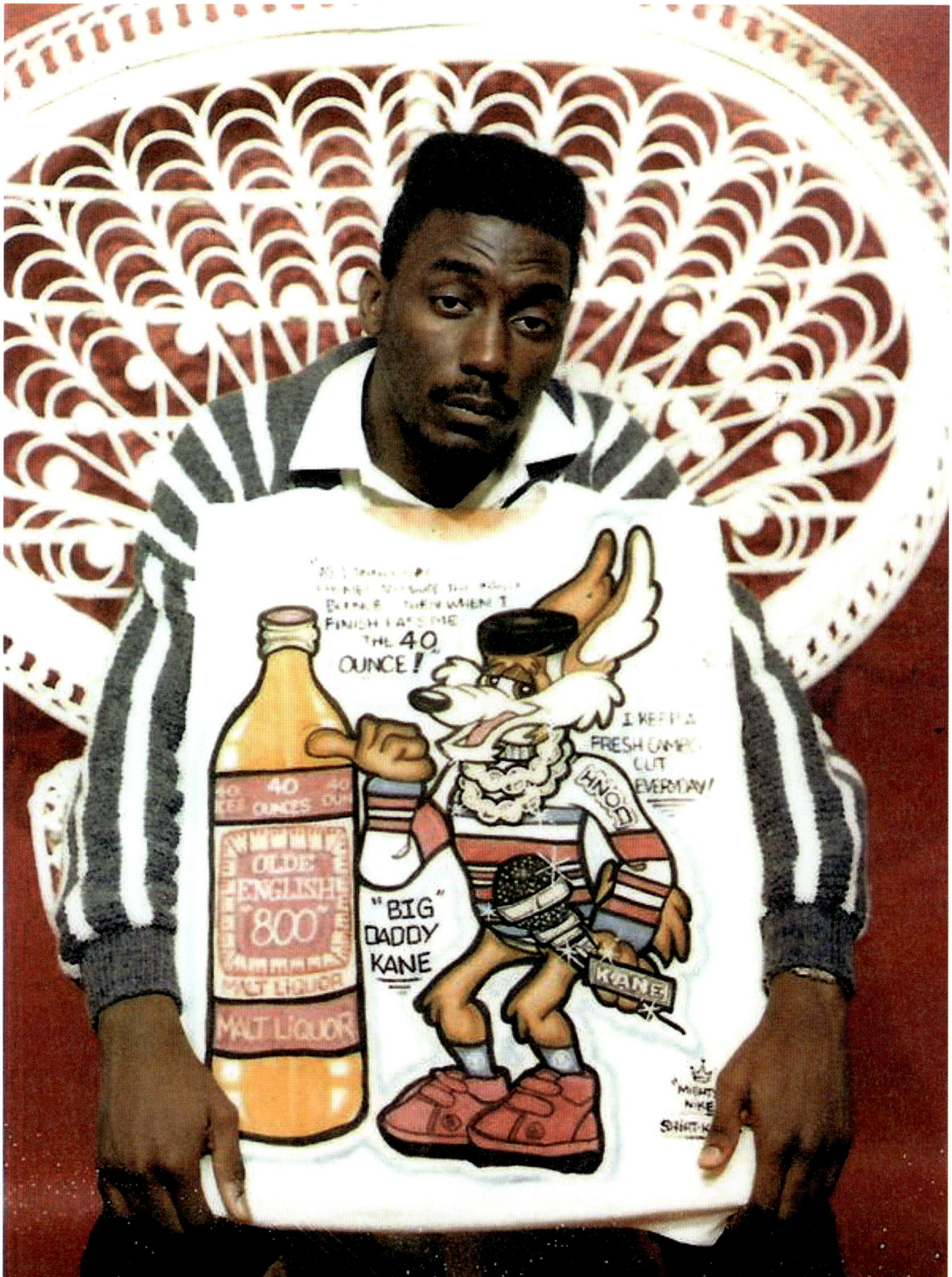

Big Daddy Kane, Jamaica Coliseum, 1987.

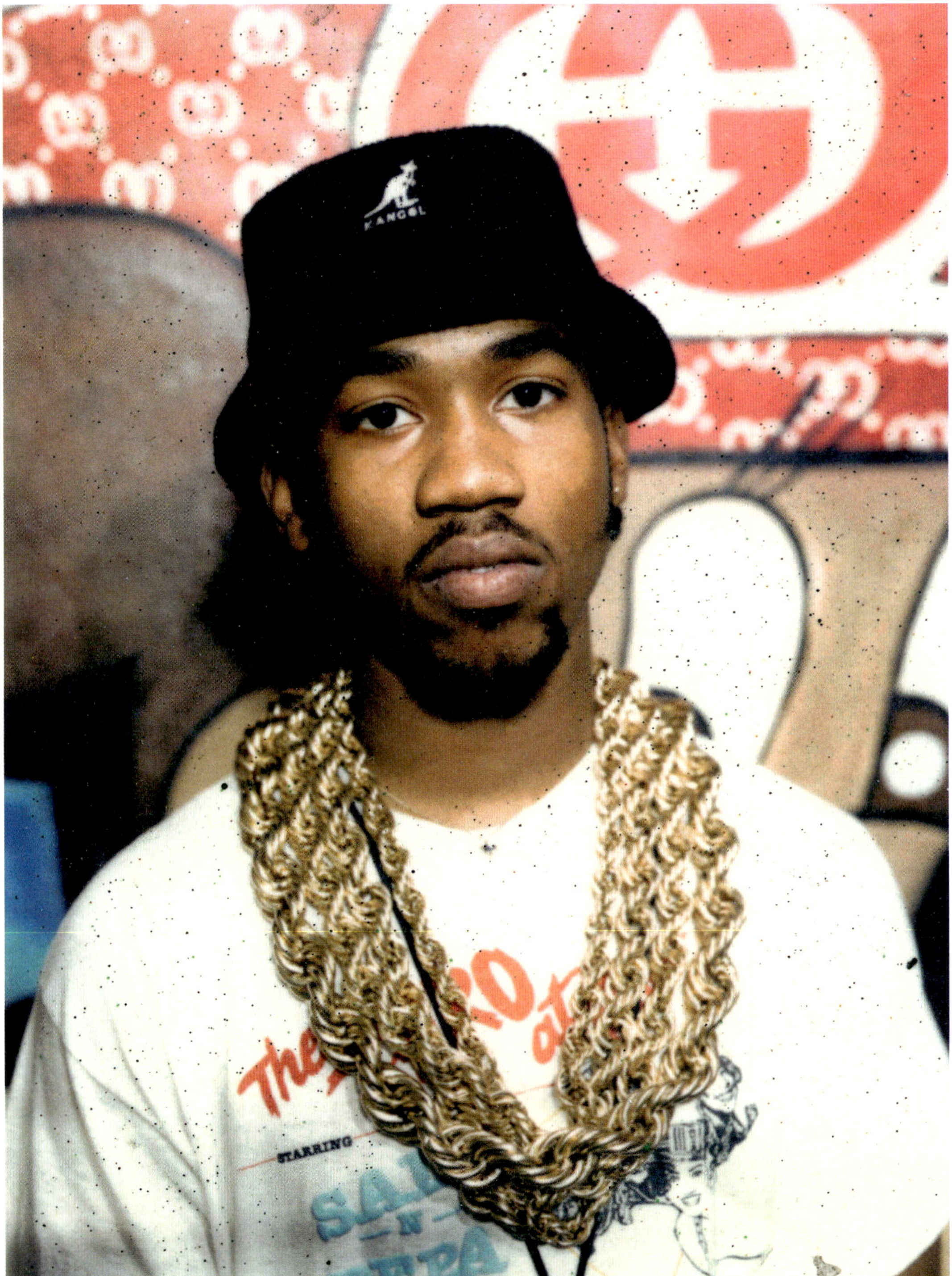

Cool V, Jamaica Coliseum, 1988.

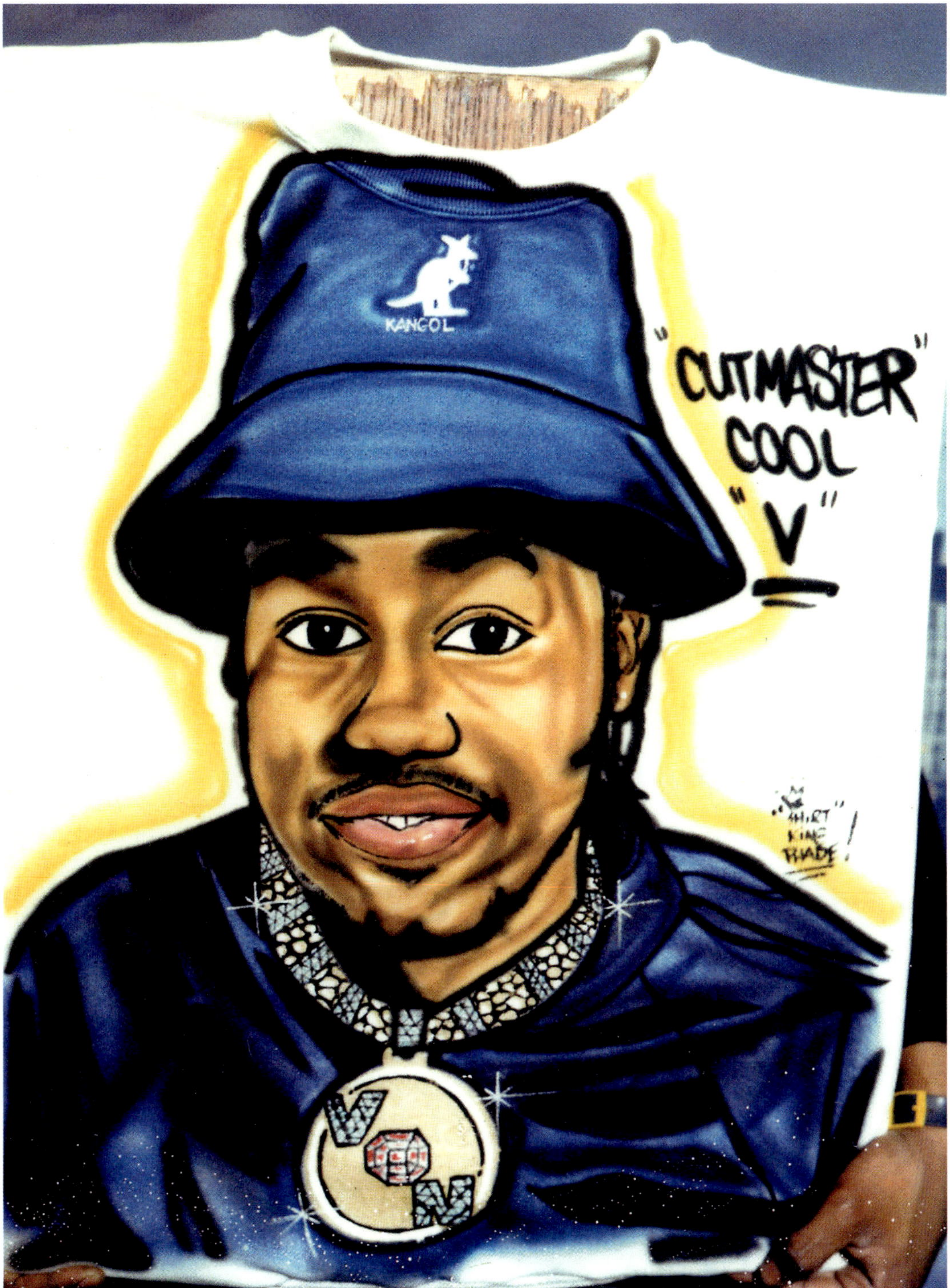

Cool V, Jamaica Coliseum, 1988.

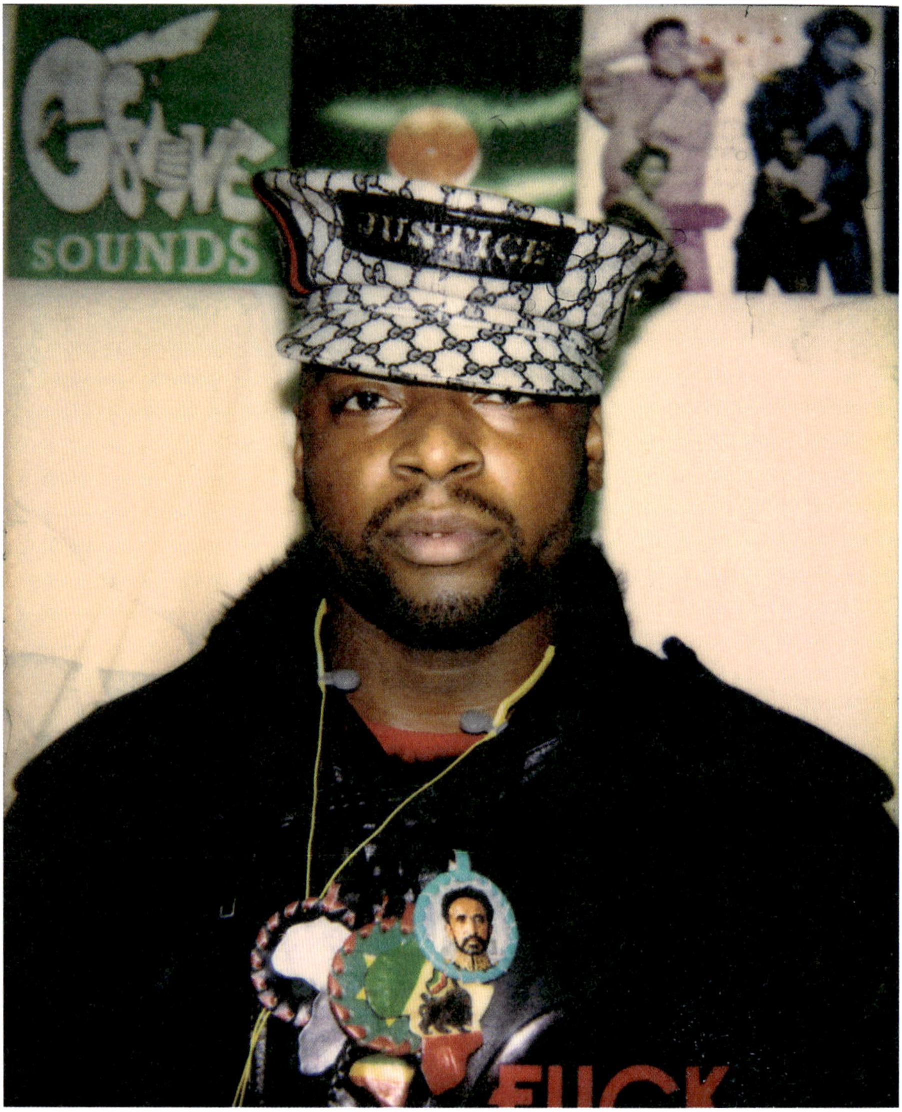

Just Ice, Jamaica Coliseum, 1987.

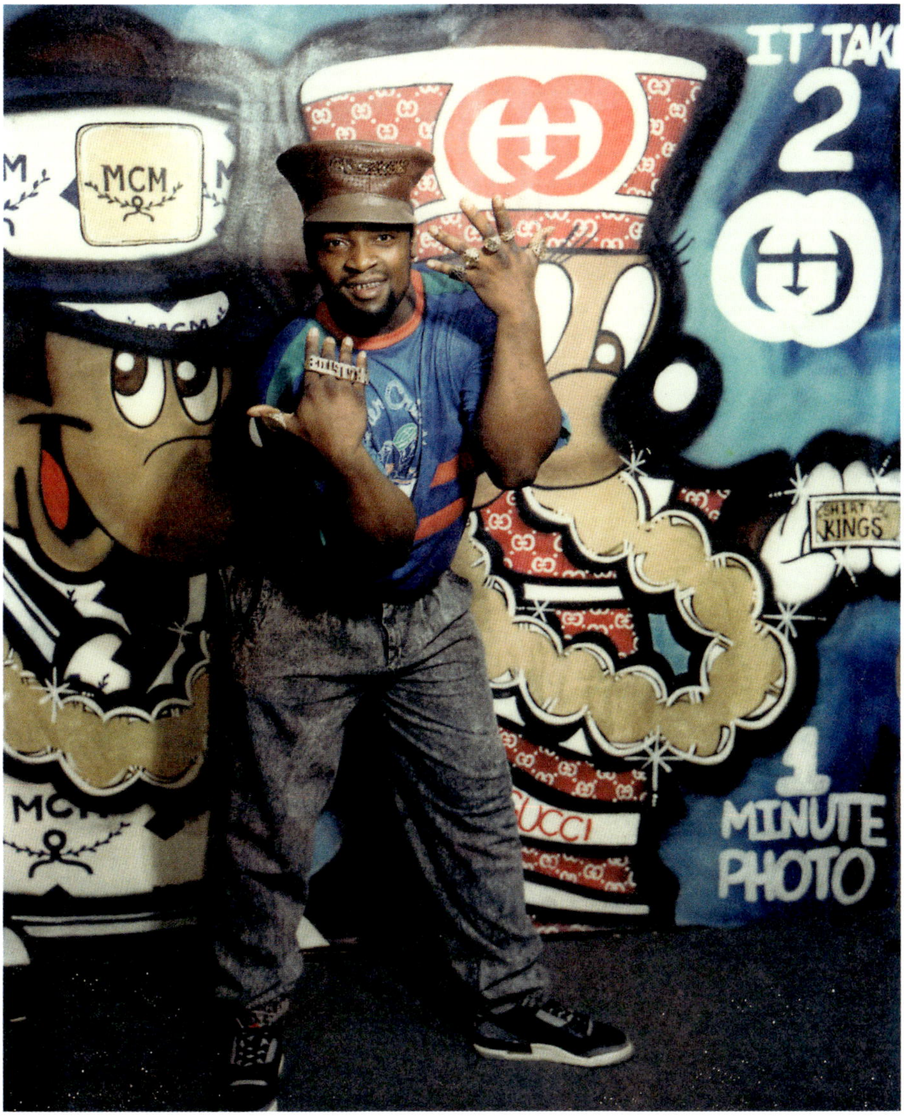

Just Ice, Jamaica Coliseum, 1987.

"Hip hop was so much a key ingredient as the elements of rap, dance, DJing, and graf work seemed to come together on a Shirt Kings blessing. I still relish the jacket and the pictures taken while my now college student oldest daughter, who was then four years old, left with a Shirt Kings special. The Shirt King's network was the fashion TV of the times, and advertising and promotion way before it became trendy."
Chuck D / Public Enemy

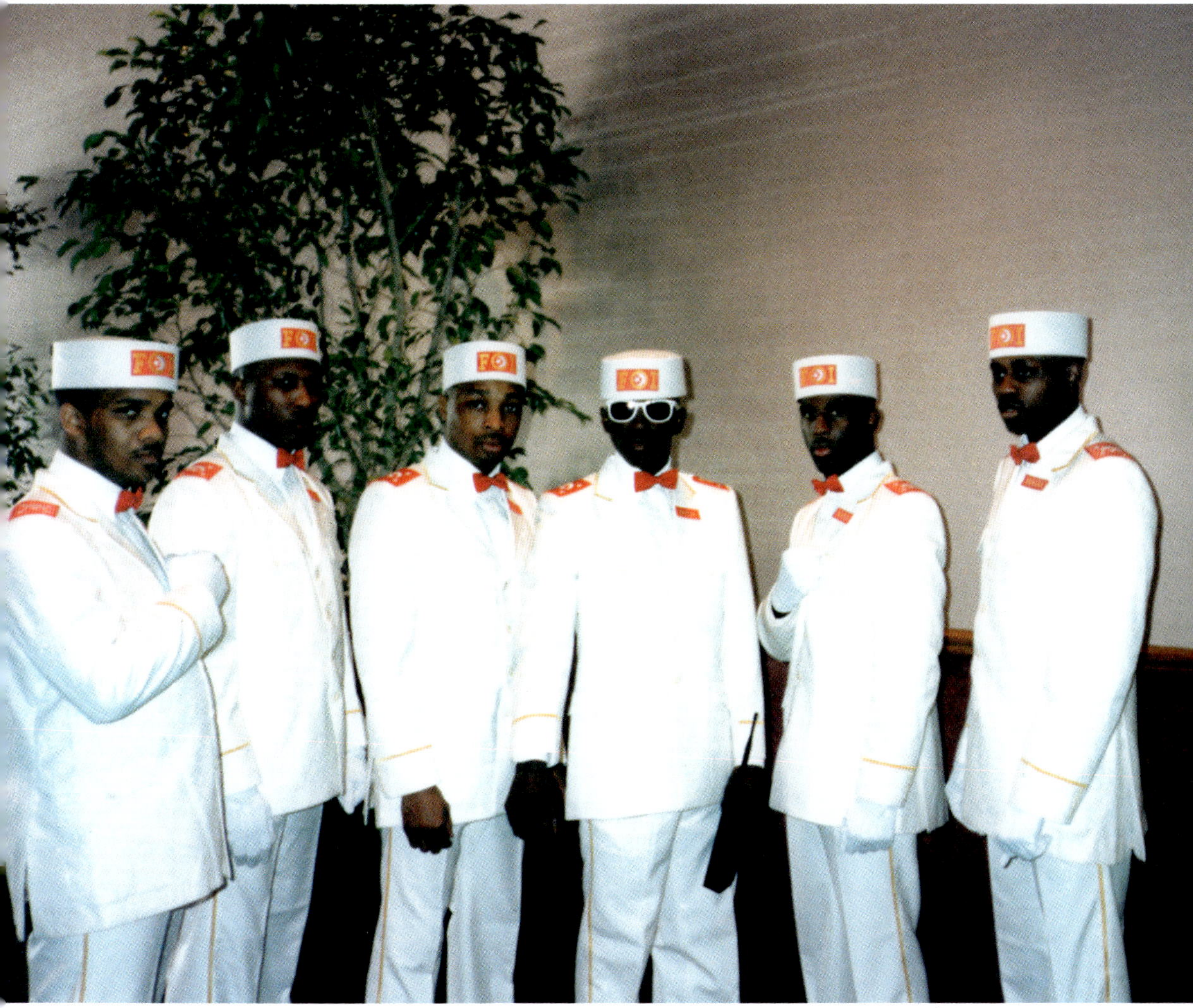

Public Enemy, Chicago, Saviour's day 1989.

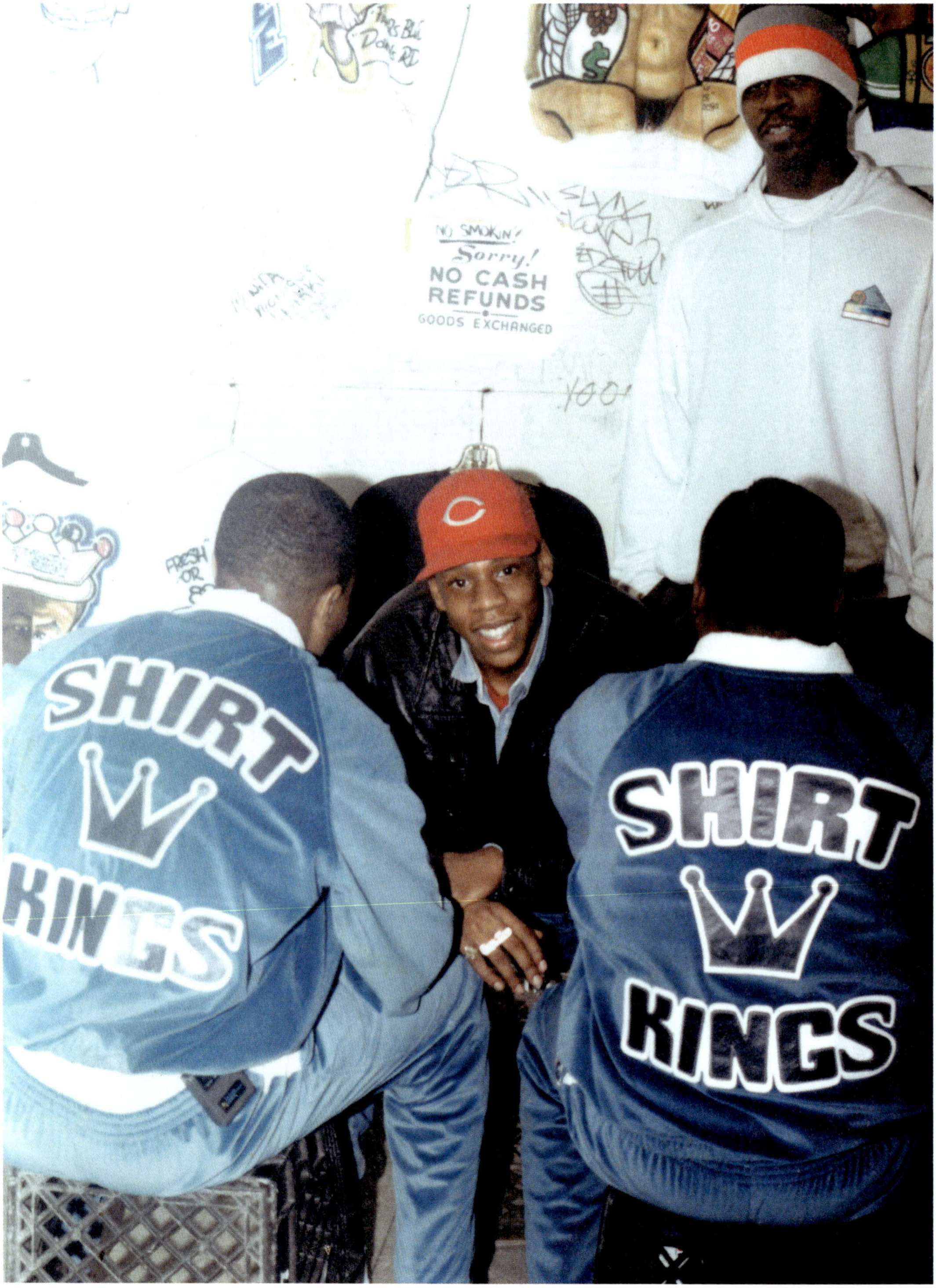

Jaz-O and Jay-Z, Jamaica Coliseum, 1988.

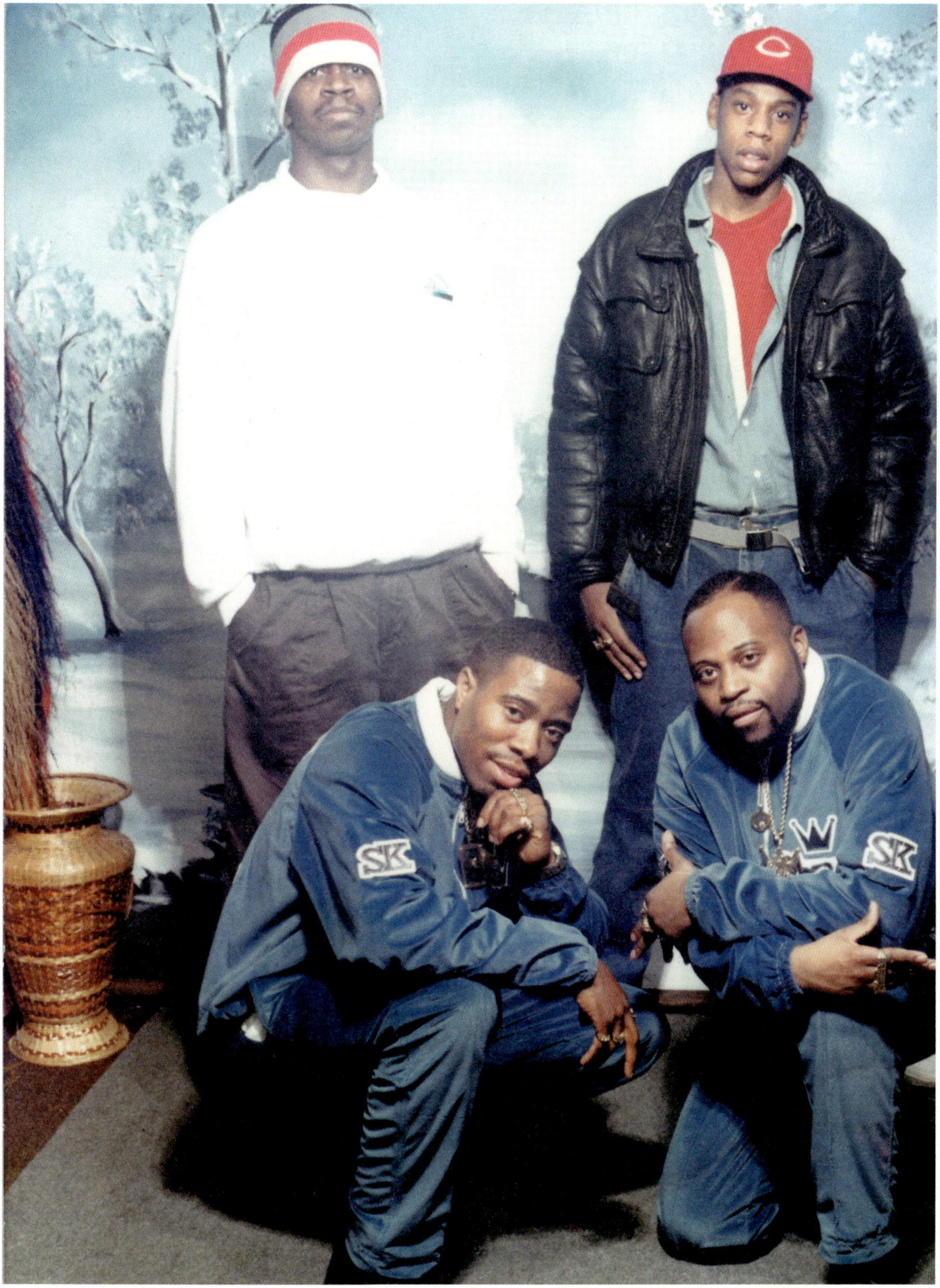

Jaz-O and Jay-Z, Jamaica Coliseum, 1988.

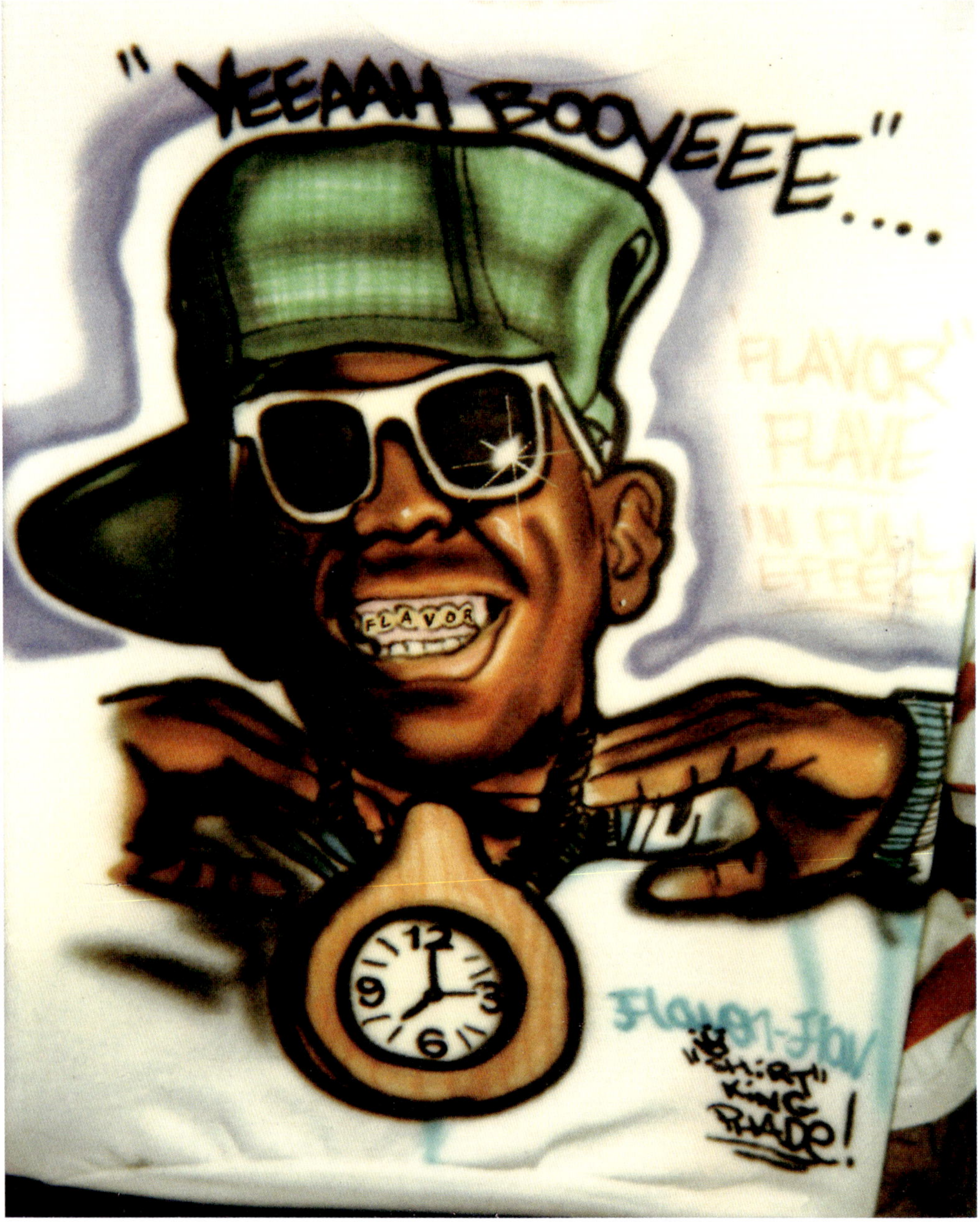

Flavor Flav, Jamaica Coliseum, 1987.

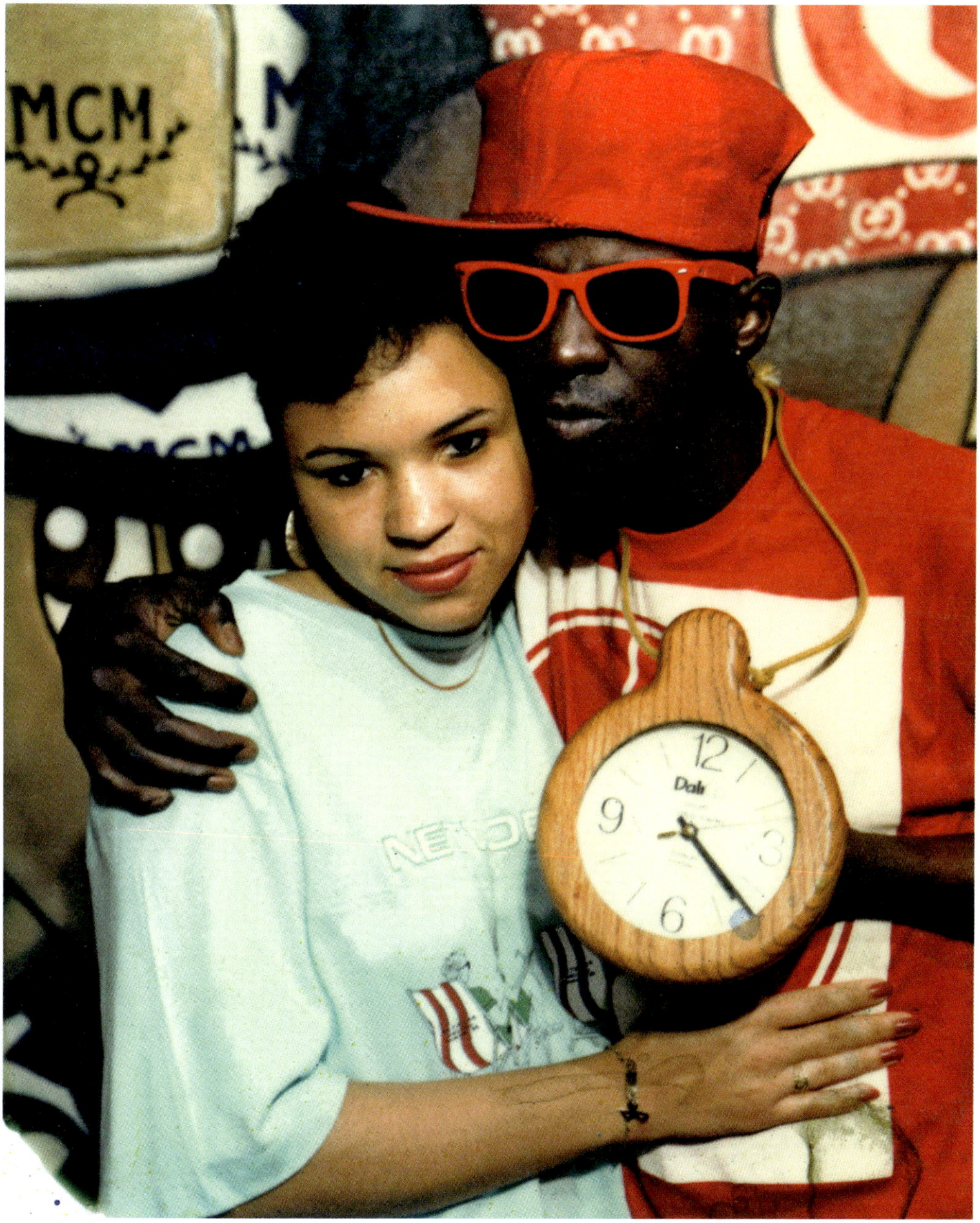

Flavor Flav, Jamaica Coliseum, 1987.

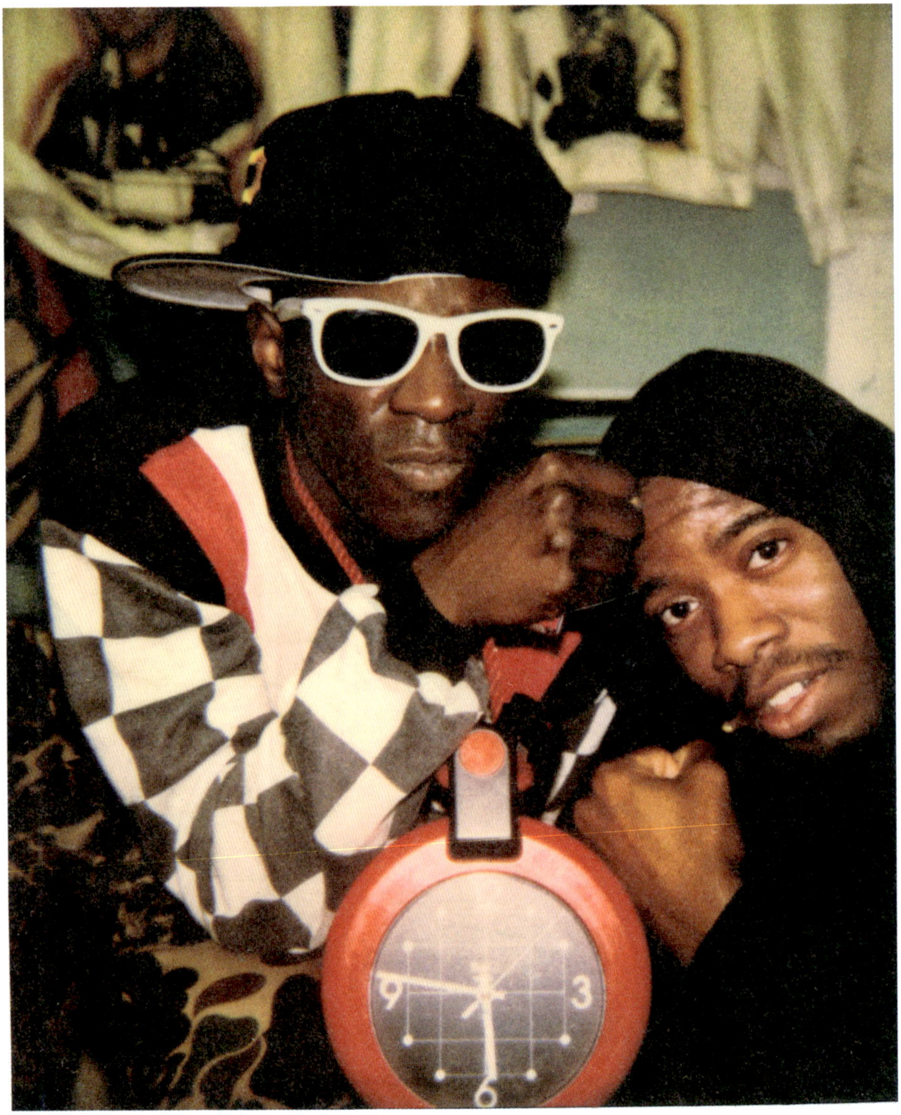

Flavor Flav and Nike, Jamaica Coliseum, 1987.

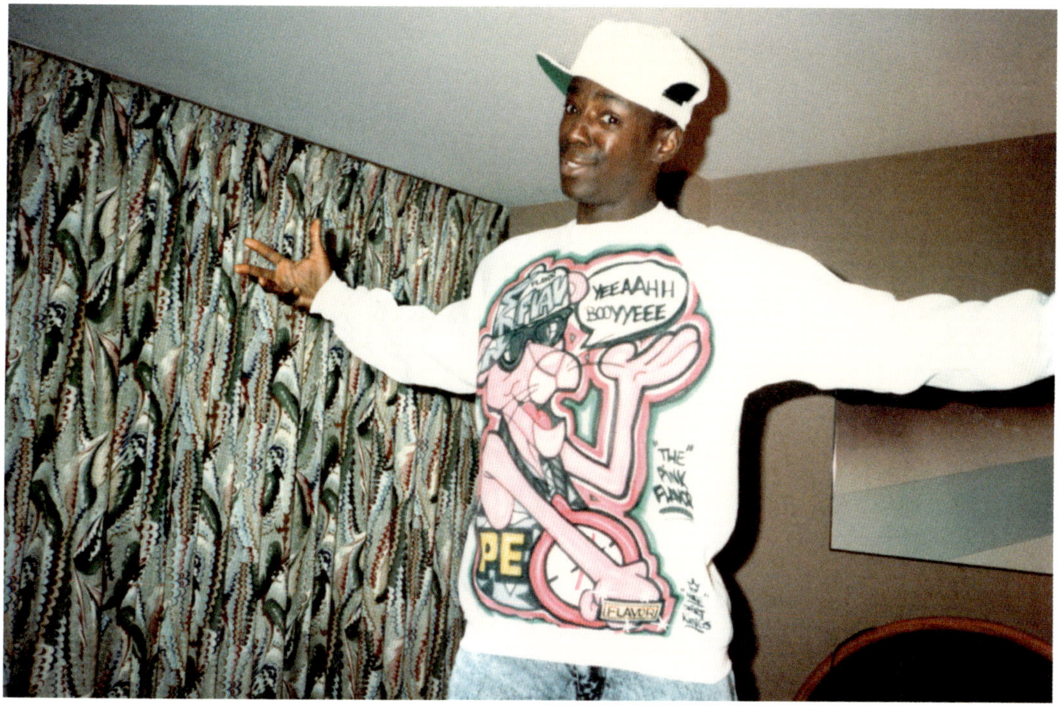

Flavor Flav, Chicago, 1989.

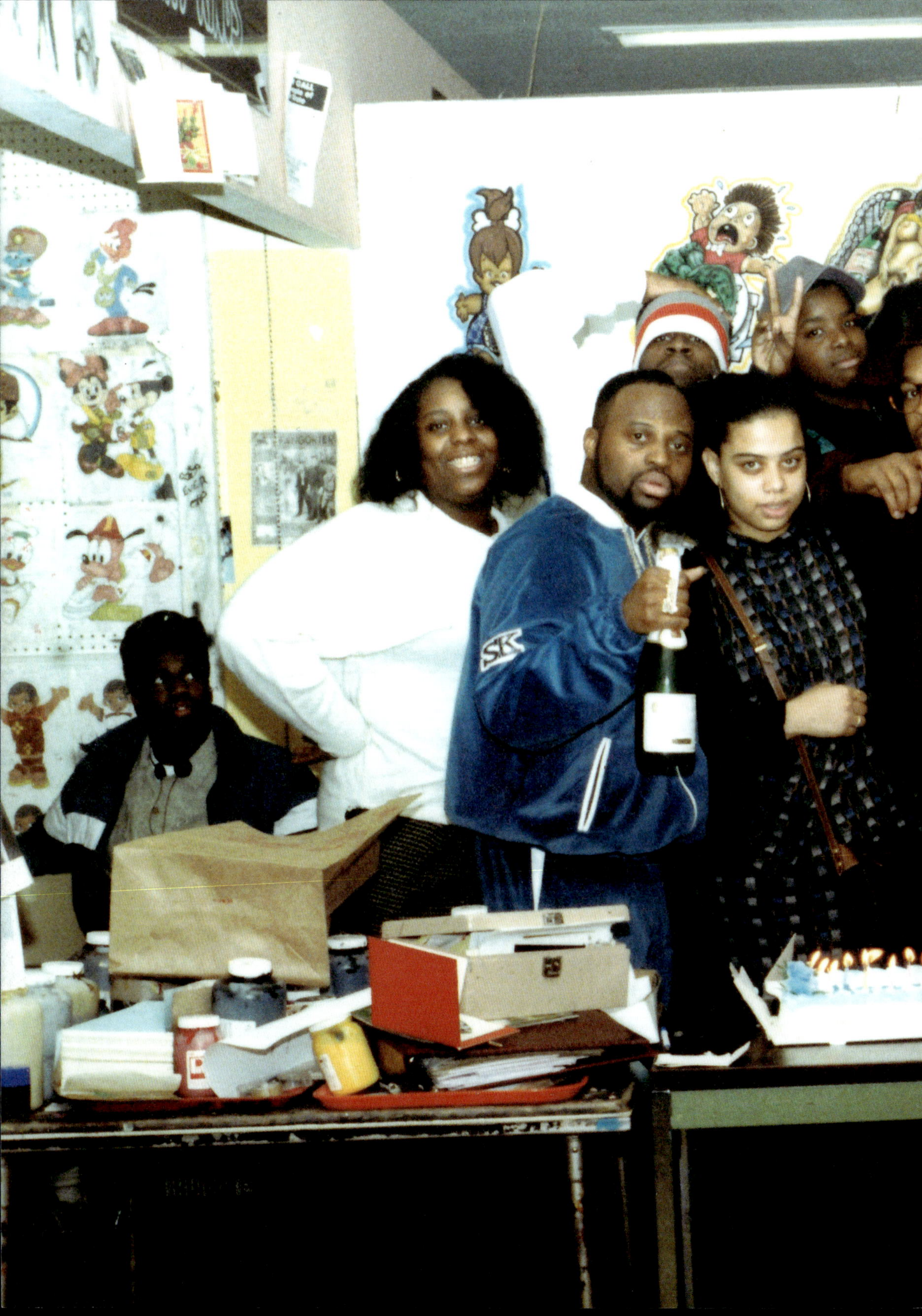

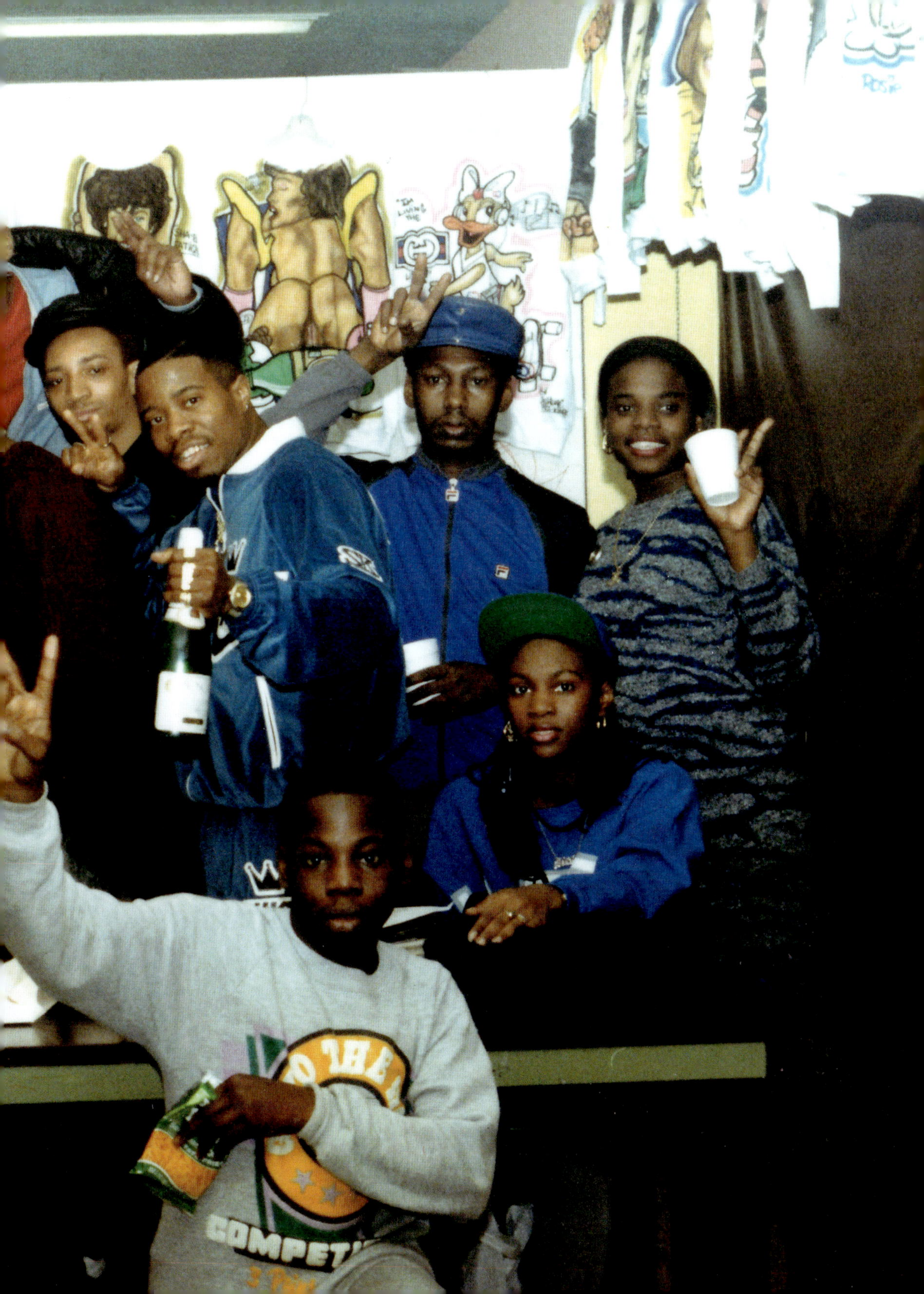

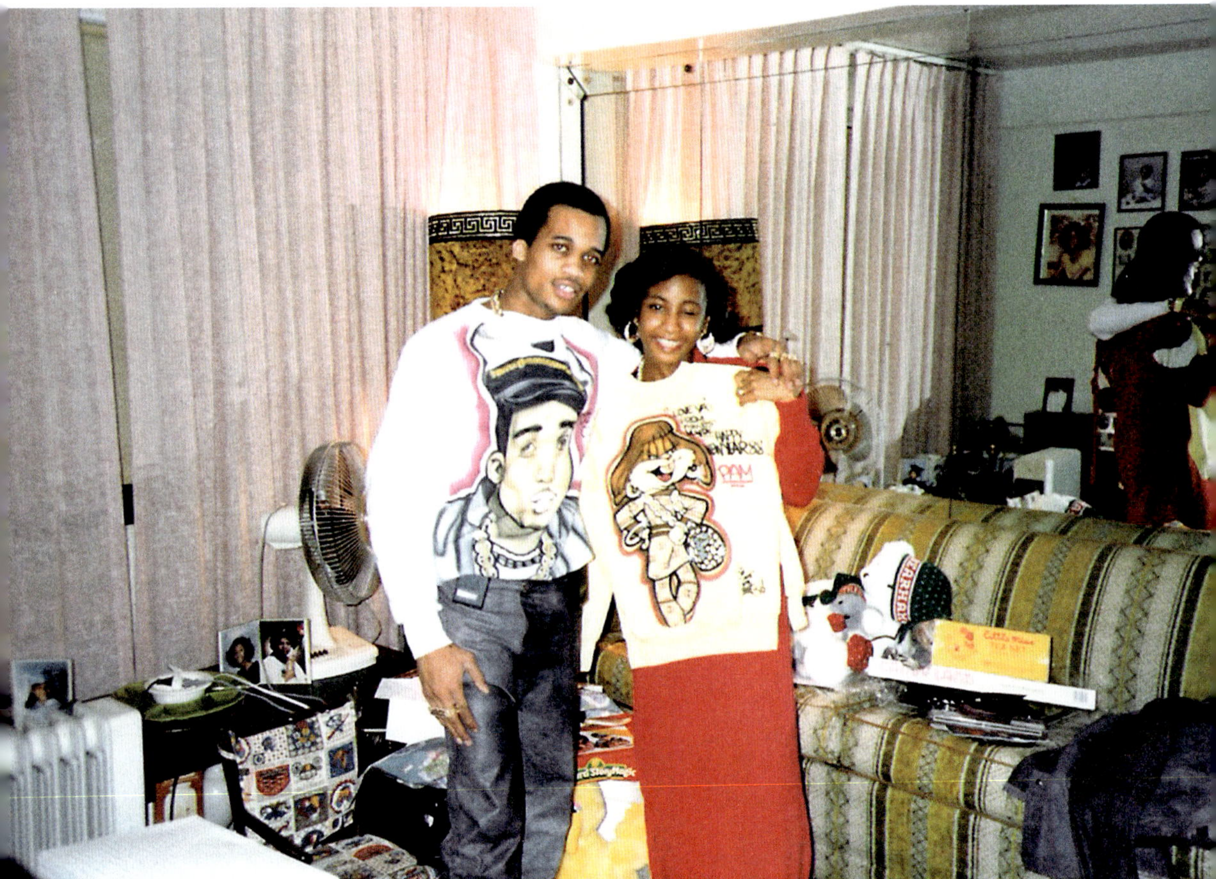

Cool Clyde, the Bronx, 1988.

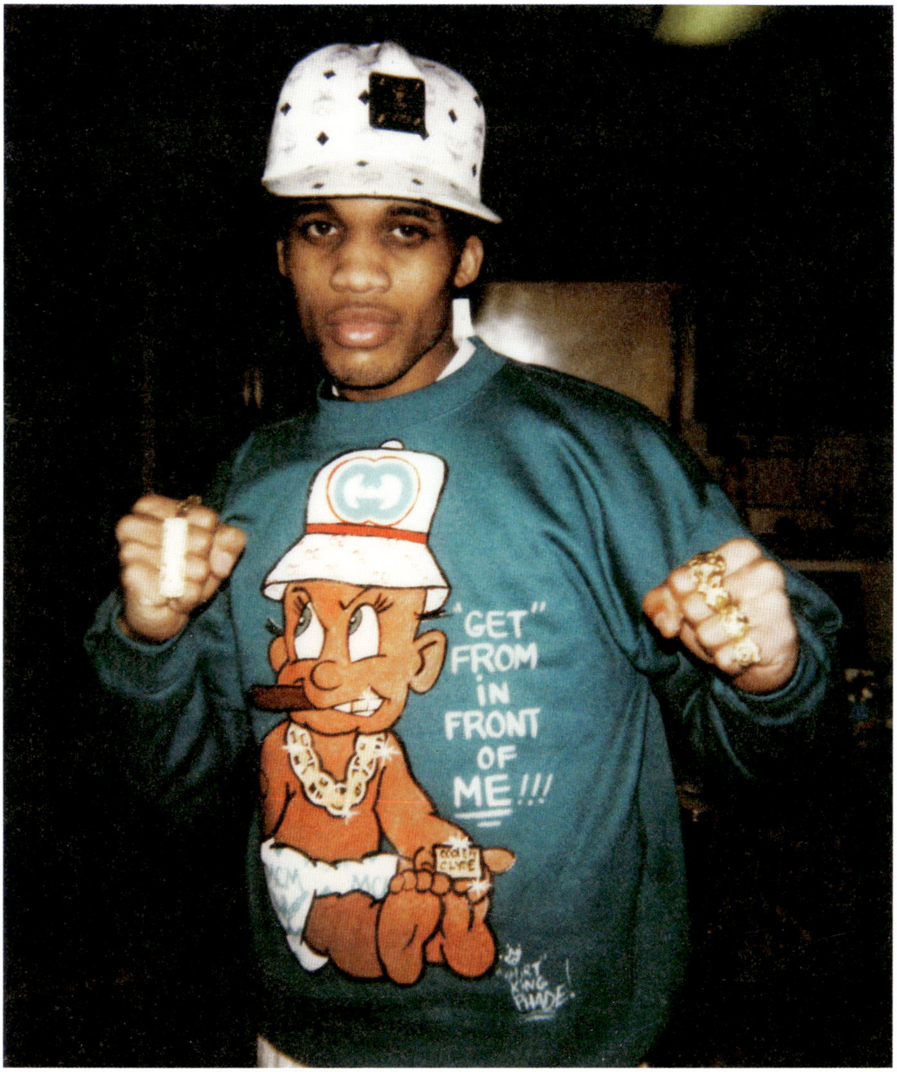

Cool Clyde, the Bronx, 1988.

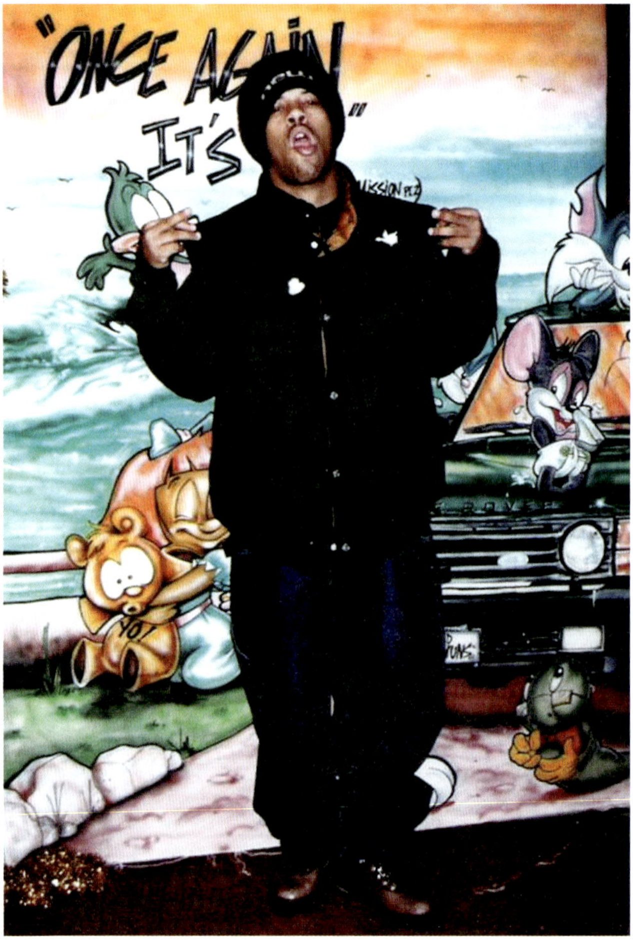

This page: Redman, Jamaica Coliseum, 1990. **Opposite page:** Marquis of the 2 Live Crew, Miami, 1988.

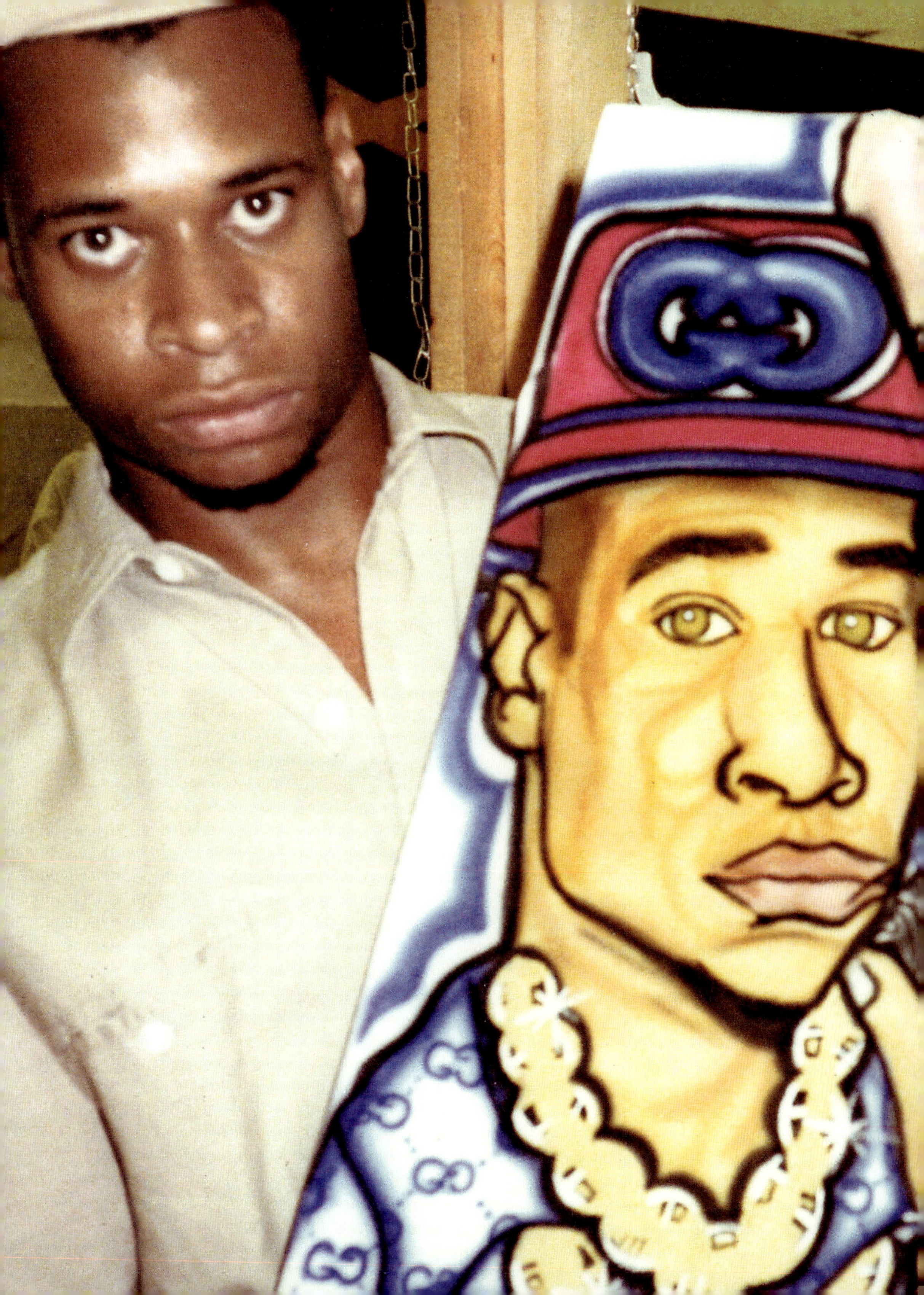

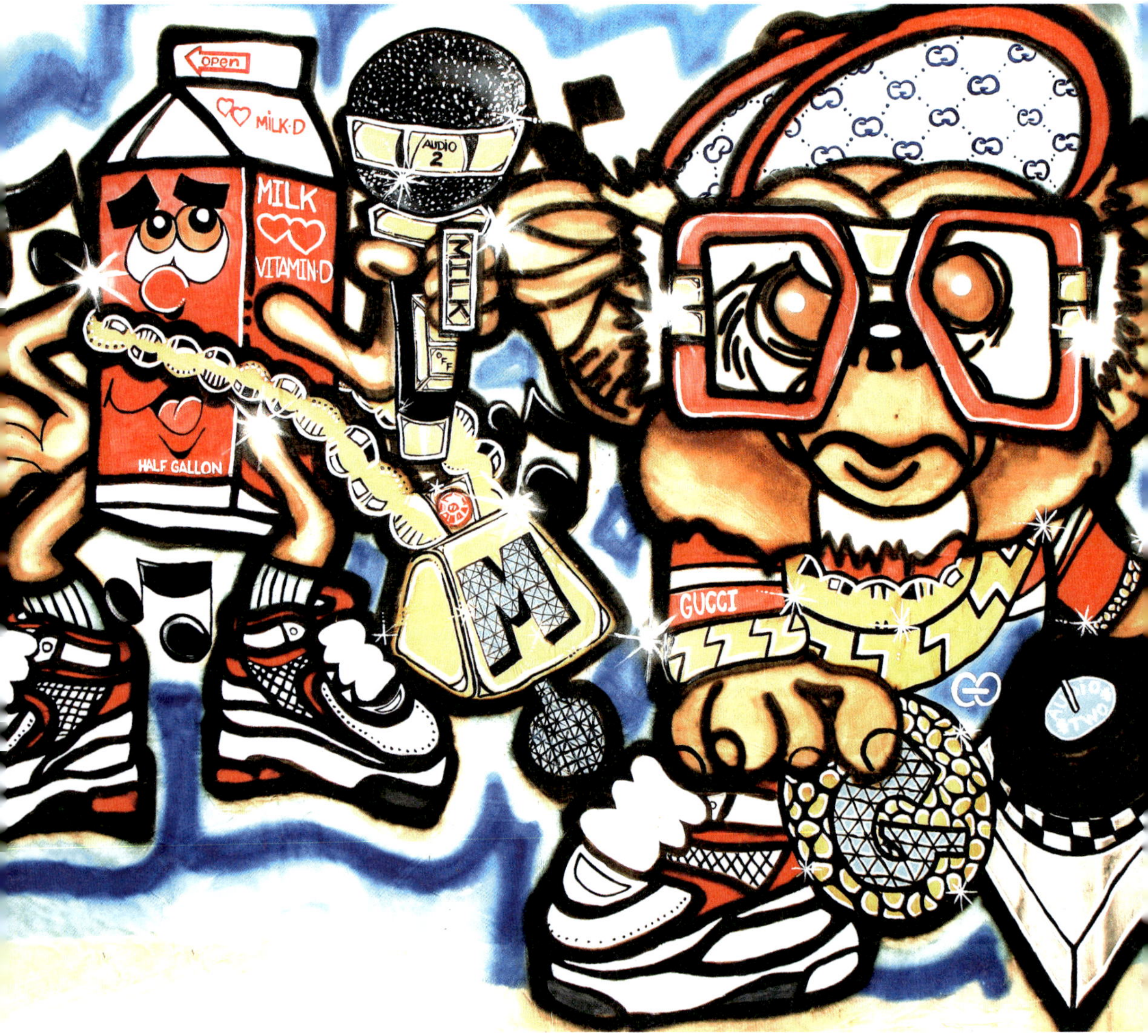

Audio Two album cover art, 1988.

"Graffiti is an essential part of hip hop culture. The Shirt Kings helped to commercialize the art form, and in turn propelling hip hop to a new plateau. Shirt Kings artwork helped make my first album, *What More Can I Say*, the classic that it is."
Milk Dee / Audio Two

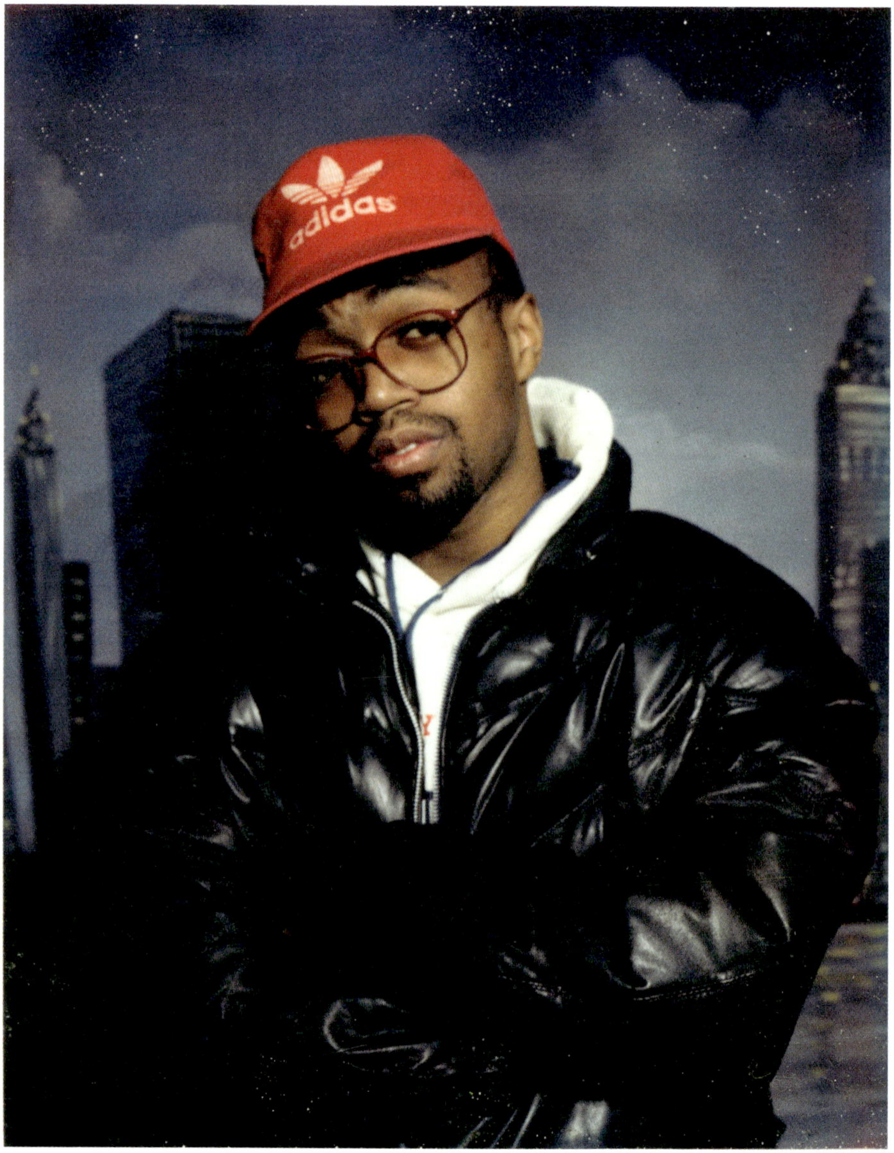

Gizmo, Jamaica Coliseum, 1987.

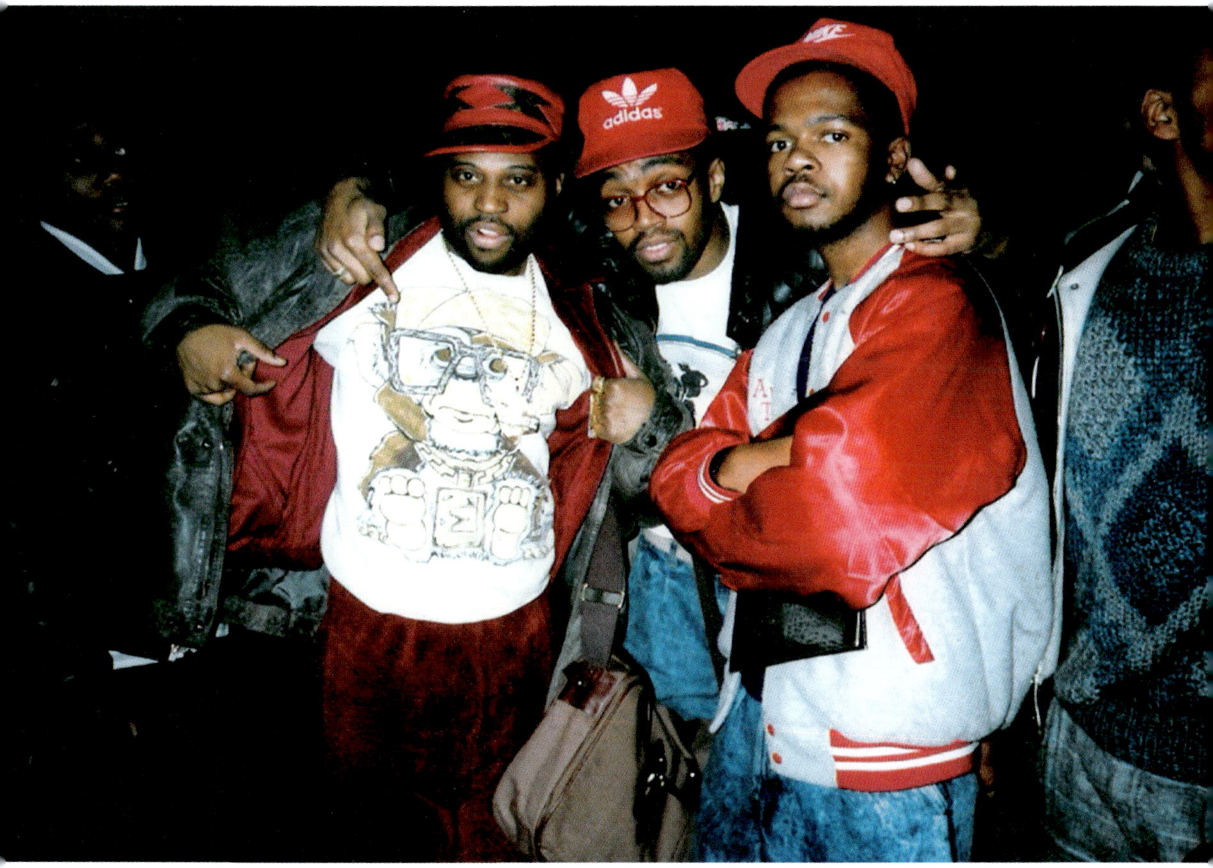

Phade, Gizmo, and Milk, Latin Quarters night club, 1987.

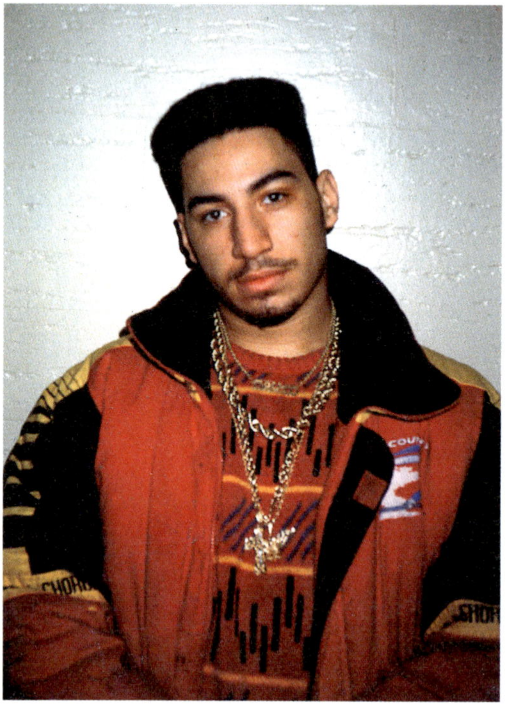

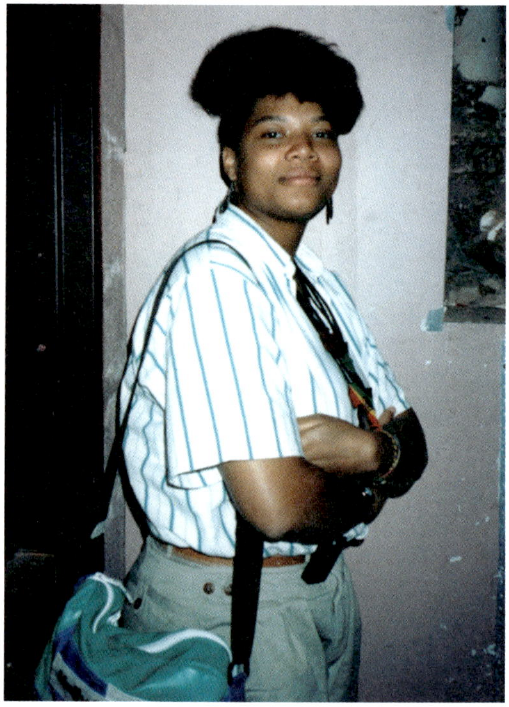

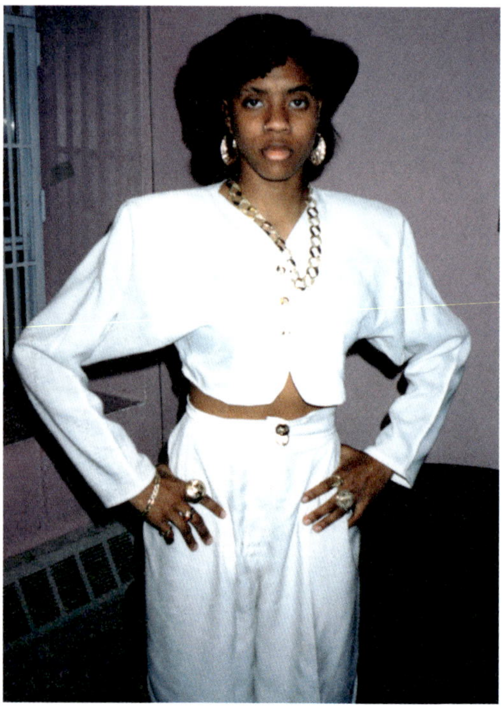

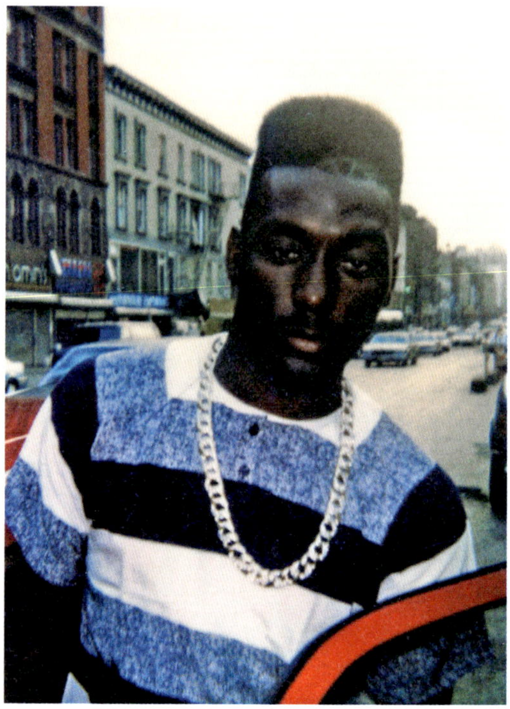

Clockwise from top left: Kid Capri, the Bronx, 1990. Queen Latifah, Apollo Theatre, 1991. Big Daddy Kane, Harlem, 1990. MC Lyte, Apollo Theatre, 1991.

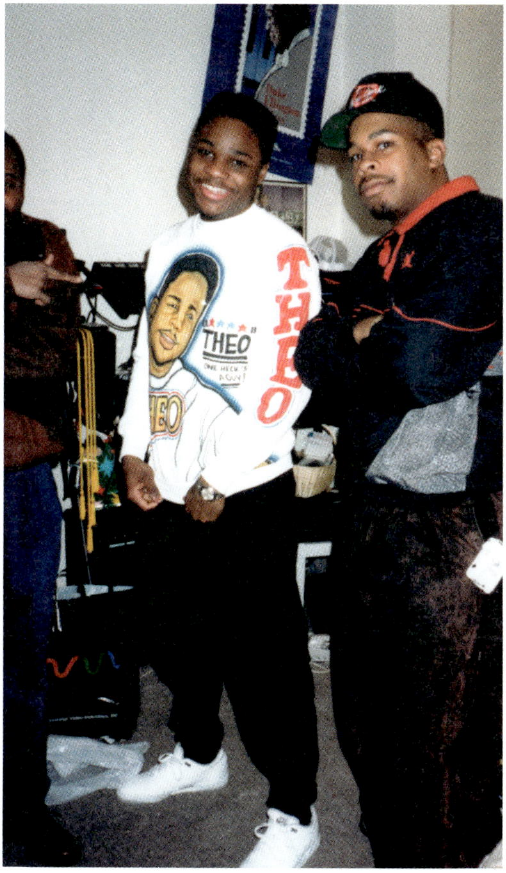

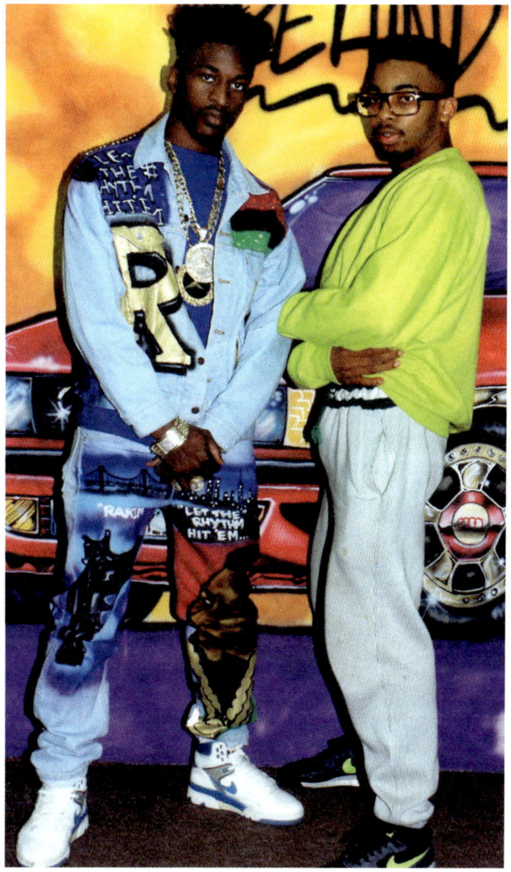

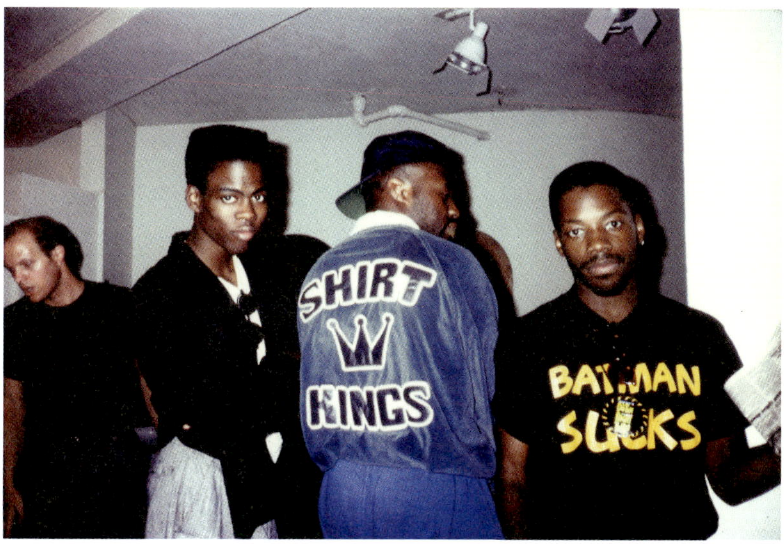

Clockwise from top left: Malcom Jamal Warner, Brooklyn, 1989. Rakim and Sike, Queens, 1992. Chris Rock, Phade, and Kadeem Hardison on the set of Big Daddy Kane's *Ain't No Half-Stepping* video shoot, 1988.

“The Shirt Kings broke a lot of ground back in the day. On a fashion level they introduced us all to a part of what was cool and what we thought was fly. By taking it from the trains and bringing it to the shirts, they were the first guys to make hip hop kids care about clothing in that way. Shirt Kings brought the Hip Hop element into the clothes for real and integrated it.”
LL Cool J

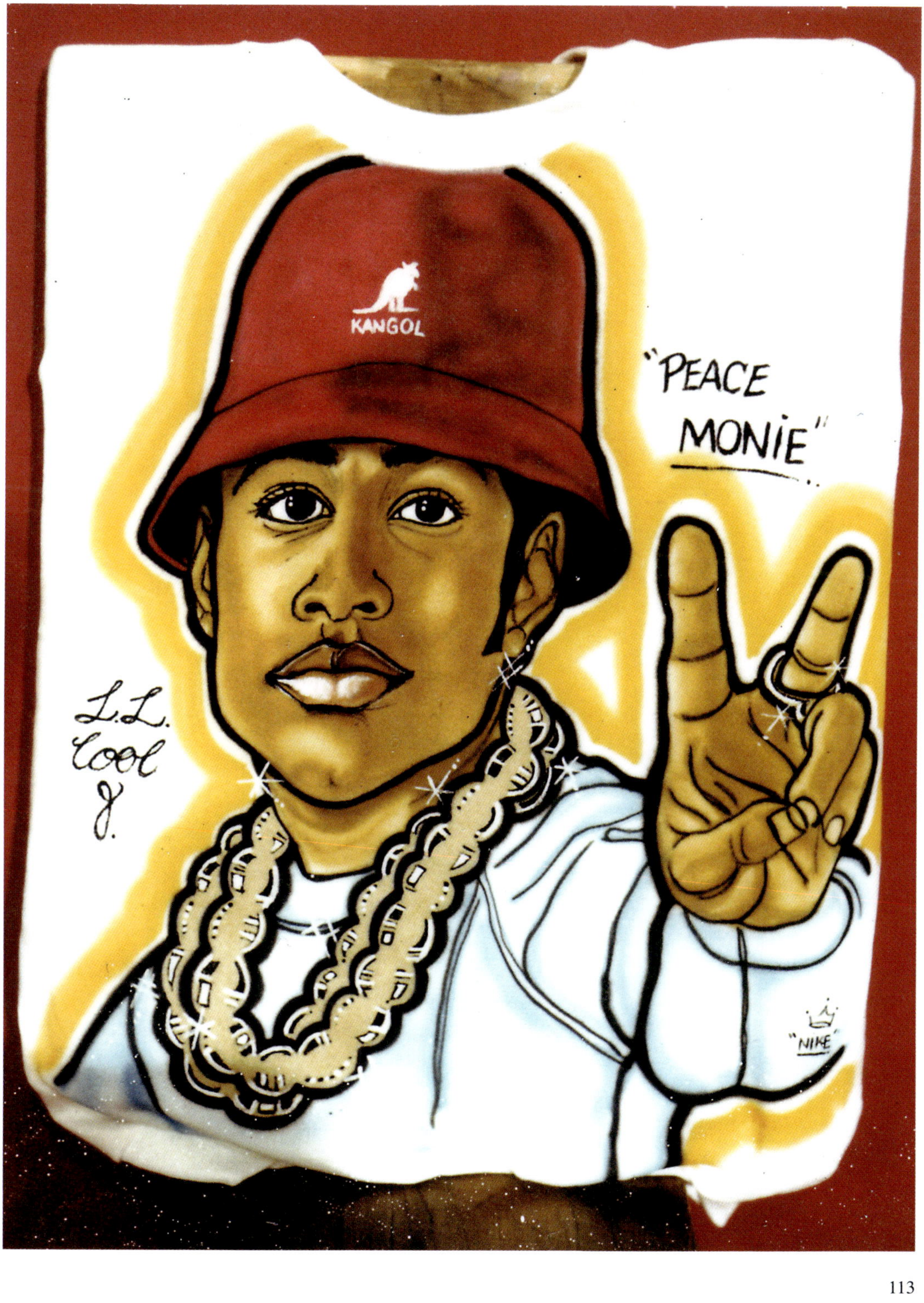
KANGOL
"PEACE
MONIE"
L.L.
Cool
J.
"NIKE"

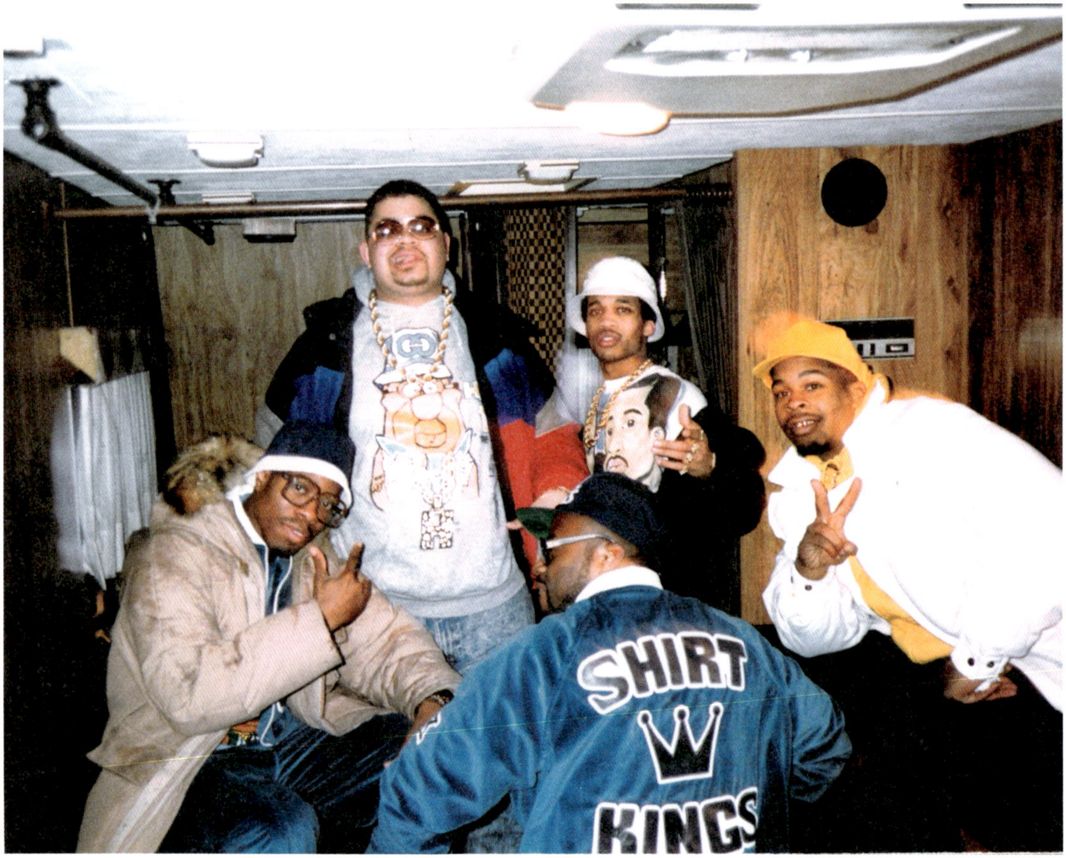

 Heavy D, Cool Clyde, and the Shirt Kings at the *Money Earning Mount Vernon* video shoot, Mount Vernon, 1989.

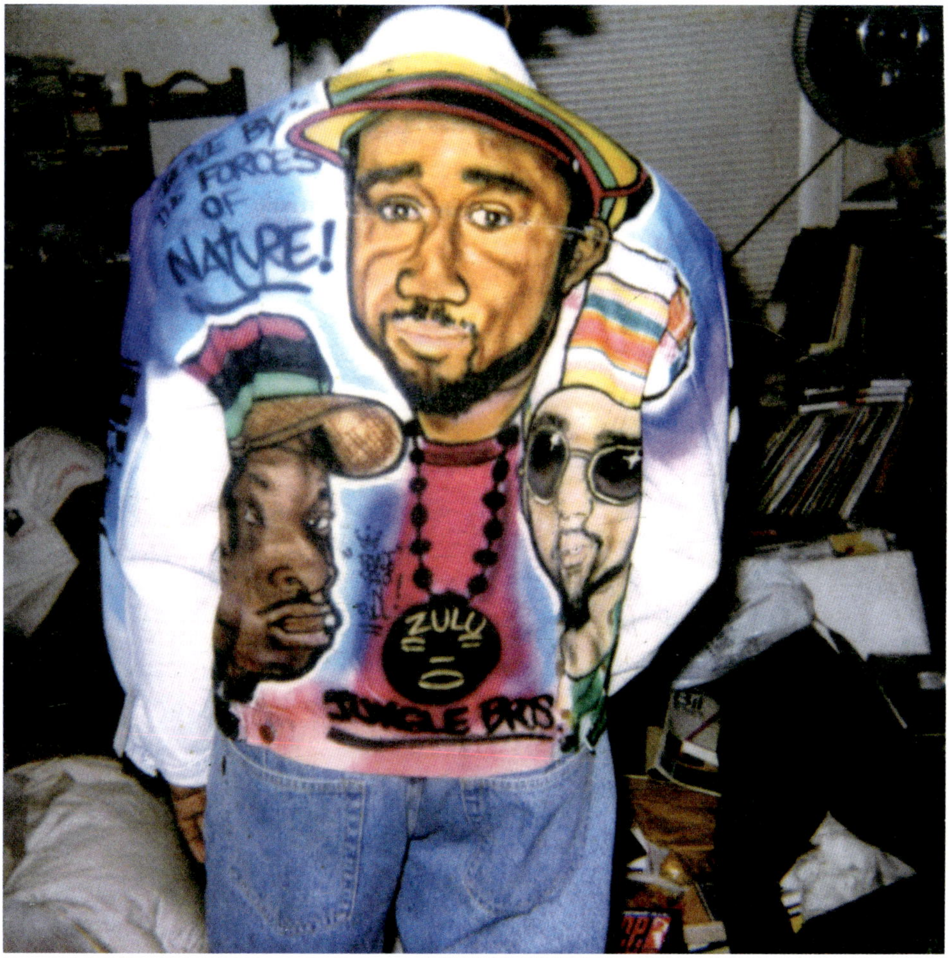

Mike Gee's jacket, Harlem, 1989.

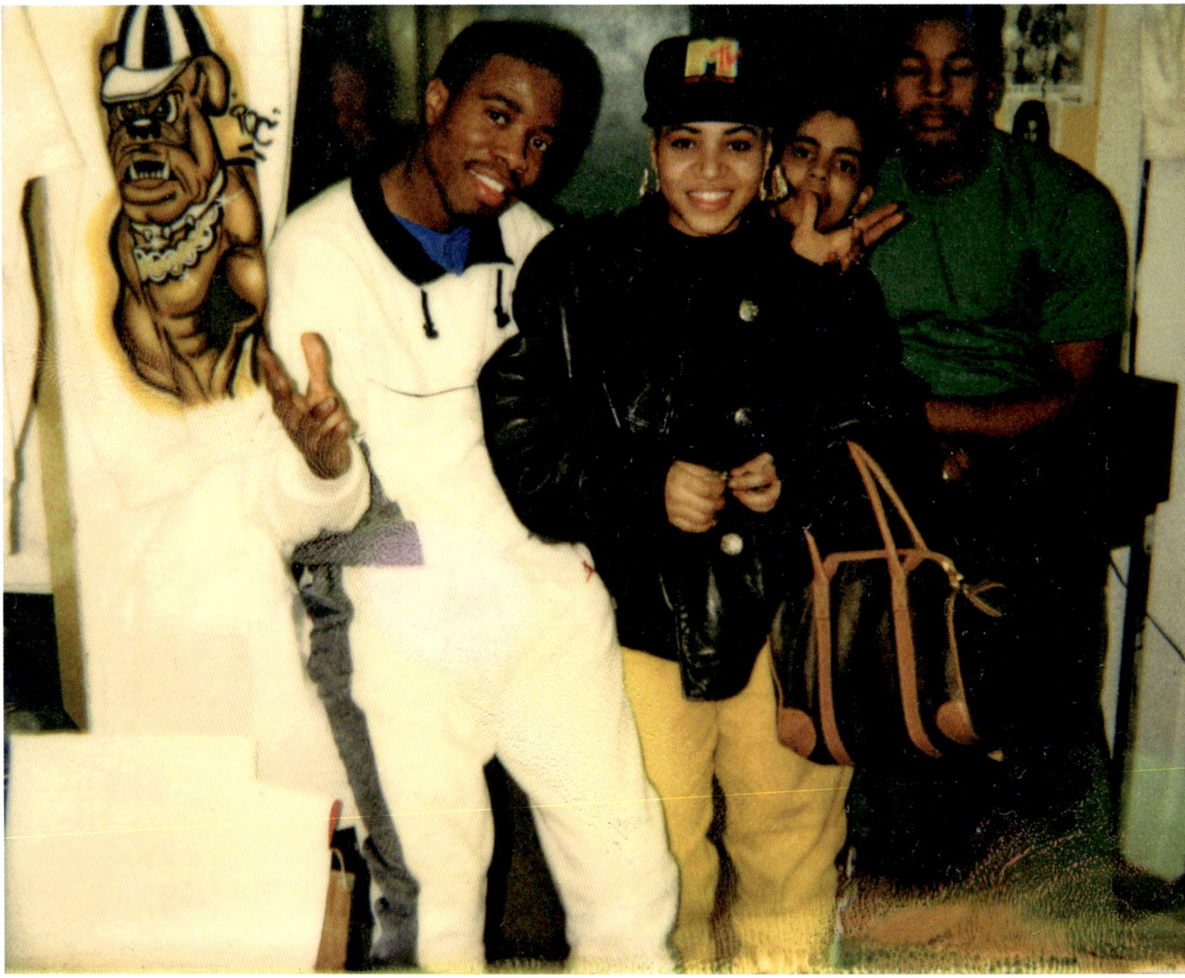

Salt and the Shirt Kings, Jamaica Coliseum, 1988.

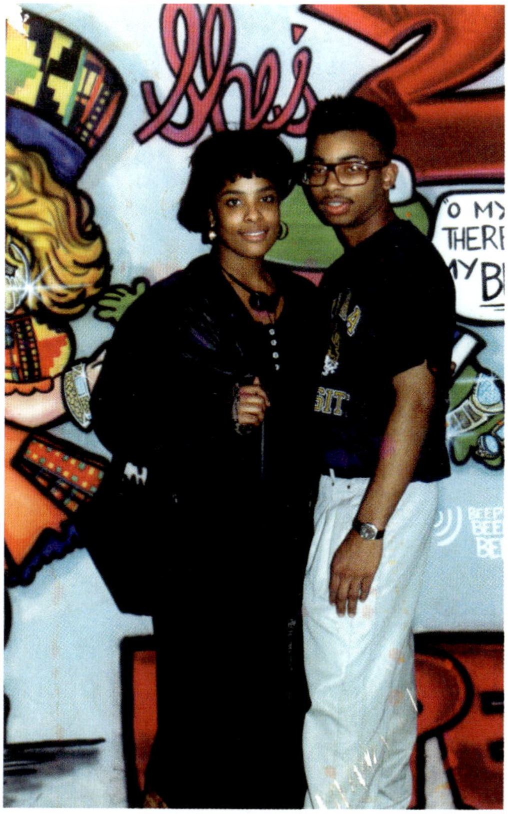

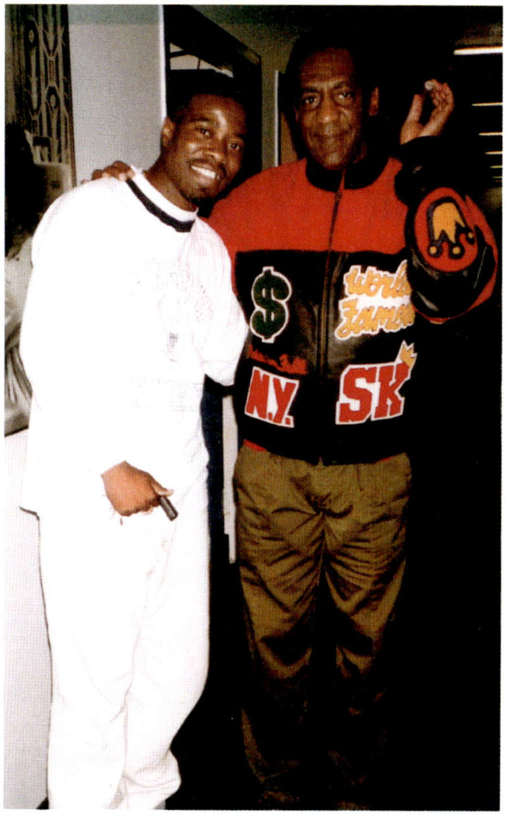

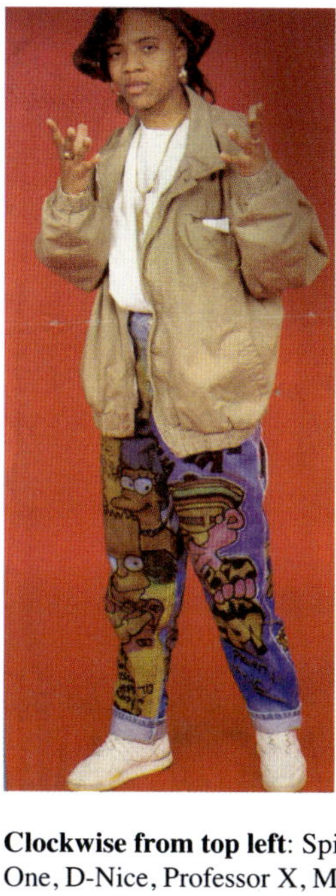

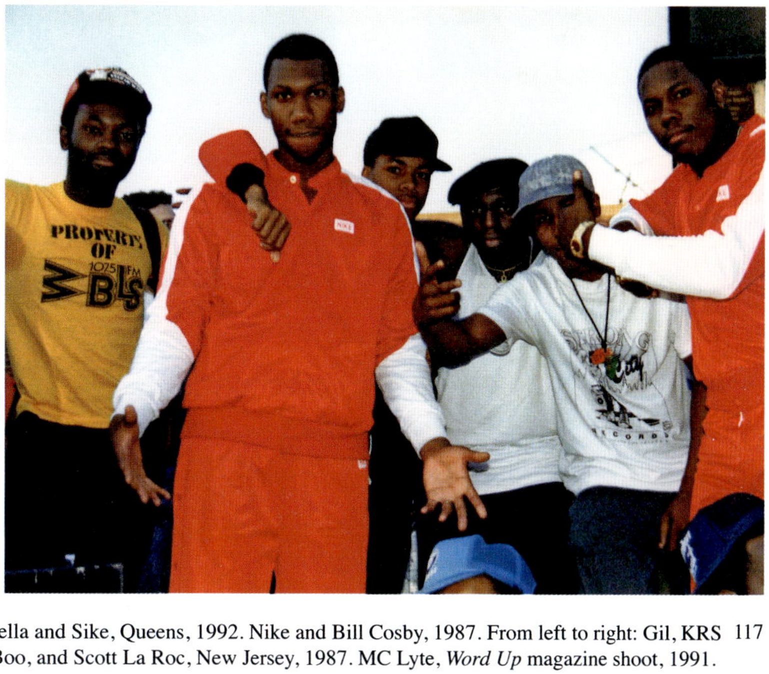

Clockwise from top left: Spindarella and Sike, Queens, 1992. Nike and Bill Cosby, 1987. From left to right: Gil, KRS One, D-Nice, Professor X, Mick Boo, and Scott La Roc, New Jersey, 1987. MC Lyte, *Word Up* magazine shoot, 1991.

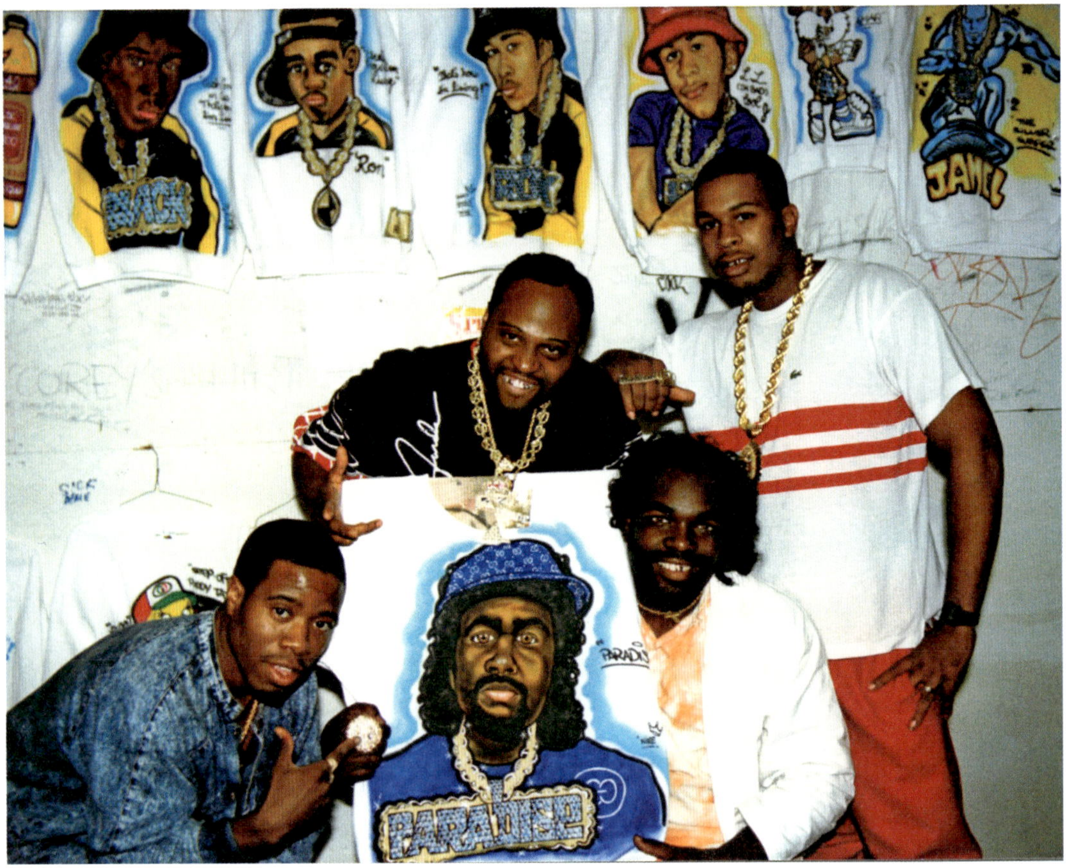

Paradise Gray with the Shirt Kings, Jamaica Coliseum, 1987.

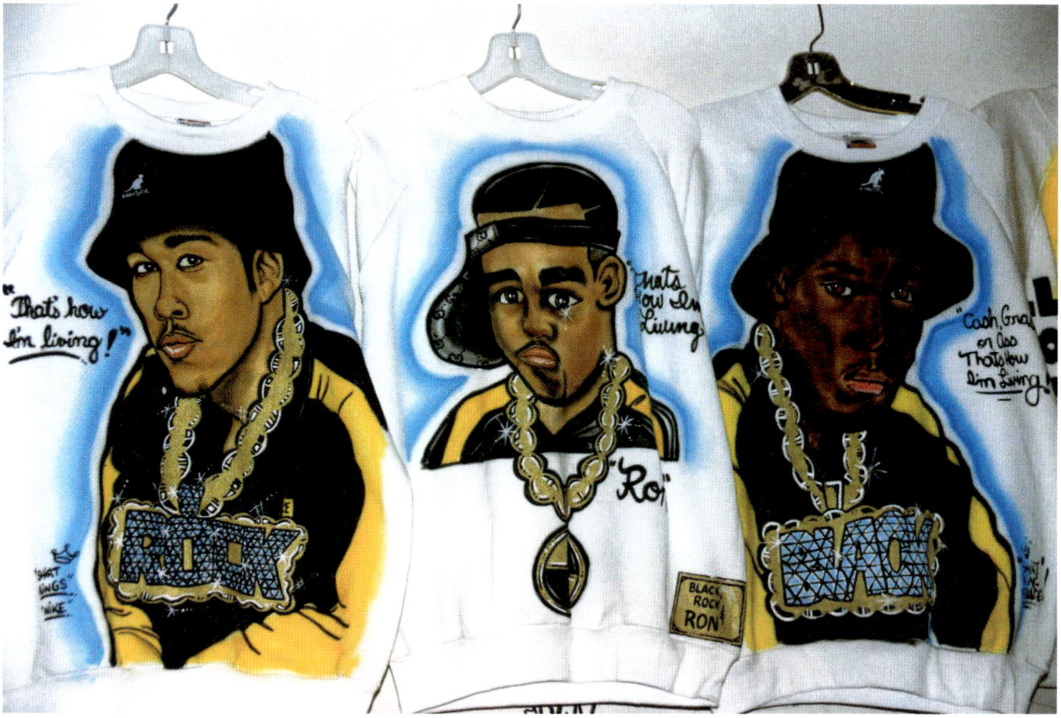

Black, Rock and Ron, Jamaica Coliseum, 1987. Photo by Paradise Gray, courtesy of the Paradise Collection.

"It's all about the Shirt Kings. The Shirt Kings! We are talking about my man Phade. We are talking about my man Nike. Rest in peace to the man Kasheme. When you see their artwork it shows the passion. Going back to 1986, Phade came across me uptown, around my way in Harlem. He let me know who he was and he said, 'Yo, come by the shop, it's out there in Queens.' At that time I used to move around and I think I was seeing a young lady about that time [in Queens]. So I took it upon myself to go out there to Jamaica Avenue. They had this big area called the Coliseum. The Coliseum is like a lot of little shops, where you could find everything, from clothes to whatever. Yeah, like my man Eddie's Gold Teeth. What they had in there was that style, that flair, whatever you were gonna portray, whatever you were gonna wear. It took me a little while to look around. I finally came around a little section where they were and I said, 'Yo, what's up?' I think they were kind of amazed, 'cause they didn't expect to see me. I started watching how they were doing their work and I was like, 'Whoa! Wow!' I asked a lot of questions 'cause I was amazed at what I saw and I asked them if they could make a shirt for me. The first shirt I had was one of the Transformers. I fell in love with that shirt. Now, I know that some people would look at the shirt and say, 'what's that grown man doing with this kid shirt on?' It wasn't like what a grown man would wear, but I felt the style, you know, airbrush of a cartoon. I know it relates more towards the kids, but I fell for it. I rocked it!

Later I got signed to a record label called Next Plateu. I was doing a compilation album, what they call a mix-tape today. I did the first early mix-tape. It wasn't mix in and out, it was song for song with inserts. The name of the compilation was *Red Alert Goes Berserk*. The Shirt Kings did the cover of me and several other people that were on the album, like Black, Rock and Ron, Ultramagnetic, a couple members of the Violators and a couple staff members of Next Plateu. I'm standing right in front, and you see me with the Transformers shirt."
Kool DJ Red Alert

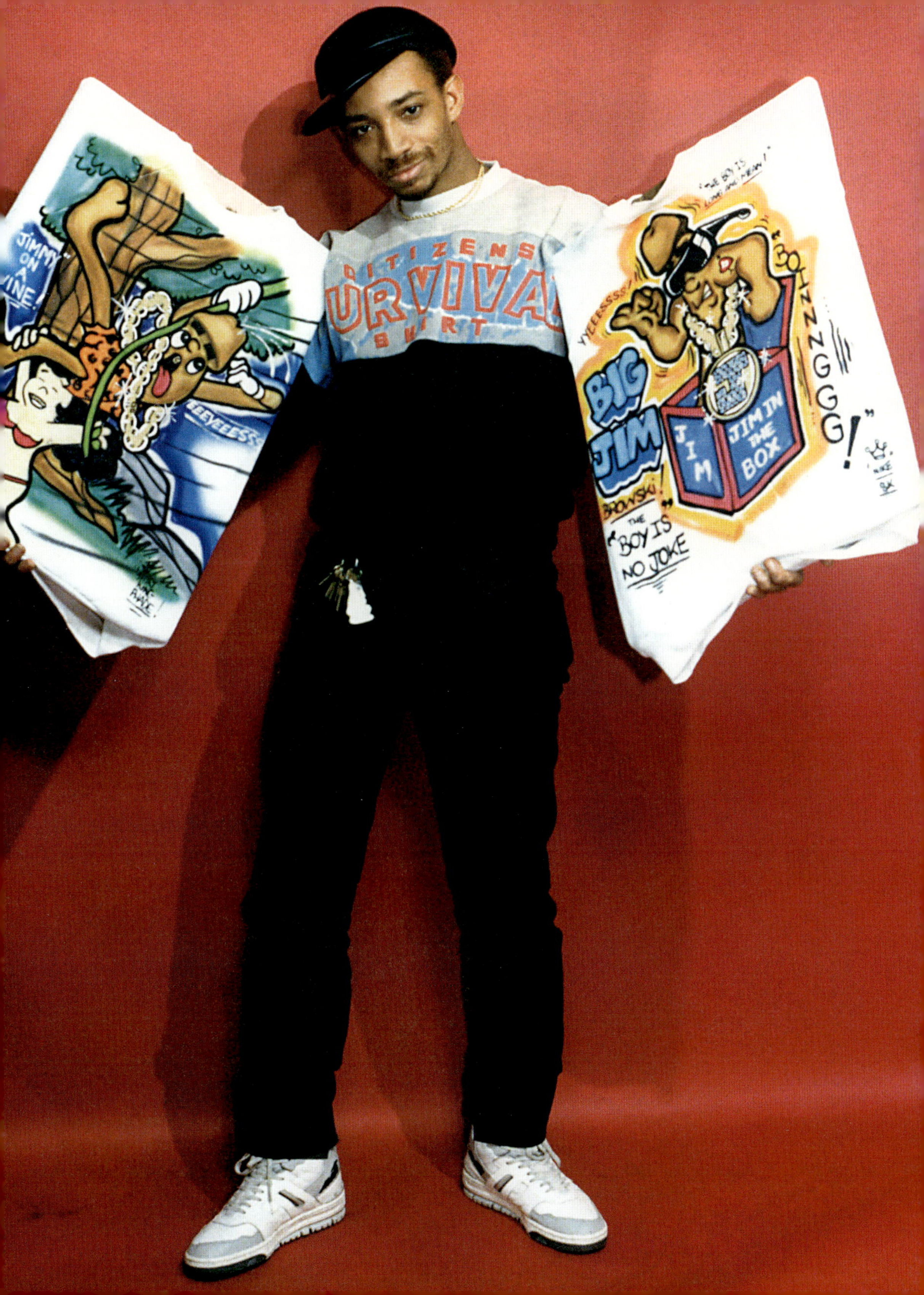

JIMMY ON A
EEEYEEESS
URVIVA
BIG JIM
JIM
JIM IN THE BOX
THE BOY IS NO JOKE

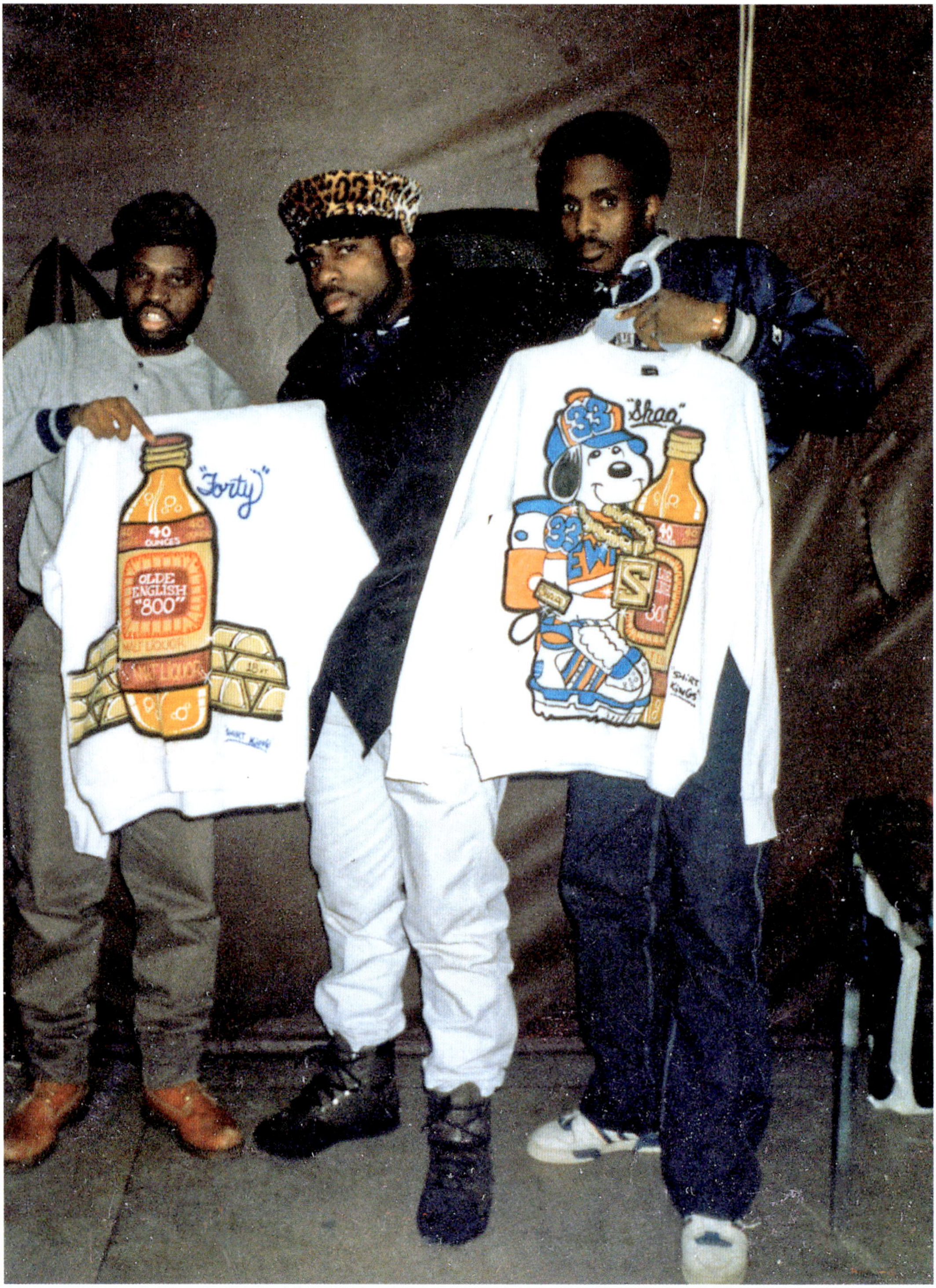

 This page: Phade, Jam Master Jay and brother, Jamaica Coliseum, 1986. **Opposite:** Stetsasonic, the Coliseum, 1986.

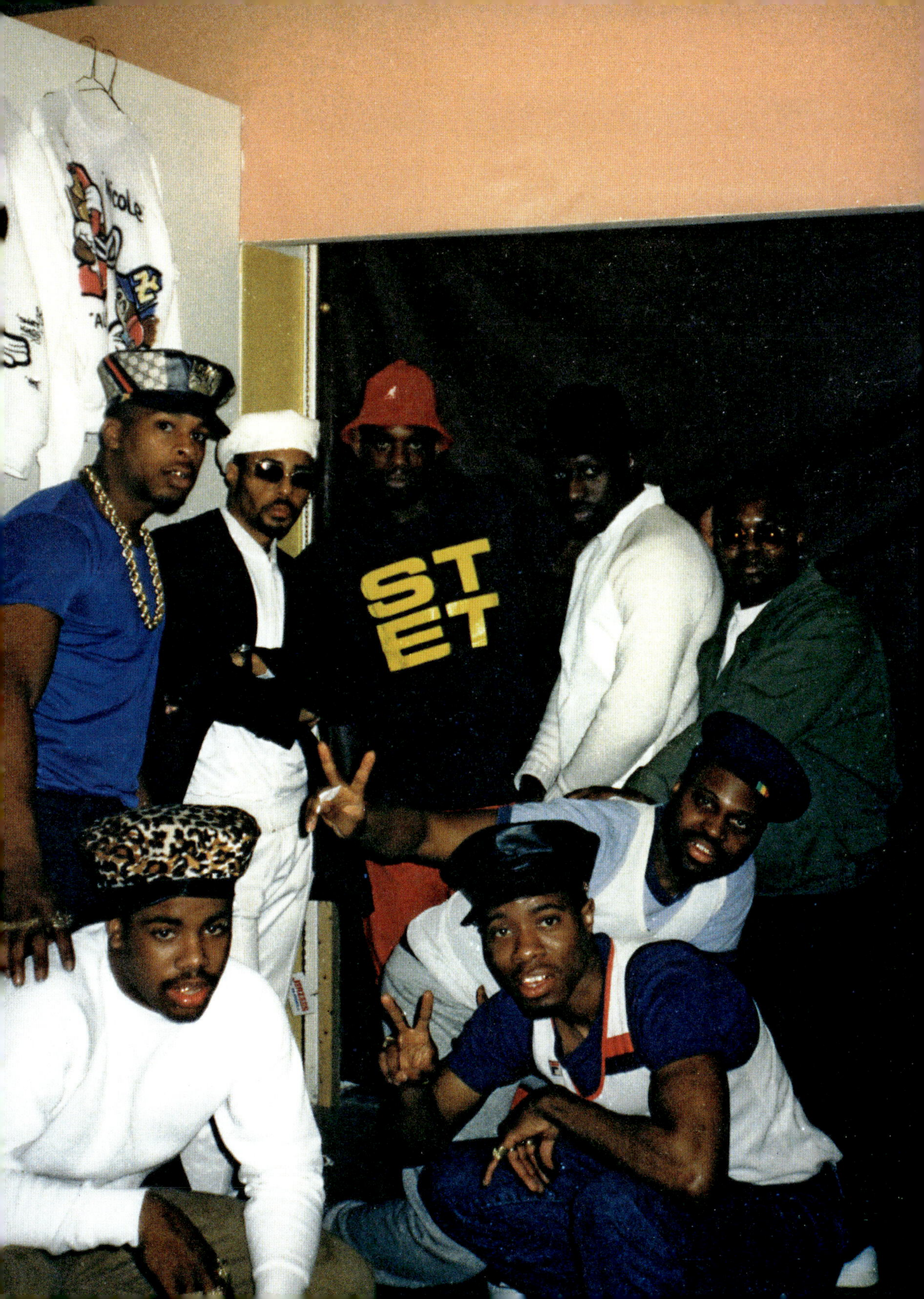
ST
ET

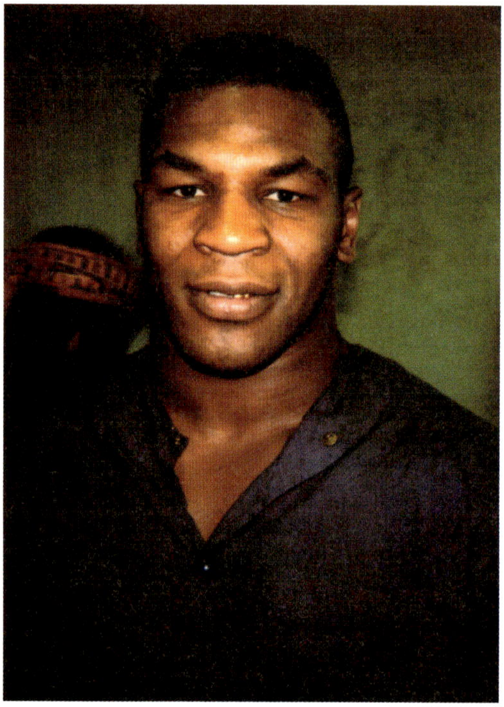

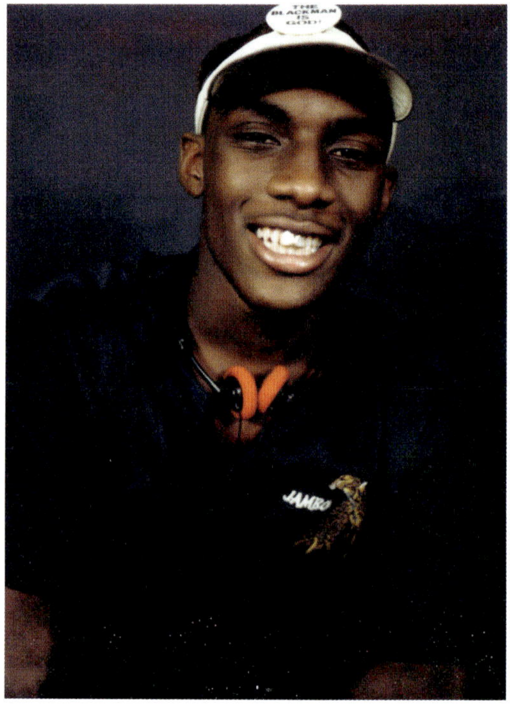

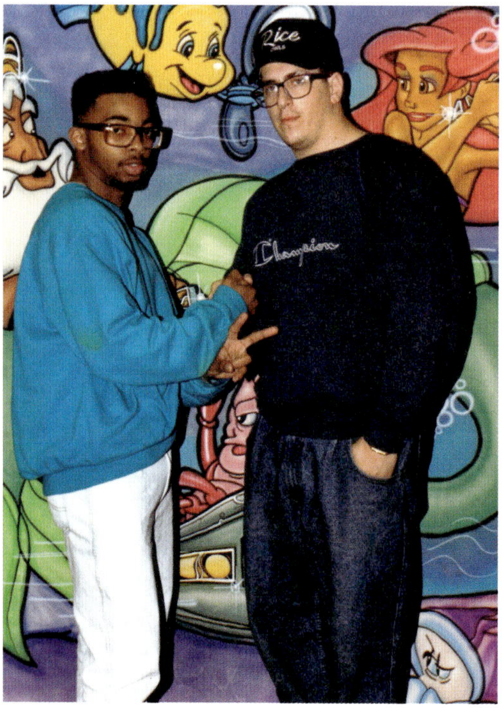

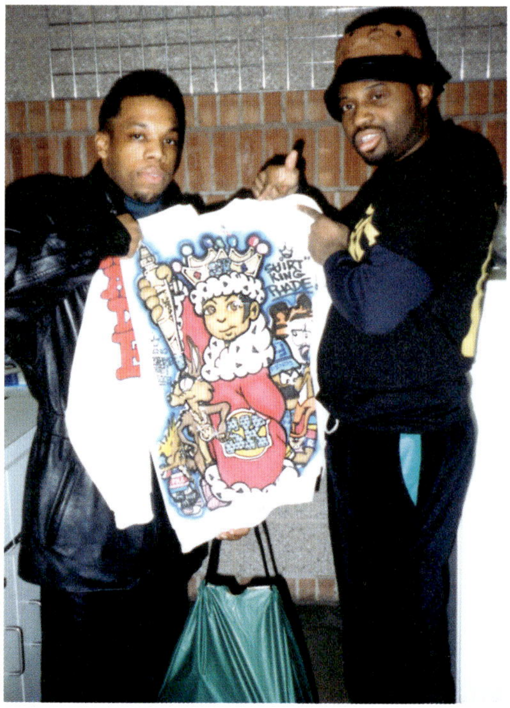

Clockwise from top left: Mike Tyson, Harlem, 1990. Lord K-Born, the Coliseum, 1987. Michael Bivens and Phade, Harlem, 1989. Sike and MC Serch, the Coliseum, 1993. **Opposite:** Kool G Rap and DJ Polo, Queens, 1990.

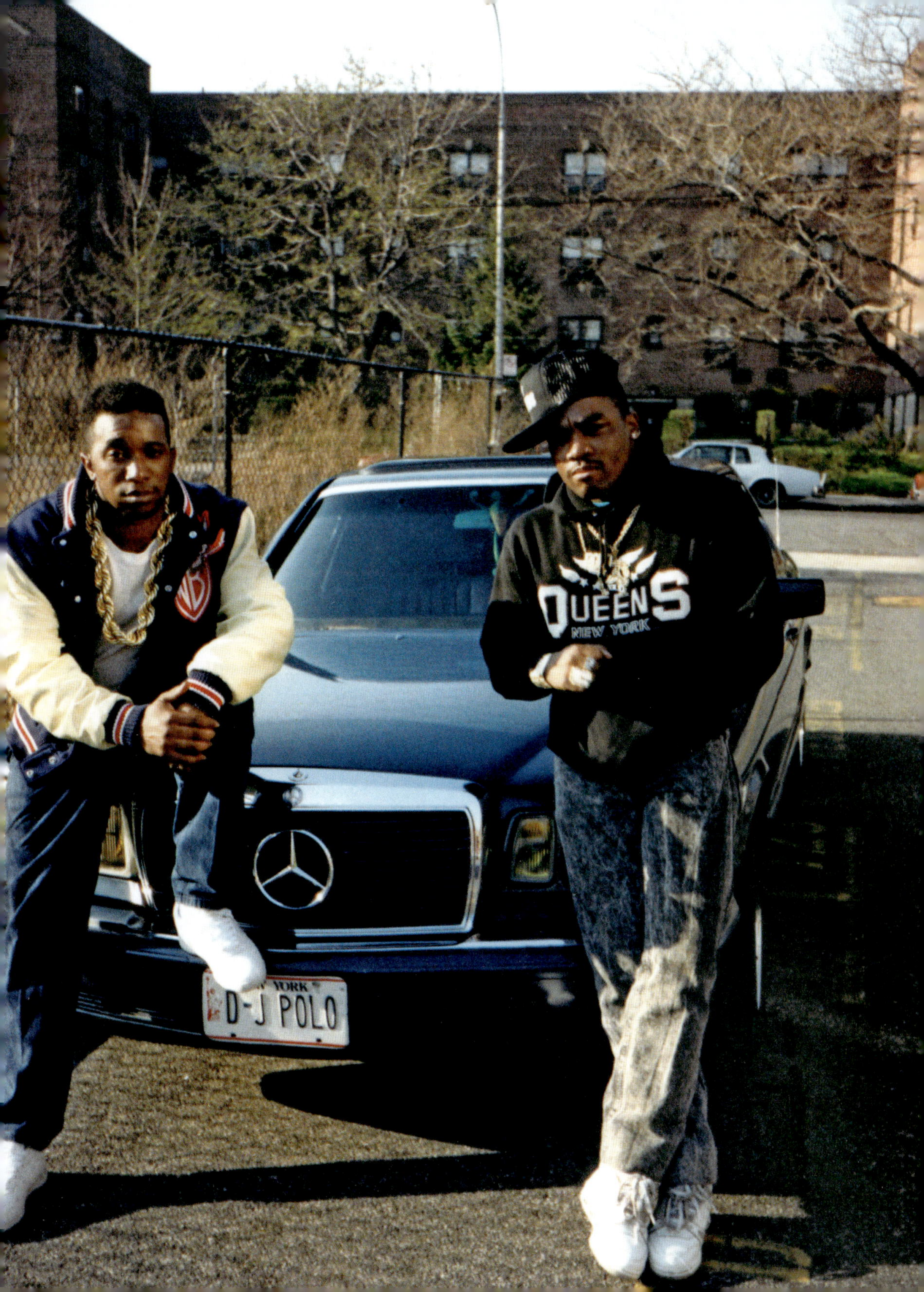
QUEENS
NEW YORK
YORK
D-J POLO

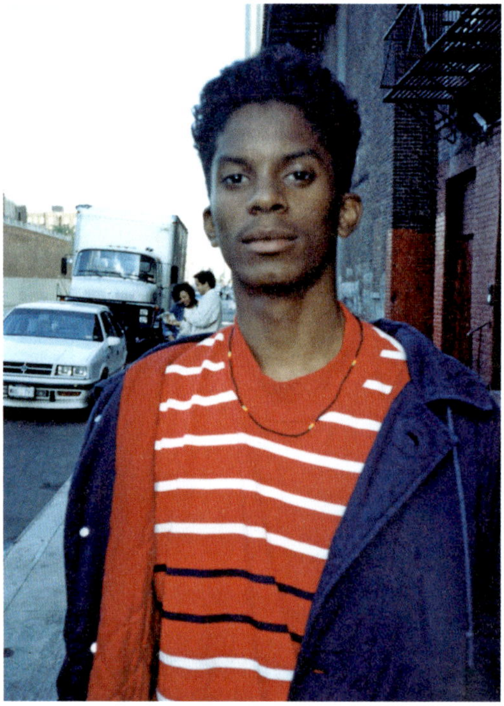

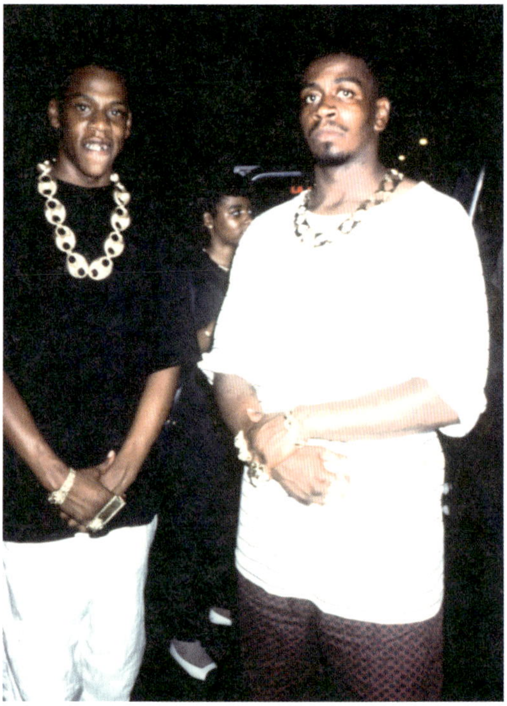

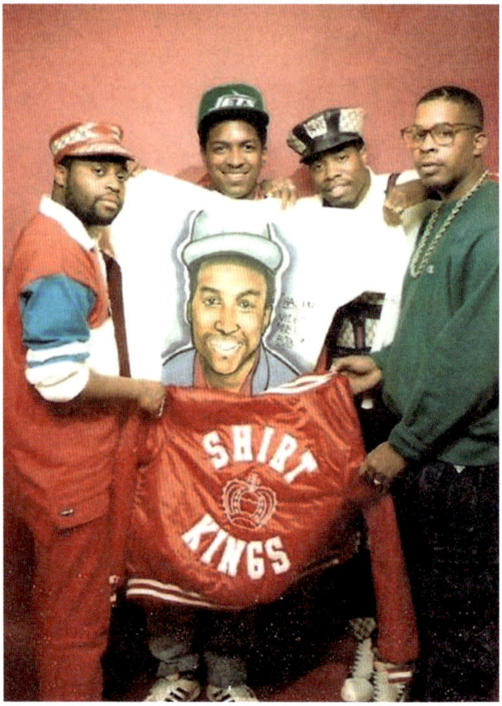

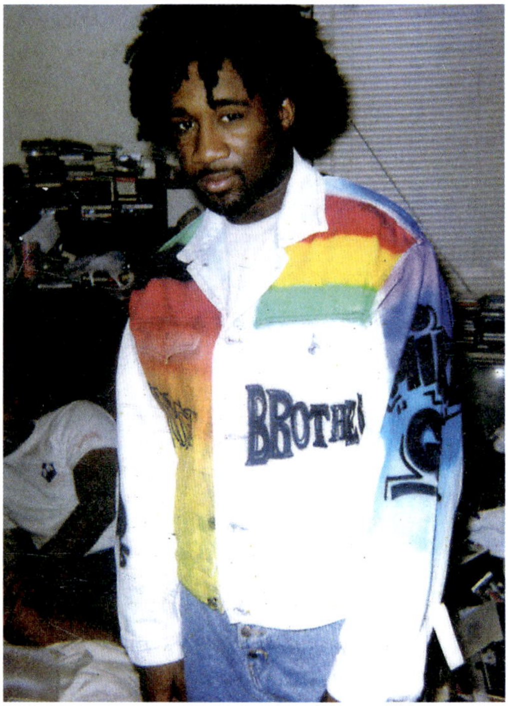

Clockwise from top left: Special Ed, Apollo Theatre, 1990. Jay-Z and Jaz-O, Harlem, 1990. Mike Gee, Harlem, 1991. Ralph McDaniels, Queens, 1987.

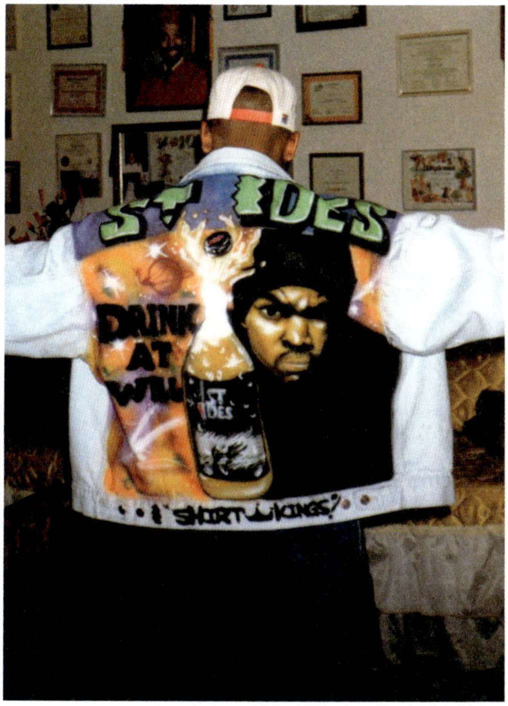

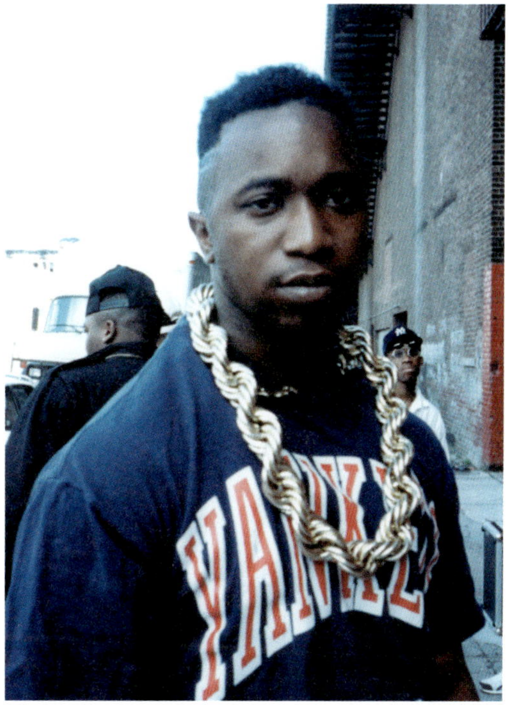

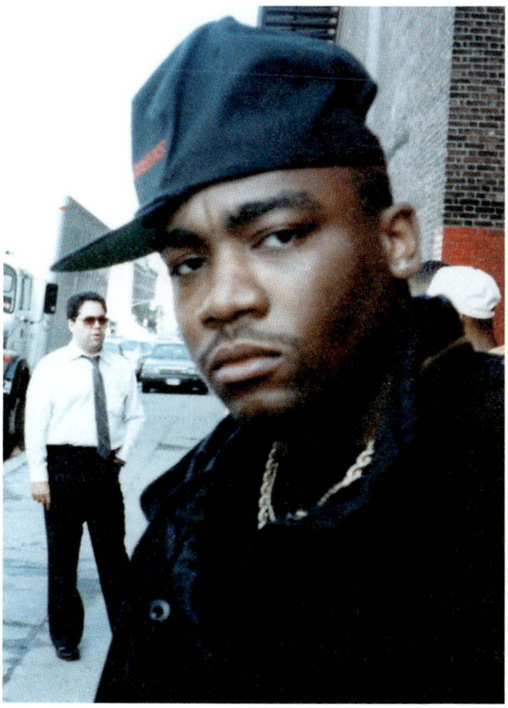

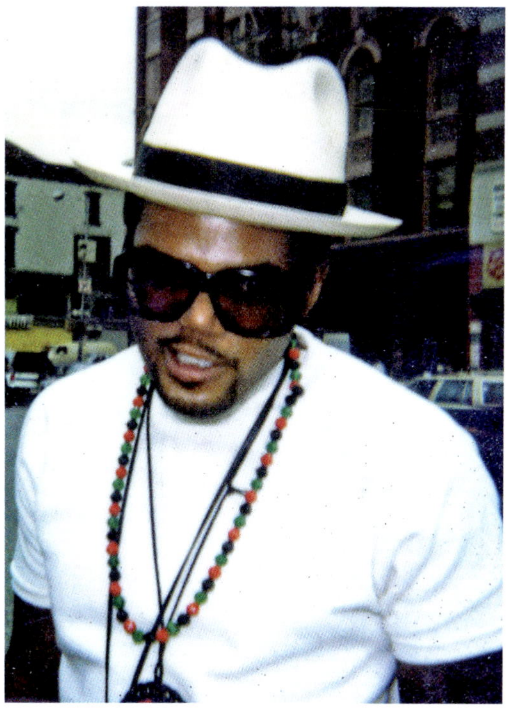

Clockwise from top left : Shirt King Sike's St. Ides jacket, Brooklyn, 1993. Kool G Rap, Apollo Theatre, 1990. DJ Polo, Apollo Theatre, Harlem, 1990. DMC, Harlem, 1990.

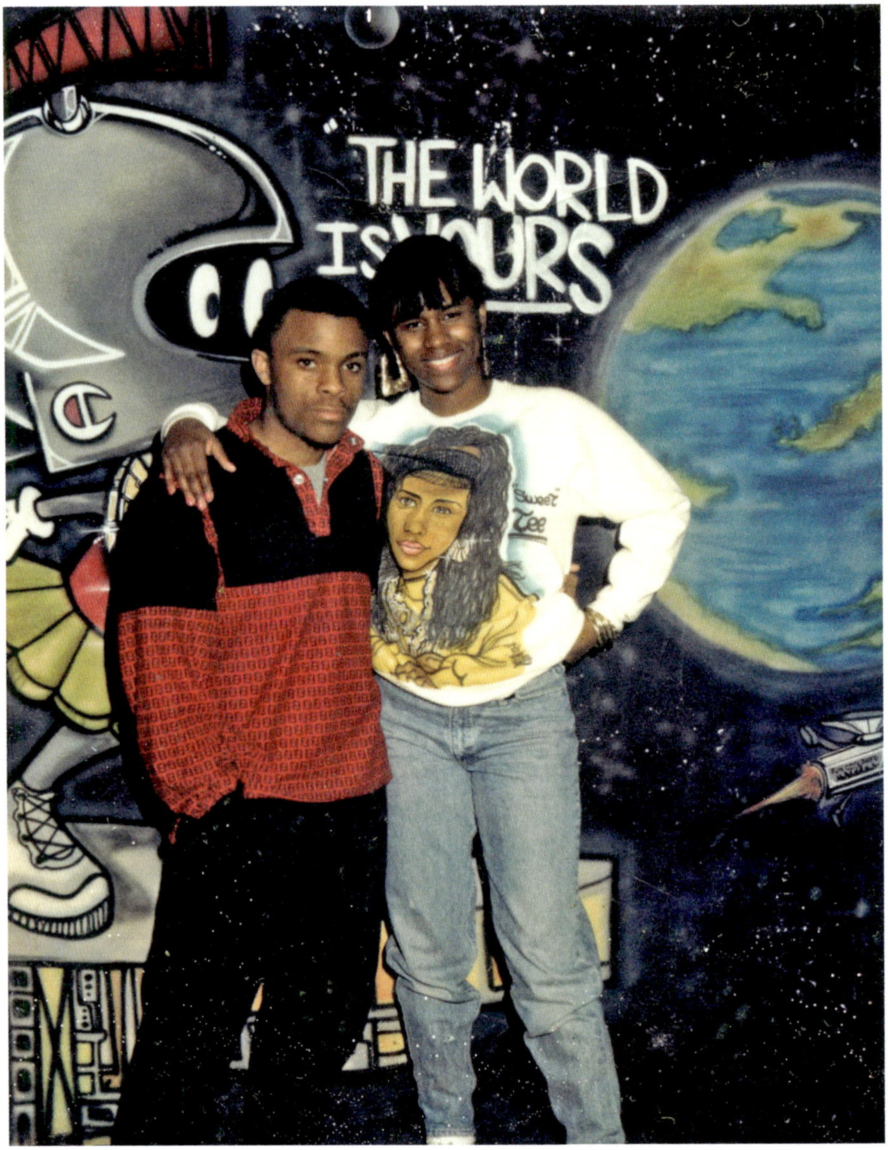

Nate from Baltimore and Sweet Tee, Jamaica Coliseum, 1990.

"Shirt Kings supplied the south side [of Queens] with artwork in motion. Shirt Kings made my signature graffiti jeans that I wore in my *On the Smooth Tip* video. They also did a beautiful portrait shirt for me. The Coliseum was a landmark that you had to pass through and you would always stop by the Shirt Kings to see what they had, that you would want."
Sweet Tee

“Everyone was doing it but Shirt Kings were doing it on another level. Everyone that had any type of fashion sense made their way to Queens and got something made by the Shirt Kings. They were official, like the real sports jersey’s of today.”
DJ Cool V

Cheryl and DJ Cool V, Miami, 1988.

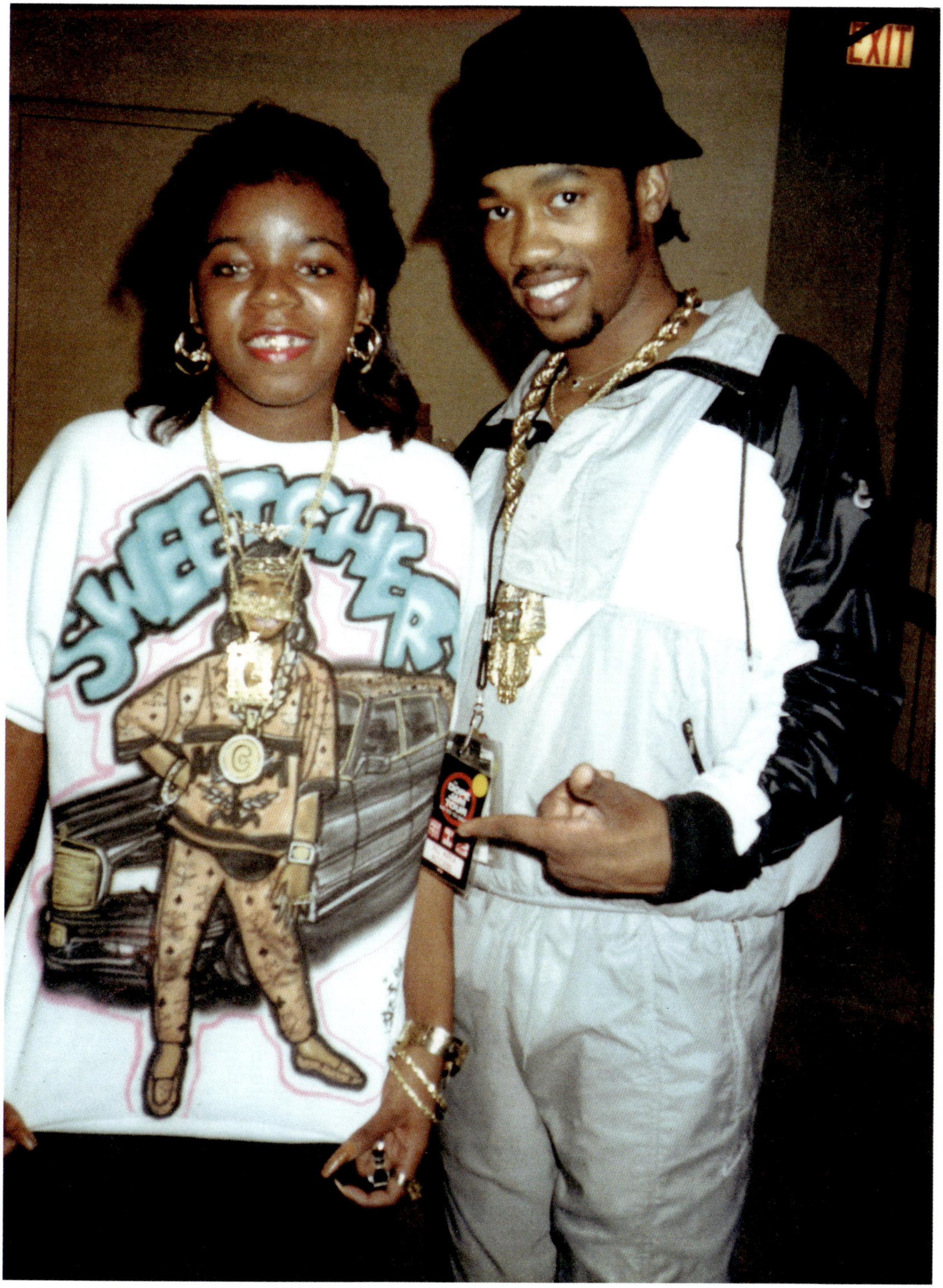
EXIT

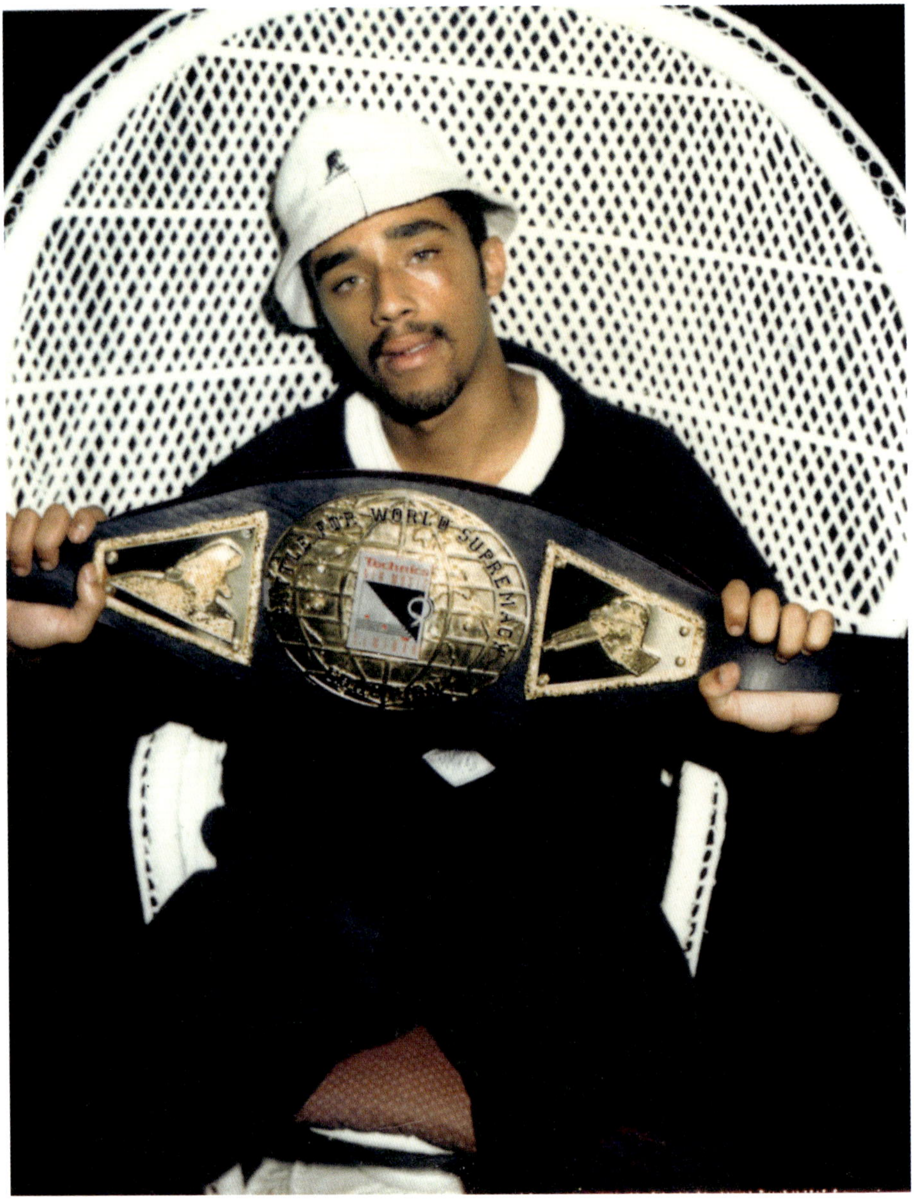

Mikey Dee with the rap supreme belt, Jamaica Coliseum, 1987.

"Mikey Dee was a freestyle king from Queens who beat out Melle Mel for the rap supremacy belt that year. Melle Mel was upset and physically took the belt back and Zulu Nation got it back for Mikey Dee."
Phade

"I remember when I first started hearing about the airbrush technique in the 80s. It was some brand new next level shit. It gave graffiti a photograph look. The Jungle Brothers first album cover for *Straight Out the Jungle* was done in airbrush. That technique was dope! I remember Uncle Red Alert breakin' out one Saturday afternoon to go to Queens to pick up his shirt that the Shirt Kings made for him. Now, I'm from Brooklyn so I'm thinking, 'what the fuck is this Harlem Zulu going all the way to Queens for?' I was like 'that's some two-fare zone shit that's gon' take you all day long to get back!' When he came back and I saw what he had on, it fucked my head up for real son! At the time we had this record out called *Jimbrowski*. It was a song about having a big dick. Red had the Shirt Kings paint the character of a big 'Jimmy' with balls and the sperm squirting out the top right on the front of the shirt! We were all cracking the fuck up. I was laughing so hard I had cramps in my stomach. While everybody in the hood was running around with the Shirt Kings Bart Simpson shirt Red Alert was showing off his Jimbrowsk. Only a Shirt King would be bold enough to draw some shit like that.

I have a rhyme I wrote that was inspired by the Shirt Kings. It goes, "...my bloodline goes back to the Zulu / I been doing this before Ecko and Fubu...." The idea of putting hip hop art on clothing made the Shirt Kings the first official hip hop clothing line in our story and in the entire universe. Phade is the Kool Herc of hip hop clothing culture.
Afrika Baby Bam / Jungle Brothers

Opposite page: Red Alert and The Jungle Brothers, Harlem, 1989.

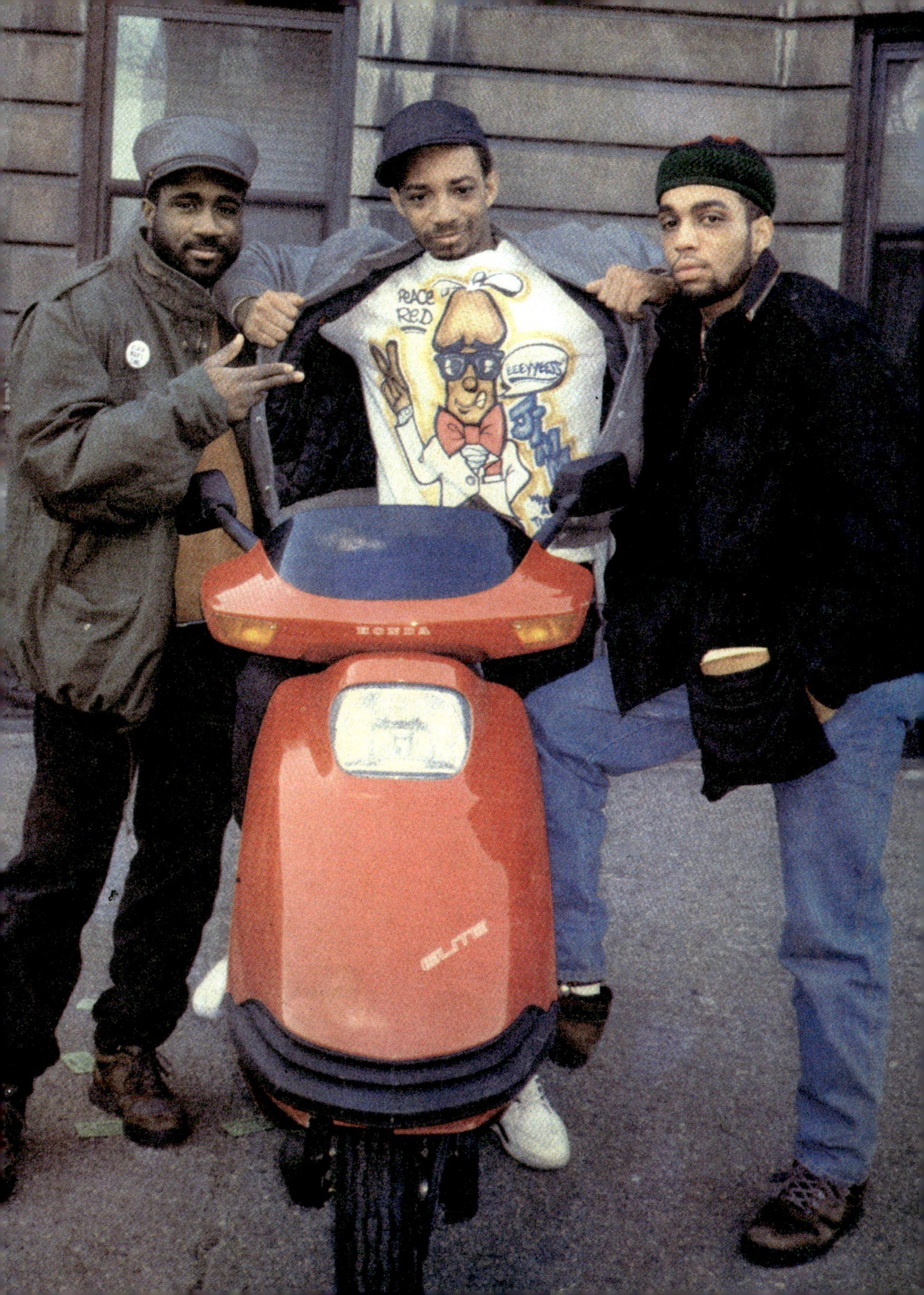
PEACE
RED
EEEYYEESS
HONDA
ELITE

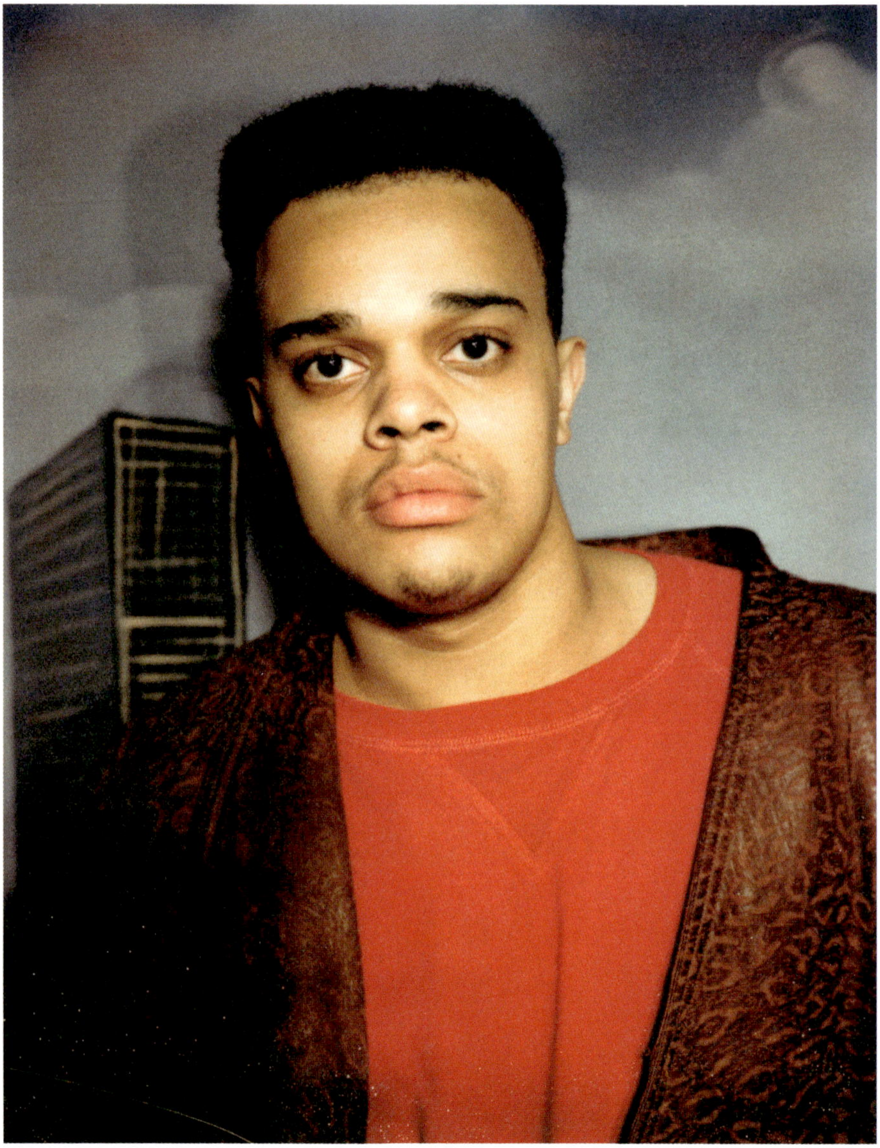

Cliff Love, Jamaica Coliseum, 1989.

"I remember going to Shirt Kings in 1987. I was on the Def Jam tour with LL, Whodini, Jazzy Jeff and Fresh Prince, Public Enemy, Eric B and Rakim and Heavy D and the Boyz. The tour was crazy. Coming home off the road I saw Biz Markie's album and I think I saw LL's Shirt Kings shirt and he told me about Nike and Phade, the Shirt Kings. I got directions and I took a cab from Brooklyn to the Coliseum, dumb excited. I gave them a picture to get my official Shirt Kings shirt. I remember the emotion I had with fashion when I was younger. I was so happy to get the sweatshirt.

They were on the same level as Dapper Dan. There was no difference between them, the same customer who rocked Dapper Dan rocked the Shirt Kings. They were genuine and real. The shirts cost paper, and for me to own one, it was like buying a pair of Gucci sneakers from Dap. They made my sweatshirt with my flat top cut by Denny Mo in Harlem. They hooked me up by painting it with a big ass flat top. It was real nice. They even added my Saint Lazarus chain that cost me $7000.

My cutie Angie from Fort Green got me for the sweatshirt. Fine ass Angie! I don't know where all my classic memorabilia is and I have tons from tours with Run DMC, but I remember for a fact that she got me for that.

Shirt King Phade and Shirt King Nike are on the same level with the respect in the streets as an Eric B and Rakim or a Public Enemy record, Whodini's *One Love*, Run DMC's *Beats to the Rhyme*, and Jazzy Jeff and Fresh Prince's *Touch of Jazz*. They are in the same lane. Period."
Cliff Love

"Shirt Kings was the official spot for all the hot rappers. You had to get your clothes tagged by them."
Frick and Frack

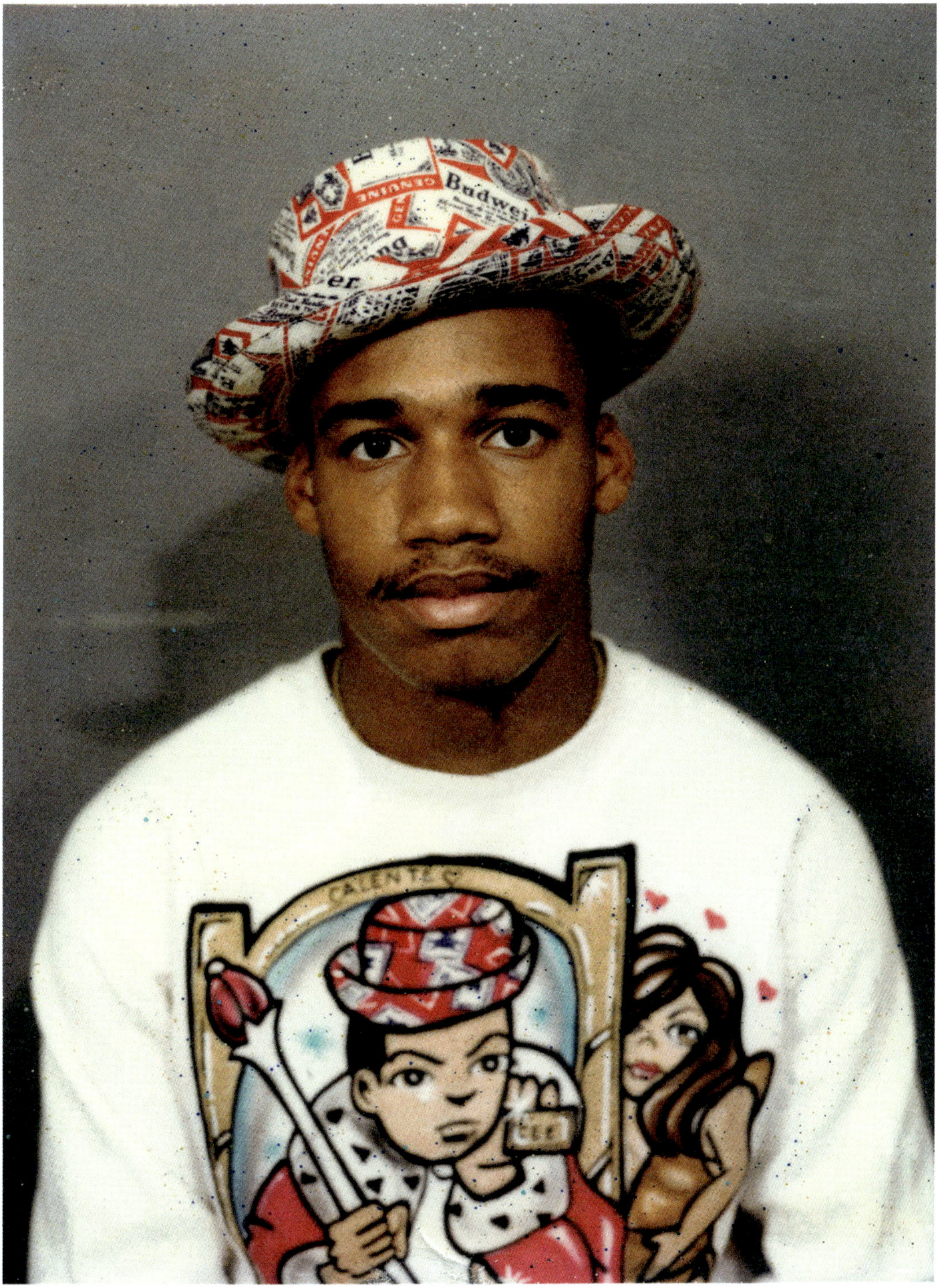

Super Lover Cee, Jamaica Coliseum, 1986.

“Shirt Kings were the first cats to do it on the shirts and on the video sets. Let it be Special Ed, let it be Heavy D and the Boys, let it be EPMD. Whatever it is, if it’s in the golden era of hip hop, these cats was putting it down, showing people how to put it on shirts and walls. Whatever it was, if I said, ‘put it on a car’, the Shirt Kings would put it on a car! The Shirt Kings, that’s what it’s all about. The Original, the blueprint for all urban clothing and all of that. Shirt Kings and Video Music Box. These cats are original cats so we relate.”
VJ Ralph McDaniels

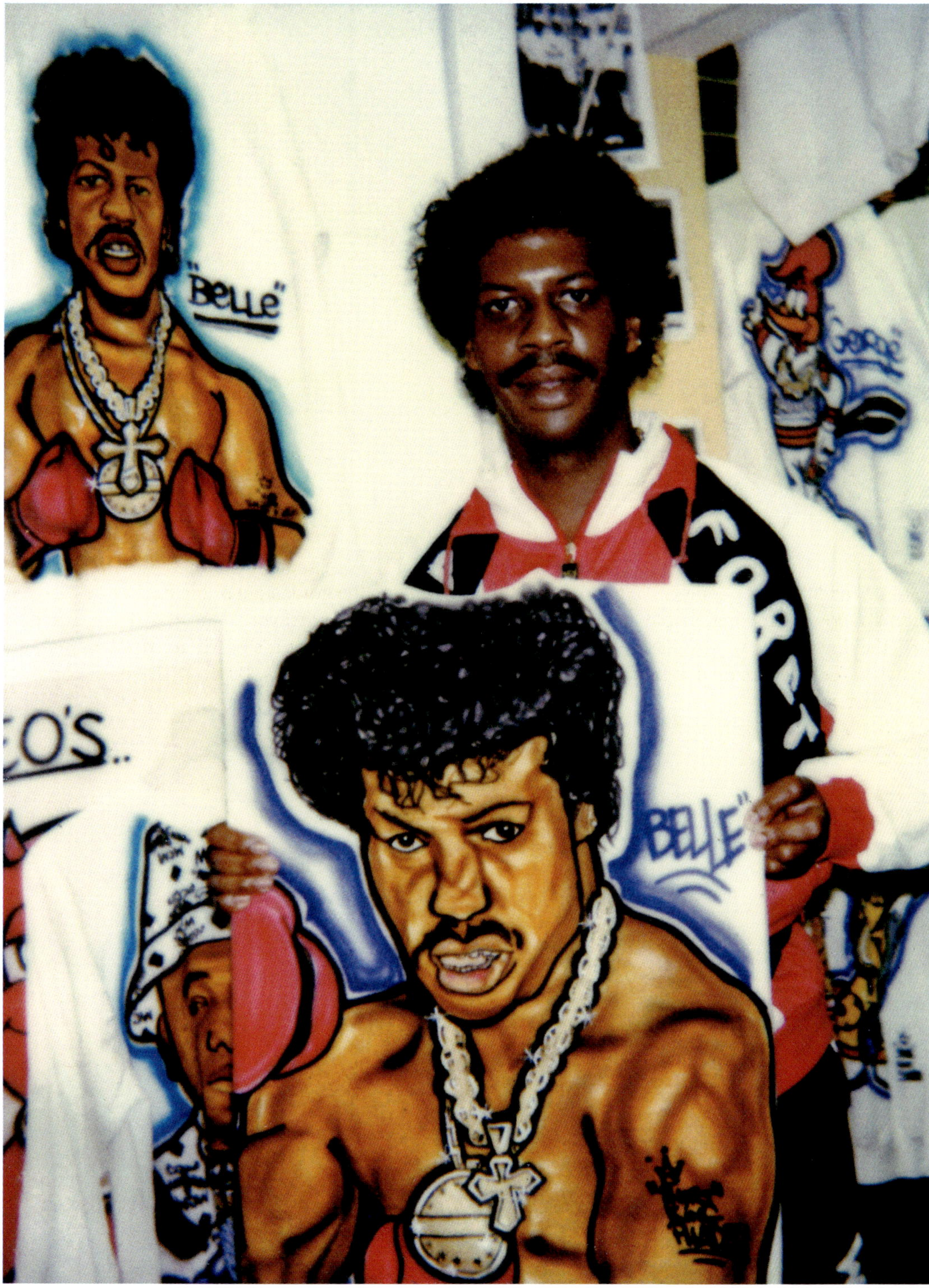

The boxer Belle, Jamaica Coliseum, 1987.

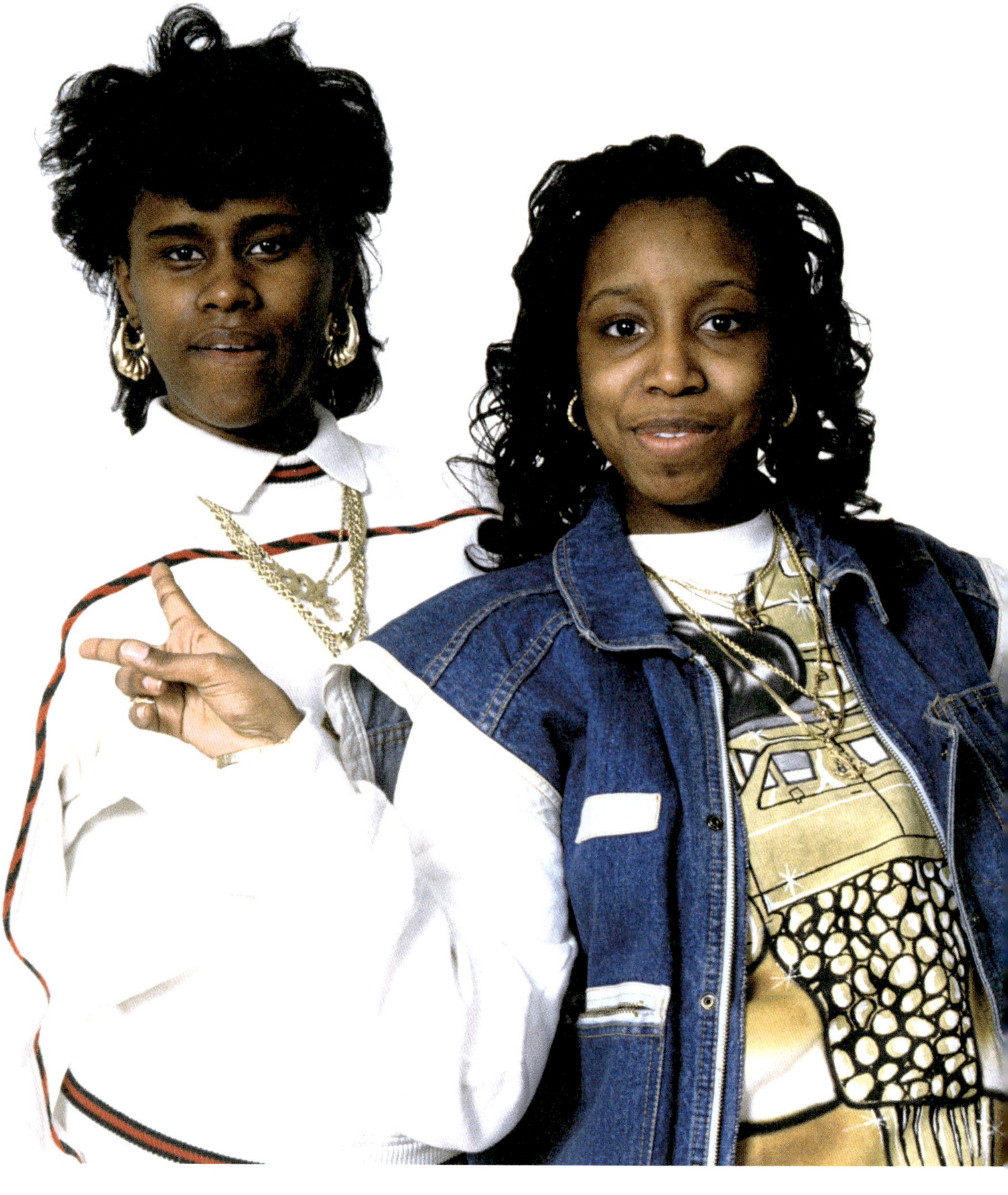

Sweet Tee and Jazzy Joyce, 1987. Photo by Janette Beckman ©.

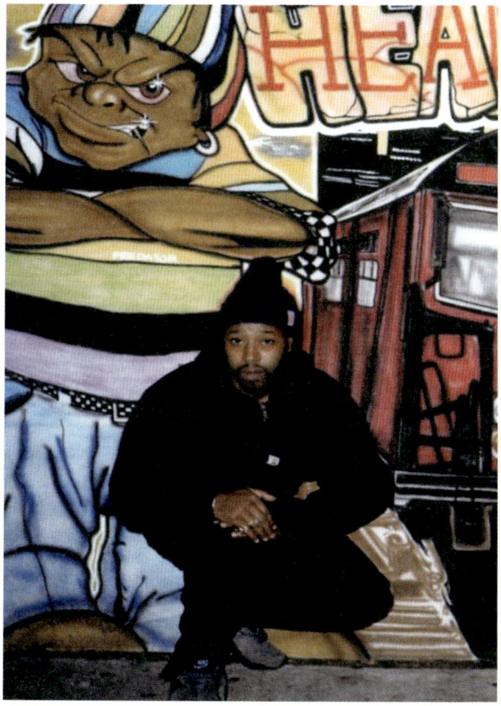

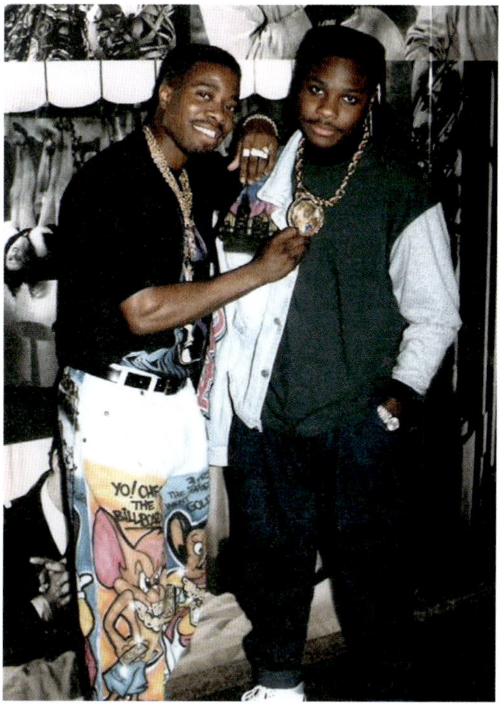

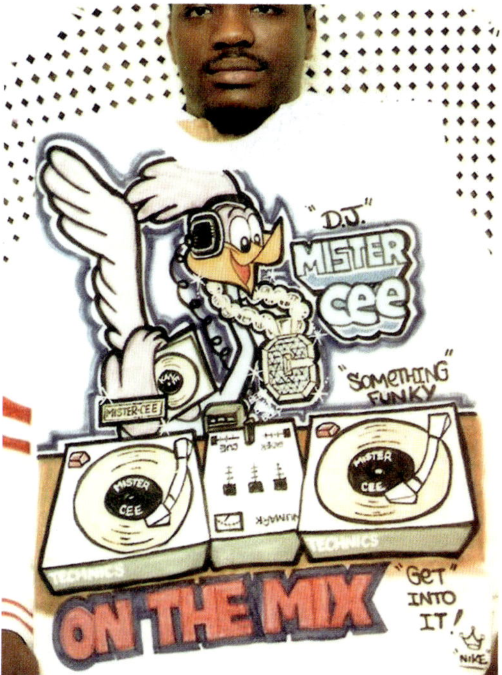

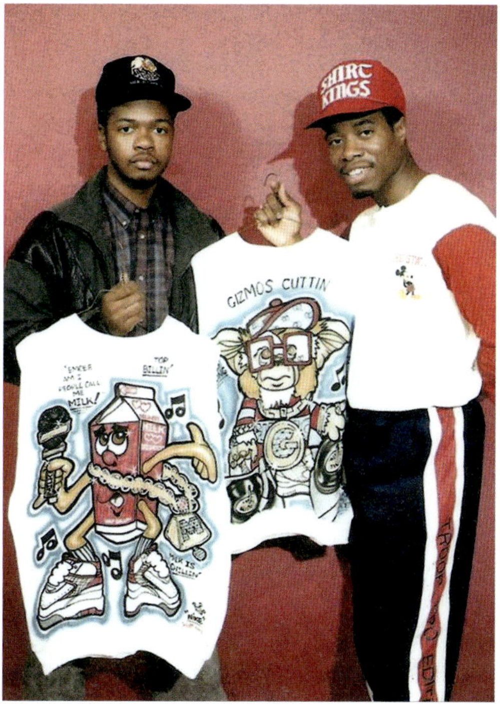

Clockwise from top left: DJ Kay Slay, 1992. Nike and Malcolm Jamal Warner, 1989. Nike and Milk D, Jamaica Coliseum, 1988. DJ Mister Cee, Jamaica Coliseum, 1987.

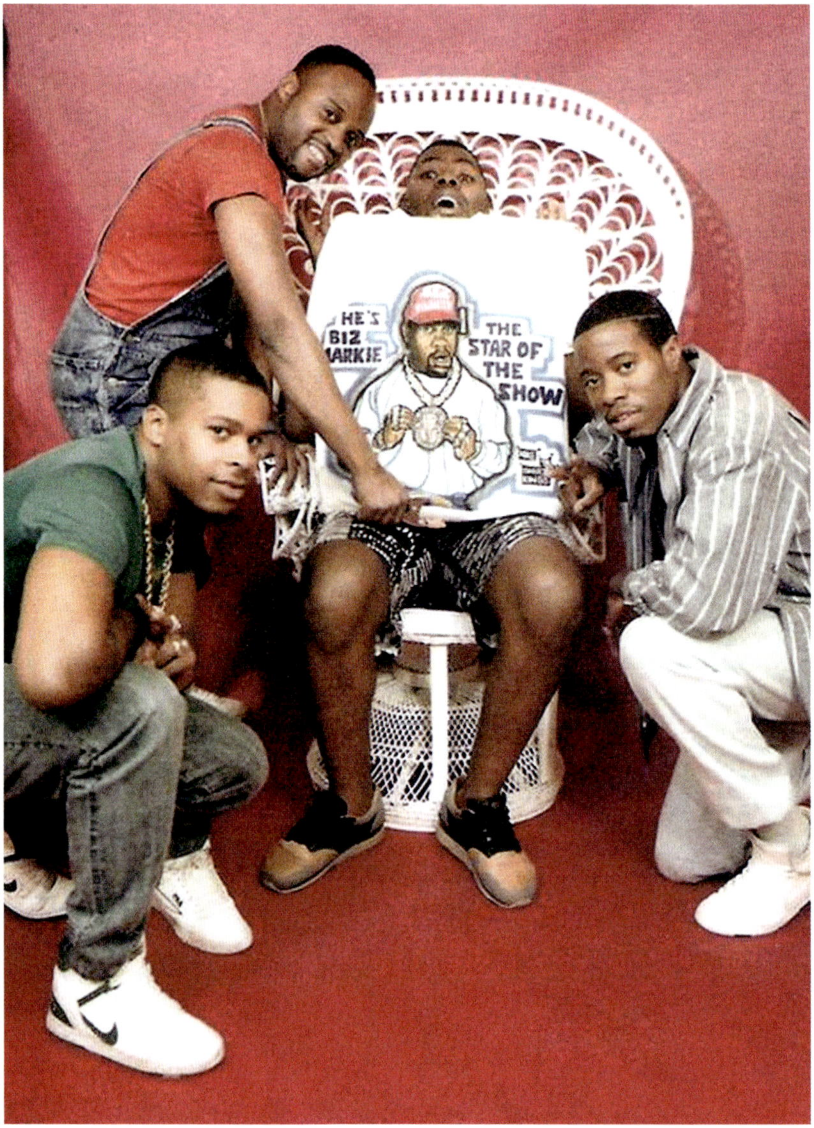

Biz Markie and the Shirt Kings, Jamaica Coliseum, 1987.